In Defense of Leon Trotsky

In Defense of Leon Trotsky

Second Edition

David North

Mehring Books

Oak Park, Michigan

2013

Published by Mehring Books
P. O. Box 48377
Oak Park, MI 48237

Printed in the United States of America

Reprinted July, 2015

Library of Congress Cataloging-in-Publication Data

North, David, 1950- author.
In defense of Leon Trotsky / David North. -- Second edition.
    pages ; cm
Includes index.
ISBN 978-1-893638-36-5 (pbk. : alk. paper) -- ISBN 978-1-893638-39-6 (ebook)
1. Trotsky, Leon, 1879-1940. 2. Swain, Geoff. Trotsky. 3. Thatcher, Ian D. Trotsky. 4. Service,
Robert, 1947- Trotsky. 5. Revolutionaries--Soviet Union--Biography. 6. Communism--
Historiography. 7. Biography--Political aspects. 8. Historiography--Political aspects. 9. Soviet
Union--History--Errors, inventions, etc. I. Title.
DK254.T6N67 2013
947.084092--dc23
                              2013020301

Contents

Part IV:

Three Lectures in Germany

Part V:

About the Author

David North has played a leading role in the international socialist movement for more than 40 years, and is presently the chairperson of the International Editorial Board of the World Socialist Web Site. An authority on the life and political ideas of Leon Trotsky, his many published works include *The Heritage We Defend*, a history of the Fourth International.

Leon Trotsky in Coyoacán, Mexico, 1940

Foreword to Second Edition

In the introduction to the first edition of *In Defense of Leon Trotsky*, I noted that even 70 years after the assassination of the great 20th century revolutionary, his life remains the subject of not only historical debate, but contemporary political controversy. Although Trotsky's political career spanned the first four decades of the 20th century, there is no indication that the passions evoked by his actions and ideas have abated even as we approach the midway point of the second decade of the 21st century. This second, expanded, edition of *In Defense of Leon Trotsky* arises out of the controversy which followed the publication of the first edition.

In Defense of Leon Trotsky was written as a response to politically-motivated anti-Trotsky diatribes, masquerading as biographies, by three British academics—Ian Thatcher, Geoffrey Swain and Robert Service. The book established that these pseudo-biographies violated basic standards of historical scholarship. They were mendacious and malicious exercises in character assassination, consisting of distortions, half-truths and outright fabrications.

None of the three writers attempted to refute my exposure of their books. Thatcher, Swain and Service assumed, in all likelihood, that they would be allowed by their professional colleagues, not to mention the press, to get away with the historiographical equivalent of murder. After all, they assured themselves, who will object to the libeling of Trotsky, whose name is synonymous with world socialist revolution? The Trotskyists, perhaps. But who in the media or the academic Establishment will pay any notice to their criticisms?

Professor Robert Service of Oxford University, the best known and least competent of the trio, seemed especially confident that little attention would be paid to the unmasking of his dishonoring of the historian's craft. His biography had been published in Britain in 2009 to great acclaim by anti-Communist critics, who were only too happy to heap praise upon an author whose book flattered their own prejudices and hatreds. The praise which spewed from Britain's right-wing gutter press went to Service's head, and so, at a London-area book launch organized in his honor, the professor incautiously acknowledged the true purpose of his work: "There's life in the old boy Trotsky yet—but if the ice pick didn't quite do its job killing him off, I hope I've managed it."[1]

But suddenly, at the height of Service's hubris, calamity struck. Nemesis appeared in the form of a review essay in the June 2011 edition of *The American Historical Review* (*AHR*). Following its release in Britain, Service's *Trotsky* had been published in the United States by the Harvard University Press. *In Defense of Leon Trotsky* had called attention to the intellectually disgraceful character of the prestigious academic publishing house's involvement in the release of Service's travesty. *The American Historical Review* apparently took the matter seriously, and assigned Stanford University historian Bertrand M. Patenaude to prepare a joint review of Service's *Trotsky* and my *In Defense of Leon Trotsky*. Patenaude's specific qualification for this assignment was that he had recently written *Trotsky: Downfall of a Revolutionary*, which dealt with the last years of Trotsky's life as an exile in Mexico.

The result of Patenaude's examination of the two books was an unequivocal endorsement of my criticisms and a devastating indictment of Service's work. Patenaude wrote:

> Given North's Trotskyism, he might reasonably be suspected of hyperbole in his brief against Service. But a careful examination of North's book shows his criticism of Service to be exactly what Trotsky scholar Baruch Knei-Paz, in a blurb on the back cover, says it is: "detailed, meticulous, well-argued and devastating."[2]

Patenaude not only summed up but also added to my indictment of Service. He described the factual errors in Service's book as "jaw-dropping," and stated, with evident contempt, that Service "is not about to let facts get in the way" of his denunciation of Trotsky. "With no way to prove his case,"

---

[1] Robert Service, speaking at Daunt Books in London's Holland Park, October 22, 2009.

[2] *The American Historical Review*, Volume 116, Number 3, June 2011, p. 900. See also Appendix I.

Patenaude wrote, "Service relies on cheap shots and slanderous asides to keep his readers convinced that Trotsky is a despicable man."[3]

Concluding his review, Patenaude wrote:

> North calls Service's biography a "piece of hack-work" (p. 140). Strong words, but entirely justified. Harvard University Press has placed its imprimatur upon a book that fails to meet the basic standards of historical scholarship.[4]

Though publicly accused in the pages of an authoritative academic journal of slovenly research and deliberate falsification of the historical record, Service offered no defense of his biography. In effect, his silence amounted to the academic equivalent of a guilty man's plea of *nolo contendere*. Service did not contest the charges against him.

Even as Service's biography was being exposed as "hack-work" in the United States, the renowned German publishing house Suhrkamp announced its intention to bring out a German-language edition of Service's *Trotsky*. That Suhrkamp was willing to associate itself with a work such as Service's was, no less than the involvement of Harvard University Press, yet another disturbing indication of the decline of intellectual standards among even the most prestigious publishing houses. For decades the imprimatur of Suhrkamp has appeared on books written by the most distinguished writers in the German language. Moreover, Suhrkamp could be justly proud of its historical association with Trotsky's literary legacy. Suhrkamp emerged out of the S. Fischer Verlag, which published Trotsky's autobiography *My Life* [*Mein Leben*] in 1931, two years before the Nazi takeover of Germany. Peter Suhrkamp, who served as editor of S. Fischer Verlag, was arrested by the Gestapo in 1944. He survived imprisonment in a concentration camp, and went on to found the publishing house bearing his name following the division of S. Fischer Verlag in 1950.

Given the remarkable history of this firm, Suhrkamp's decision to publish Service's discredited biography aroused consternation among a group of 14 distinguished German, Austrian and Swiss historians specializing in the field of Soviet studies. Thanks to my comrades in the Partei für Soziale Gleichheit, the historians had been sent the German-language edition of *In Defense of*

---

[3] Ibid, p. 901.

[4] Ibid, p. 902.

Leon Trotsky [*Verteidigung Leo Trotzkis*, Mehring Verlag, 2010]. They also received Professor Patenaude's review of Service's travesty.

On July 30, 2011, the 14 historians sent a letter to Suhrkamp, urging it to reconsider its decision to publish the biography. They stated:

> North and Patenaude have pointed out a host of factual errors by Service (including false information regarding biographical facts and historical events, incorrect names of places and persons, up to blatant misrepresentations—e.g., Trotsky's position regarding autonomy and "partiality" in art and literature). Service's sources are unreliable. Sources that are very difficult to access and hardly verifiable for most readers often have nothing to do with the claims made, or demonstrate the opposite. Contrary to the announcement of the book made by Suhrkamp, Service has not sought to deal with Trotsky and Stalin in an "impartial and genuine" manner. Instead, the aim of his work is to discredit Trotsky, and unfortunately he often resorts to the formulas associated with Stalinist propaganda.[5]

The historians chose not to make their letter public for several months, in order to give Suhrkamp time to consider their objections and submit Service's text to a careful re-examination. Receiving no reply from Suhrkamp, the historians released their letter to the public in November 2011. However, despite

---

[5]   Letter from historians to German publisher Suhrkamp on Robert Service's biography of Trotsky (*World Socialist Web Site*, November 23, 2011, http://www.wsws.org/en/articles/2011/11/lett-n23.html). The signatories included:

Hermann Weber, Professor of Political Science and Contemporary History, Mannheim University

Helmut Dahmer, Professor of Sociology, Technical University, Darmstadt

Bernhard Bayerlein, Centre for Contemporary Research, Potsdam

Heiko Haumann, Professor of East European History, University of Basel

Wladislaw Hedeler, Historian and author, Berlin

Andrea Hurton, Historian and author, Vienna

Mario Kessler, Professor at the Centre for Contemporary Research, Potsdam

Hartmut Mehringer, Institute for Contemporary History, Berlin

Oskar Negt, Professor of Sociology, University of Hanover

Hans Schafranek, Historian and author, Vienna

Oliver Rathkolb, Professor at the Institute for Contemporary History, University of Vienna

Peter Steinbach, Professor at the University of Mannheim, Director of The German Resistance Memorial Center

Reiner Tosstorff, University of Mainz

Rolf Wörsdörfer, Technical University of Darmstadt

Suhrkamp's silence, the historians' letter was not without effect. Suhrkamp delayed the publication of Service's biography. In response to inquiries from the press, the publisher claimed that it had asked an outside editor to review the manuscript.

Despite the condemnation of his biography by 14 highly respected European historians and the postponement of the release date, Service offered no public defense of his book. However, a political campaign was launched in the bourgeois press to pressure Suhrkamp to go ahead with the publication of Service's biography. A leading role in this effort was played by the *Neue Zürcher Zeitung*. In the war against Trotsky and Trotskyism, Switzerland decided not to observe its traditional policy of neutrality. Professor Ulrich Schmid of St. Gallen University was invited by the *NZZ* to contribute two articles defending Service. Schmid made light of the "little mistakes" in Service's book. While acknowledging that Service had provided an "inexact description of historical events," cited "unreliable footnotes," and demonstrated a "selective preference for memoirs that show Trotsky in an unfavorable light," such errors, claimed Schmid, did not detract from the overriding value of the book. "[N]either North nor Patenaude," wrote the St. Gallen historian, "have been able to advance arguments that undermine Service's fundamental critique of Trotsky's revolutionary fanaticism and his willingness to use violence."[6]

Schmid defended Service's book on purely political and ideological grounds. Whether Service observed accepted standards of scholarship was, as far as Schmid was concerned, irrelevant. All that mattered was Service's denunciation of Trotsky's "revolutionary fanaticism."

In July 2012, after a delay of nearly one year, Suhrkamp finally published Service's *Trotsky*. Except for a few minor cosmetic changes, the Suhrkamp edition hardly differed from the original English-language version.

Of the four new chapters in this expanded edition of *In Defense of Leon Trotsky,* three were prepared as lectures for German audiences in Berlin, Leipzig and Mainz. They were written as answers to Schmid and other apologists for Service's execrable work. The one paper that was presented in the United States—at the 2010 conference in Los Angeles of the Association of Slavic, East European and Eurasian Studies—offered an assessment of Trotsky as a historical figure seventy years after his assassination. It was no more possible to avoid a polemical tone in this lecture than in the other three.

---

[6] *Neue Zürcher Zeitung,* 21 February, 2012.

I was compelled to answer yet another barrage of anti-Trotsky falsifications written by the Russian historian, Roy Medvedev. In the three decades that preceded the dissolution of the Soviet Union in 1991, Medvedev had established an international reputation as a dissident historian. While never a Trotskyist, Medvedev had in his earlier work—most notably in *Let History Judge*—acknowledged, however cautiously, Trotsky's outstanding role in the 1917 October Revolution, the Russian Civil War and the struggle against Stalinism. But by 2010 Medvedev had adapted himself to the reactionary climate of Putin's Russia. He abandoned the principles he had once upheld and denounced Trotsky in the crudest terms.

It would not be unreasonable to hope that with the publication of this second edition, it will not be necessary to devote further efforts to defending Trotsky against defamatory lies. But it would be politically naïve. Trotsky's life will remain the subject of the bitterest controversy as long as his ideas retain the power to influence the outcome of on-going political and social struggles. The attacks directed against Trotsky are aimed not only against a figure in history, but against a man whose vision of world socialist revolution remains to this day, a source of inspiration and hope for the future of humanity. The polemics, arising from and expressing the interests of opposing class forces, will continue.

David North
Detroit
7 March 2013

Introduction

It is difficult to think of another figure in the twentieth century, and perhaps in world history, whose life has been the subject of such unrelenting vilification and falsification as Leon Trotsky. The peculiar intensity of the hatred directed against Trotsky, which persists even 70 years after his death, is bound up with his unique historical role. Trotsky was both the leader of the first socialist revolution and also the implacable opponent of the Stalinist regime that subsequently betrayed that revolution. The Soviet Union no longer exists and the Stalinist regime has disappeared into the "dustbin of history." But Trotsky remains a relentlessly contemporary political figure. The significance of his life in world history transcends his role in the Russian Revolution. Leon Trotsky was, above all else, the great tribune and theoretician of world socialist revolution. The passions evoked by his name testify to the enduring significance of Trotsky's ideas. Arguments about Trotsky are never simply about what happened in the past. They are just as much about what is happening in the world today, and what is likely to happen in the future.

In October 1917 Trotsky played, next to Lenin himself, the most important role in the Bolshevik seizure of power. His role in the overthrow of the bourgeois Provisional Government was not limited to his operational leadership of the revolutionary insurrection in Petrograd. Though it was Lenin who, between April and October 1917, politically directed the Bolshevik Party toward the conquest of state power, Lenin's strategic line drew heavily on the theory of Permanent Revolution elaborated by Trotsky. Moreover, the Soviet regime's survival and ultimate victory in the civil war that raged between 1918 and 1921 owed a great deal to Trotsky's activities as principal commander of the Red Army.

But the end of the Civil War marked a turning point in Soviet history and in Trotsky's position in the Bolshevik leadership. Though it was not immediately apparent, the adoption of the market-oriented New Economic Policy in 1921—a necessary response by the Soviet regime to the calamitous conditions that existed in the country after seven years of world war, revolution and civil war—strengthened more conservative political tendencies within the Russian Communist Party. This process was exacerbated by the absorption of large sections of party cadre, including many "Old Bolsheviks," into the rapidly expanding state and party bureaucracy. The setbacks suffered by revolutionary movements in central and Western Europe between 1919 and 1923, especially in Germany, foreclosed the possibility that the massive social and economic problems confronting the Bolshevik regime would be alleviated through the timely establishment of friendly socialist regimes.

Beneath unrelenting domestic and international pressure, the political constituency within the party grew for a redefinition of the basic aims of the Soviet regime—away from the world revolutionary perspective that had inspired the October Revolution, and with which Trotsky was indelibly identified. Prior to 1923 it had been accepted, as a basic premise of Marxist theory, that the development of socialism in Russia could not be achieved on a national basis. Russia, with its predominantly peasant population and limited industrial base, lacked the resources for a socialist reorganization of its economy. While it was necessary for the Soviet government to work patiently for the development of the economic foundations of a socialist economy, the success of the revolutionary project depended on the victory of the working class in the advanced centers of capitalism. However, this internationalist perspective gave way to an essentially autarkic conception of the economic development of the USSR as a national state. The new outlook found expression in the program of "socialism in one country" advanced in 1924 by Stalin and Bukharin. This nationalist reorientation intersected with the bureaucracy's growing identification of its own privileged social position with national state power.

Trotsky's efforts in the autumn of 1923 to draw attention to the symptoms of bureaucratization within the Communist Party and Soviet state immediately evoked a bitter political response, a sure sign that his criticisms impinged on significant material interests. The incurable final illness of Lenin, who died in January 1924, deprived Trotsky of his irreplaceable political ally. From its earliest stages, the campaign against Trotsky assumed the form of historical falsifications. His factional opponents within the ruling Politburo began misrepresenting old pre-1917 political disputes between Lenin and Trotsky. The theory of Permanent Revolution, which, as every party leader understood, formed the basis of the Bolshevik seizure of power, was denounced as Trotsky's original heresy. As the struggle against Trotsky and "Trotskyism" developed, every contribution made by Trotsky to the victory of the October Revolution was denied. In 1918 Stalin had written:

> All the work of practical organization of the insurrection was carried out under the direct leadership of the Chairman of the Petrograd Soviet, comrade Trotsky. We can say with certainty that the swift passing of the garrison to the side of the Soviet and the bold execution of the work of the Military Revolutionary Committee the party owes principally and above all to comrade Trotsky.[1]

But only six years later, in November 1924, Stalin claimed that "neither in the Party, nor in the October uprising, did Trotsky play any *special* role, nor could he do so, for he was a relatively new man in our Party in the period of October."[2] Such brazen lies were not the product of mere political rivalries and petty jealousies. Concealed within the lies were the material and political interests of the new bureaucratic elite. The Stalinist regime was compelled to falsify history to mask the contradiction between the publicly-proclaimed revolutionary pretensions and its real defense of material interests, incompatible with socialism. Thus, as Trotsky later wrote, the lies of the Stalinists served "as the fundamental ideological cement of bureaucracy."[3]

Trotsky was expelled from the Communist Party and the Stalinized Communist International in late 1927, and sent into exile in Alma-Ata, near the Soviet-Chinese border. In January 1929 he was expelled from the Soviet Union. Stalin's efforts to suppress Trotsky's immense political influence and eradicate his enduring prestige among the Soviet masses required the systematic falsification of revolutionary history. Within little more than one decade, the early anti-Trotsky falsifications of 1923–1924 metastasized into the monstrous frame-ups of the Moscow Trials, whose nightmarish accusations against Trotsky and all the other principal leaders of the October Revolution

---

[1] Cited by Trotsky in *The Stalin School of Falsification* (London: New Park, 1974), pp. 69-70.

[2] J. V. Stalin, "Trotskyism or Leninism," in *On the Opposition* (Peking: Foreign Language Press, 1974), p. 110.

[3] *Stalin School of Falsification*, p. xiii.

provided Stalin with a pretext for the murder of hundreds of thousands of the finest representatives of the revolutionary socialist intelligentsia and working class within the Soviet Union. No allegation was too hideous or farfetched for the Stalinist regime. Trotsky was denounced as the arch-enemy of the Soviet people, a murderous conspirator who organized acts of sabotage and terror against the USSR. Depending on Stalin's own political alliances, Trotsky was presented as an agent of fascist Germany at one moment, and an agent of British imperialism at another.

In exile in Mexico, Trotsky remained unyielding in his struggle against Stalin's totalitarian regime. Calling in early 1937 for the establishment of an international commission of inquiry into the Moscow Trials, Trotsky explained what was at stake in the refutation of Stalin's lies:

> The Moscow trials are perpetrated under the banner of socialism. We will not concede this banner to the masters of falsehood! If our generation happens to be too weak to establish socialism over the earth, we will hand the spotless banner down to our children. The struggle which is in the offing transcends by far the importance of individuals, factions, and parties. It is the struggle for the future of all mankind. It will be severe. It will be lengthy. Whoever seeks physical comfort and spiritual calm, let him step aside. In time of reaction it is more convenient to lean on the bureaucracy than on the truth. But all those for whom the word *socialism* is not a hollow sound but the content of their moral life—forward! Neither threats, nor persecutions, nor violations can stop us! Be it even over our bleaching bones, the truth will triumph! We will blaze the trail for it. It will conquer! Under all the severe blows of fate, I shall be happy, as in the best days of my youth! Because, my friends, the highest human happiness is not the exploitation of the present but the preparation of the future.[4]

Trotsky was assassinated three years later, in August 1940, by an agent of the Soviet secret police. But the state-sponsored campaign of falsification, in which the Stalinist satellite parties of the Kremlin participated with enthusiasm, continued for decades. Even after Khrushchev denounced Stalin's crimes in 1956, the Soviet Union did not lift its anathema against Trotsky.

---

[4] *I Stake My Life*, Speech by Leon Trotsky, February 9, 1937 (New York: Labor Publications, 1977), p. 26.

Rather, the radicalization of workers and youth in the 1960s, which was accompanied by a renewal of interest in Trotsky's life and ideas, provoked an intensification of the Kremlin bureaucracy's political and ideological campaign against Trotskyism. This continued almost until the dissolution of the Soviet Union. Only in the final convulsive years of Mikhail Gorbachev's tenure in the Kremlin did the depiction of Trotsky as the arch-enemy of socialism break down beneath a flood of newly-published historical documents. His decisive role in the victory of the October Revolution was acknowledged, albeit grudgingly and with many caveats. However, in contrast to every other Bolshevik leader sentenced to death at the Moscow Trials, the Soviet government never officially rehabilitated Trotsky. But, despite the continued, though somewhat subdued, official hostility of the Soviet regime, interest in Trotsky's life and writings grew rapidly within the Soviet Union. For the first time, Soviet historians were able to conduct research within long-buried Soviet archives and begin to write about Trotsky. The most outstanding product of this new situation was the work of the Soviet sociologist and historian, the late Vadim Z. Rogovin (1937–1998), whose seven-volume study of the Trotskyist opposition to Stalinism between 1923 and 1940 ranks as the masterpiece of Soviet/Russian historical literature.

It might have been expected that the dissolution of the Soviet Union in 1991 would finally bring an end to the decades-long era of anti-Trotsky slanders. If nothing else, Trotsky's indictment of Stalinism had been vindicated in virtually every detail. Even the circumstances of the USSR's dissolution, in which the ruling bureaucracy sponsored the reintroduction of capitalism and exploited the process to enrich strategically-placed party functionaries, followed closely the political and economic scenario anticipated by Trotsky more than a half-century earlier in his prophetic *The Revolution Betrayed*.

However, the new political situation worked against an honest evaluation of Trotsky's historical role. Within the "new" Russia, no small number of Stalinist functionaries—who had previously denounced Trotsky as an enemy of the October Revolution—transformed themselves into virulent anti-Communists and denounced Trotsky for having led the October Revolution. Moreover, the dissolution of the USSR released former state and party functionaries from even a ceremonial commitment to Marxian socialism. The Stalinist ideology and political outlook completed its natural evolution into an avowedly right-wing nationalistic Russian chauvinism. Among the elements who assemble in Moscow for demonstrations in which portraits of Stalin are held aloft alongside banners emblazoned with the fascist swastika, hatred of Trotsky and socialist internationalism is the critical link between their political past and present.

The present volume is concerned with a related but different phenomenon: the emergence, outside the former Soviet Union, of a new campaign of anti-Trotsky historical falsification. Within little more than five years, three prominent British historians—Ian Thatcher of Brunel College, Geoffrey Swain of Glasgow University, and Robert Service of St. Antony's College in Oxford—have published biographies of Trotsky. If these works had arrived at their conclusions based on an objective presentation of well-established facts, the argument with Thatcher, Swain and Service would be over interpretation. However, the biographies make a travesty of the historical record. Not one of these works observes the standards of serious scholarship. This appalling and inexcusable deficiency arises from the fundamental purpose of these books: to completely discredit Trotsky as a historical figure.

In a brief aphorism, Chekhov deplores the apologetic attitude that allows lies, especially those that have been long in circulation, to go unchallenged. The correct attitude is one that declares openly, "This is a lie, therefore it must not exist." This attitude is especially necessary when confronted with lies about the most important events of the twentieth century. Even if what was involved here were merely the misguided works of three poorly-trained historians, it would be necessary to protect the historical record against its debasement. But here, in any case, more is involved. The historians are not novices but well-known professionals who occupy prestigious positions in major British institutions. Their biographies have been brought out and promoted by major publishers in Britain and the United States. Their works have received, for the most part, respectful and even enthusiastic reviews. Most of the acclaim is, quite plainly, politically motivated. The identification of Stalinism with Marxism, which is an indispensable element of efforts to discredit socialism and the possibility of an alternative to capitalism, is contradicted by the life and ideas of Leon Trotsky. Therefore, both the facts of his life and the content of his ideas must be falsified. This work of historical defamation requires little originality. The biographers whose books are examined in this volume draw liberally from the old anti-Trotsky lies of the Stalinist bureaucracy. They recirculate the slanders of the past with the knowledge that in the prevailing environment of intellectual reaction, there simply does not exist any standard of scholarship to which they will be held accountable.

A few words about the organization of this book. The first part consists of two lectures, delivered in 2001 and 2008, on the subject of Trotsky's historical significance. The second part consists of an examination, written in 2007, of the Trotsky biographies of Thatcher and Swain. When I completed that work, I hardly imagined that within two years I would again find myself compelled to refute yet another exercise in historical falsification. But that was precisely the unpleasant challenge posed by the publication of Professor Service's biography of Trotsky in the autumn of 2009. My analysis of this work unfolded over the course of several months. The initial review, published on the *World Socialist Web Site* in November 2009, was followed by three lectures. The first lecture was in London in December 2009, the second in Sydney, Australia in February 2010, and the third at St. Catherine's College in Oxford in May 2010. The review and the three lectures comprise the third part of this volume. While there is unavoidably a certain amount of overlapping material in these presentations, the sprawling character of Service's falsifications enabled me to speak and write at length about his biography without excessive repetition.

Leon Trotsky in Coyoacán, Mexcio, 1940

Part I

Two Lectures
on Leon Trotsky's
Life & Ideas

Photograph of Trotsky taken in 1919 by the distinguished
portrait photographer Moisei Nappelbaum. From the David King Collection.

Toward a Reconsideration of Trotsky's Place in the History of the 20th Century[1]

Sixty years ago, on August 21, 1940, Leon Trotsky died from wounds that had been inflicted by an agent of the Soviet secret police one day earlier. The Stalinist regime hoped that this murder would not only end the political activities of its greatest opponent, but also eradicate his place in history. Totalitarian pragmatism proved to be shortsighted in its calculations. The killer ended Trotsky's life. But the ideas and the writings of the great revolutionary lived on. Murdering Trotsky did not bring to an end the political work of the world movement that he had founded. The Fourth International, as it turned out, lived to see the collapse of the Stalinist regime. It follows, of course, that the assassination failed to remove Trotsky from history. As historians study and interpret the twentieth century, the figure of Leon Trotsky looms ever larger. In few other lives were the struggles, aspirations and tragedies of the last century reflected so profoundly and nobly as in that of Trotsky. If we accept as true the observation of Thomas Mann that, "In our time the destiny of man presents itself in political terms," then it can be said that in the sixty years of Trotsky's life, destiny found its most conscious realization. The biography of Leon Trotsky is the concentrated expression of the vicissitudes of the world socialist revolution during the first half of the twentieth century.

Three years before his death, in a discussion with a skeptical American journalist, Trotsky explained that he saw his life not as a series of bewildering and ultimately tragic episodes, but as different stages in the historical

---

[1] Lecture given on January 21, 2001 at an international school held in Sydney by the Socialist Equality Party of Australia.

3

trajectory of the revolutionary movement. His rise to power in 1917 was the product of a revolutionary upsurge of the working class. For six years his power depended on the social and political relations created by that offensive. The decline in Trotsky's personal political fortunes flowed from the ebbing of the revolutionary wave. Trotsky lost power not because he was less skilled a politician than Stalin, but because the social force upon which his power was based—the Russian and international working class—was in political retreat. Indeed, Trotsky's historically conscious approach to politics—so effective during the revolutionary years—placed him at a disadvantage vis-à-vis his unscrupulous adversaries during a period of growing political conservatism. The exhaustion of the Russian working class in the aftermath of the Civil War, the growing political power of the Soviet bureaucracy and the defeats suffered by the European working class—particularly in Germany—were, in the final analysis, the decisive factors in Trotsky's fall from power.

The defeats suffered by the international working class were recorded in Trotsky's personal fate: the political demoralization provoked by the defeat of the Chinese Revolution in 1927 provided Stalin with the opportunity to expel the Left Opposition from the Communist International and to exile Trotsky, first to Alma-Ata and, not long after, outside the borders of the USSR. The victory of Hitler in 1933—made possible by the policies of the Stalinist-led German Communist Party—set into motion a chain of events that led to the Moscow Trials, the political catastrophes of Stalinist Popular Frontism and the final expulsion of Trotsky from Europe to distant Mexico.

It was there in Coyoacán, a suburb of Mexico City, that Trotsky was murdered by a Stalinist agent, Ramon Mercader. Trotsky's death came at the highpoint of the fascist and Stalinist counterrevolution. By 1940 virtually all of Trotsky's old comrades had been liquidated in the Soviet Union. All four children of Trotsky were dead. The two older daughters had died prematurely as a result of the hardships caused by the persecution of their father. The two sons, Sergei and Lev, were murdered by the Stalinist regime. At the time of his death in Paris in February 1938, Lev Sedov was, next to his father, the most important political figure in the Fourth International. Other exceptional figures in the secretariat of the Fourth International—Erwin Wolf and Rudolf Klement—were assassinated in 1937 and 1938.

By 1940 Trotsky believed his own assassination to be all but inevitable. This does not mean that he was resigned to his fate. He did all that he could to delay the blow being prepared by Stalin and his agents in the apparatus of the GPU/NKVD. But he understood that Stalin's actions were determined by the needs of the Soviet bureaucracy. "I live on this earth," he wrote, "not in accordance with the rule, but as an exception to the rule."[2] He predicted that Stalin would take advantage of the eruption of a shooting war in Western Europe during the spring and summer of 1940 to strike a blow. Trotsky was proved correct.

The first major assassination attempt, on the evening of May 24, 1940, took place as the world's attention was focused on Hitler's rout of the French army. The second and successful attempt occurred during the Battle of Britain in the late summer of the same year.

Why was Trotsky, in exile and apparently isolated, so feared? Why did Stalin consider his death necessary? Trotsky himself offered a political explanation. In the autumn of 1939, several weeks after the signing of the Stalin-Hitler Pact (which he had predicted) and the outbreak of World War II, Trotsky called attention to a conversation, reported in a Parisian newspaper, between Hitler and the French ambassador Robert Coulondre. As Hitler boasted that his treaty with Stalin would give him a free hand to defeat Germany's enemies in the west, Coulondre cut the Führer short with a warning: "The real victor (in case of war) will be Trotsky. Have you thought this over?" Hitler voiced agreement with the assessment of the French ambassador, but blamed his adversaries for forcing his hand. Citing this amazing report, Trotsky wrote: "These gentlemen like to give a personal name to the specter of revolution ... Both of them, Coulondre and Hitler, represent the barbarism which advances over Europe. At the same time neither of them doubts that their barbarism will be conquered by socialist revolution."[3]

Nor had Stalin forgotten that the defeats suffered by the Russian armies during the First World War had discredited the tsarist regime and set the masses into motion. Did there not exist a similar danger should war break out again, notwithstanding the agreement with Hitler? As long as Trotsky lived he would remain the great revolutionary alternative to the bureaucratic dictatorship, the embodiment of the program, ideals and spirit of October 1917. That is why Trotsky was assassinated.

But even in death, the fear of Trotsky did not abate. It is hard to think of another figure who, not only in his lifetime but even decades after his death, retains his power to frighten the powers that be. The historical legacy of Trotsky resists any form of assimilation and cooptation. Within 10 years of Marx's

---

[2] *Writings of Leon Trotsky [1939-40]* (New York: Pathfinder Press, 2001), p. 298.

[3] Leon Trotsky, *In Defence of Marxism* (London: New Park Publications, 1971), p. 39.

death, the theoreticians of the German Social Democracy had found ways to adapt his writings to the perspective of social reform. The fate of Lenin was even more terrible—his remains were embalmed and his theoretical legacy was falsified and remade into a bureaucratically sanctioned state religion. This has not proved to be possible with Trotsky. His writings and actions were too precise in their revolutionary implications. Moreover, the political problems that Trotsky analyzed, the socio-political relations that he defined, and even the parties that he so aptly and scathingly characterized, persisted for most of the remainder of the century.

In 1991, Duke University published a 1,000-page study of the International Trotskyist movement by Robert J. Alexander. In his introduction, Alexander observes:

> As of the end of the 1980s the Trotskyists have never come to power in any country. Although International Trotskyism does not enjoy the support of a well-established regime, as did the heirs of Stalinism, the persistence of the movement in a wide variety of countries together with the instability of the political life of most of the world's nations means that the possibility that a Trotskyist party might come to power in the foreseeable future cannot be totally ruled out.[4]

That "well-established regime" disappeared not long after the publication of Alexander's book. The Soviet bureaucracy never rehabilitated Leon Trotsky. History, as has often been noted, is the greatest of all ironists. For decades the Stalinists claimed that Trotsky had sought the destruction of the Soviet Union, that he had entered into conspiracies with the imperialists to dismember the USSR. For these alleged crimes Trotsky had been sentenced to death in absentia by the Soviet regime. But in the end, it was the Soviet bureaucracy itself, as Trotsky had warned so presciently, that liquidated the USSR. And it did so without ever repudiating, openly and forthrightly, the charges leveled against Trotsky and his son, Lev Sedov. Instead, it was easier for Gorbachev and Yeltsin to sign the death warrant of the USSR than to acknowledge the utter falsity of all the charges against Trotsky.

Despite the vast economic and social changes in the last 60 years, we are not so far removed from the problems, issues and themes with which Trotsky dealt. Even after the collapse of the Soviet Union, Trotsky's writings retain, to

---

[4] Robert J. Alexander, *International Trotskyism, 1929-1985: A Documented Analysis of the Movement* (Durham: Duke University Press, 1991), p. 32.

an extraordinary degree, a contemporary character. A study of Trotsky's writings is essential not only for an understanding of the politics of the twentieth century, but also for the purpose of orienting oneself politically in the very complex world of the twenty-first century.

If the greatness of a political figure is measured by the extent and enduring relevance of his legacy, then Trotsky must be placed in the very first rank of twentieth century leaders. Let us for a moment consider the political figures that dominated the world stage in 1940. It is difficult even to mention the names of the totalitarian leaders of that era—Hitler, Mussolini, Stalin, Franco—without uttering an obscenity. They left nothing behind but the memory of their unspeakable crimes. As for the "great" leaders of the imperialist democracies, Roosevelt and Churchill, no one would deny that they were striking personalities and displayed skill within the framework of conventional parliamentary politics. Churchill, more brilliant than the American president, was a talented orator and displayed some skill as a writer. But can one really speak of either man's legacy? Churchill's hymns to the fading British Empire were regarded as anachronistic even by many of his admirers. His writings are of interest as historical documents, but have very limited contemporary relevance. As for Roosevelt, he was the consummate political pragmatist, who reacted with a combination of guile and intuition to the problems of the day. Would anyone suggest seriously that one would find in the speeches and/or books of Churchill and Roosevelt (the latter, by the way, did not write any) analyses and insights that would contribute to an understanding of the political problems that we confront at the outset of the twenty-first century?

Even in their own day, Trotsky towered over his political contemporaries. The influence of all his adversaries was directly bound up with, and dependent upon, their control over the instruments of state power. Separated from that power, they could hardly have commanded world attention. Stalin, separated from the Kremlin and its apparatus of terror, would have been no more than he was before October 1917: "a grey blur."

Trotsky was deprived of all the official instruments of power in 1927. He was, however, never powerless. Trotsky was fond of quoting the famous sentence, spoken by Dr. Stockman, with which Ibsen closes his *Enemy of the People*: "The most powerful man is he who stands alone." The insight of the great Norwegian dramatist was realized in the life of the greatest of all the Russian revolutionists. Trotsky provided a timeless demonstration of the power of ideas and ideals that correspond to and articulate the progressive strivings of humanity.

Trotsky as a Writer

When speaking of Trotsky's ideas, it is difficult to resist the temptation to quote at length from his writings. At the very least, one would certainly succeed in providing one's audience with an exceptional aesthetic experience. Putting aside for a moment one's political sympathies, any reader capable of rendering objective judgment would be hard pressed to deny that Trotsky ranks among the greatest writers of the twentieth century. Some 30 years have passed since I first read a book by Trotsky—his monumental *History of the Russian Revolution*. I am sure that I am not the only person who still recalls the emotional and intellectual impact of his first encounter with Trotsky's prose. Reading Trotsky in translation, I wondered what estimate of his stature as a writer would be made by those able to read his work in the original Russian. Unexpectedly, an opportunity arose for me to satisfy my curiosity. I attended a lecture on Russian literature by an aged specialist who had fled his homeland in the aftermath of the October Revolution. This was not a man from whom one would expect the slightest sympathy for Trotsky. At the conclusion of his lecture, a survey of Russian literature in the twentieth century, I asked him to give his opinion of Trotsky as a writer. I recall vividly both his answer and the thick accent with which it was delivered: "Trotsky," he replied, "was the greatest master of Russian prose after Tolstoy." Many years later, this assessment was echoed in a remark made by a student I met during my first visit to the Soviet Union in 1989. He confessed that reading Trotsky was for him a very difficult experience. Why was this so? "When I read Trotsky," he explained, "I am forced to agree with him—but I don't want to!"

The range of Trotsky's writings—on art, literature and culture, scientific developments, problems of life, and, of course, politics—almost defies comprehension. We lesser mortals, forced to make do with far more modest talents, can only be amazed by Trotsky's literary output. How, one asks oneself, did he do it—before the age of word-processors and spell check? Perhaps part of the answer lies in Trotsky's remarkable ability to speak *ex tempore* almost as beautifully and cogently as he wrote. His dictation, by all accounts, reads better than the polished drafts of even very skilled writers.

A major figure in the literature of the twentieth century, Trotsky owed a great deal to the great Russian masters of the nineteenth century, particularly Turgenev, Tolstoy, Herzen and Belinsky. The same man who wrote proclamations and battle orders in unyielding martial prose that stirred millions could also produce passages of haunting beauty, as, for example, when he recalled one moment during his 1907 escape from Siberian exile:

> The sleigh skidded along smoothly and noiselessly, like a boat on the glassy surface of a pond. In the gathering darkness the forest looked even more gigantic than before. I could not see the road and hardly felt the motion of my sleigh. It was as though the trees were under a spell and came running towards us, bushes slipped away, old tree stumps covered with snow flew past—everything seemed filled with mystery. The only sound was the fast, regular chu-chu-chu-chu of the reindeer's breathing. Thousands of long-forgotten sounds filled my head in the midst of the silence. Suddenly I heard a sharp whistle in the depth of the dark forest. It seemed mysterious and infinitely remote. Yet it was only our Ostyak signaling to his reindeer. Then silence once more, more whistling far away, more trees rushing noiselessly out of darkness into darkness.[5]

Trotsky possessed an exceptional sensitivity to the paradoxes and contradictions of politics. Writing of his own trial after the defeat of the 1905 Revolution, Trotsky describes the contrast between the harsh and threatening official environment of the court building—crowded with "gendarmes with drawn sabers"—and the "infinite quantities of flowers" that had been delivered to the courtroom by admirers and supporters of the revolutionary defendants:

> There were flowers in buttonholes, flowers held in hands and on laps, finally flowers simply lying on the benches. The president of the court did not dare to remove these fragrant intruders. In the end, even gendarmerie officers and officers of the court, totally "demoralized" by the prevailing atmosphere, were handing flowers to the defendants.[6]

It was, I believe, no less a writer than George Bernard Shaw who once observed that when Trotsky used his pen to cut off the head of an opponent, he could not resist the opportunity to pick it up and show, to one and all, that it had no brains. Yet, the power of Trotsky's polemics lay in the brilliance with which he exposed the incongruity between the subjective aims of this

---

[5] Leon Trotsky, *1905* (New York: Vintage, 1971), pp. 459-460.

[6] Ibid., p. 356.

or that politician and the objective development of social contradictions in a revolutionary epoch. Using the necessary unfolding of the historic process as his measuring rod, Trotsky's withering criticisms were not cruel. They were simply on the mark. Thus, of the principal leader of the bourgeois Provisional Government in 1917:

> Kerensky was not a revolutionist; he merely hung around the revolution ... He had no theoretical preparation, no political schooling, no ability to think, no political will. The place of these qualities was occupied by a nimble susceptibility, an inflammable temperament, and that kind of eloquence which operates neither upon mind or will, but upon the nerves.[7]

And of the leader of the Socialist Revolutionaries, Viktor Chernov:

> A well-read rather than educated man, with a considerable but unintegrated learning, Chernov always had at his disposal a boundless assortment of appropriate quotations, which for a long time caught the imagination of the Russian youth without teaching them much. There was only one single question which this many-worded leader could not answer: Whom was he leading and whither? The eclectic formulas of Chernov, ornamented with moralisms and verses, united for a time a most variegated public who at all critical moments pulled in different directions. No wonder Chernov complacently contrasted his methods of forming a party with Lenin's "sectarianism."[8]

And finally, of the once-formidable theoretician of German Social-Democracy:

> Kautsky has a clear and solitary path to salvation: democracy. All that is necessary is that every one should acknowledge it and bind himself to it. The Right Socialists must renounce the sanguinary slaughter with which they have been carrying out the will of the bourgeoisie. The bourgeoisie itself must abandon the idea of using its Noskes and Lieutenant Vogels to defend its privileges to the last breath. Finally, the proletariat must once and for all reject the idea

---

[7] Leon Trotsky, *History of the Russian Revolution* (London: Pluto Press, 1977), p. 201.

[8] Ibid., p. 247.

of overthrowing the bourgeoisie by means other than those laid down in the Constitution. If the conditions enumerated are observed, the social revolution will painlessly melt into democracy. In order to succeed it is sufficient, as we see, for our stormy history to draw a nightcap over its head, and take a pinch of wisdom out of Kautsky's snuffbox.[9]

One could without difficulty spend an entire day quoting passages in which Trotsky's literary genius finds brilliant expression. But this genius was not simply, nor primarily, a matter of style. There is a deeper and more profound element in Trotsky's literary work that raises him above any other political thinker of his time. To the extent that history can find conscious articulation in the course of its own immediate unfolding, that process is manifested in the writings of Leon Trotsky. In general, there is nothing more ephemeral than political commentary. The half-life of even a well-written newspaper column is generally no longer than the time it takes to drink a cup of coffee—it passes straight from the breakfast table to the wastepaper basket.

That is not the case with the writings of Trotsky—and I am speaking not of his major works, but even commentary he produced for newspapers. The writings and, I must add, speeches of Leon Trotsky, appear at times to represent history's first attempt to explain as best as it can what it is doing and attempting. The purpose of Trotsky's greatest political writings—to locate the latest events in the world historical trajectory of socialist revolution—was reflected in the titles he chose: "Through What Stage are We Passing?," "Where is Britain Going?," "Whither France?," "Towards Capitalism or Socialism?" Lunacharsky once said of Trotsky: He is always aware of his position in history. This was Trotsky's strength—the source of his political resistance against opportunism and all manner of pressures. Trotsky conceived of Marxism as the "science of perspective."

A consequence of the destruction of revolutionary cadre by Stalinism and the consequent erosion of Marxism as a theoretical weapon of the emancipatory struggle of the working class has been the celebration of all sorts of people unconnected with this struggle as great Marxists: Marxist economists, Marxist philosophers, Marxist aestheticists, etc. Yet, when they have attempted to apply their supposed mastery of the dialectic to political analysis of the events of their times, they have proven to be incompetent. Trotsky was

[9] Leon Trotsky, *Terrorism and Communism* (Ann Arbor: University of Michigan Press, 1969), p. 28.

the last great representative of a school of Marxist thought—let us call it the classical school—whose mastery of the dialectic revealed itself above all in a capacity to assess a political situation, to advance a political prognosis and to elaborate a strategic orientation.

Reassessing Trotsky

Among the most important tasks of the Fourth International throughout its history has been the defense of Trotsky's historical role against the calumny of the Stalinists. This task involved the defense not only of an individual, but also of the entire programmatic heritage of international Marxism and the October Revolution. In defending Trotsky, the Fourth International has upheld historical truth against the falsification and betrayal of the principles upon which the Bolshevik Revolution was based.

And yet, notwithstanding its intransigent defense of Leon Trotsky, did the Fourth International do full justice to the political and historical legacy of the "Old Man"? There is good reason to believe, now that the century in which Trotsky lived is behind us, that a richer appreciation of his political legacy and historical stature is possible. Let us begin this task by subjecting to critical re-examination a well-known passage in which Trotsky assessed his own contribution to the success of the October Revolution of 1917.

In an entry into his diary dated March 25, 1935, Trotsky wrote:

> Had I not been present in 1917 in Petersburg, the October Revolution would still have taken place—*on the condition that Lenin was present and in command.* If neither Lenin nor I had been present in Petersburg, there would have been no October Revolution: the leadership of the Bolshevik Party would have prevented it from occurring—of this I have not the slightest doubt! If Lenin had not been in Petersburg, I doubt whether I could have managed to overcome the resistance of the Bolshevik leaders. The struggle with "Trotskyism" (i.e., with the proletarian revolution) would have commenced in May, 1917, and the outcome of the revolution would have been in question. But I repeat, granted the presence of Lenin the October Revolution would have been victorious anyway. The same could by and large be said of the Civil War, although in its first period, especially at the time of the fall of Simbirsk and Kazan, Lenin wavered and was beset by doubts.

But this was undoubtedly a passing mood which he probably never even admitted to anyone but me... Thus I cannot speak of the "indispensability" of my work, even about the period from 1917 to 1921.[10]

Is this assessment accurate? In this passage, Trotsky is referring principally to the political struggle within the Bolshevik Party. Quite correctly, he takes as his point of departure the crucial significance of the reorientation of the Bolshevik Party in April 1917. Lenin's greatest achievement in 1917, upon which the success of the Revolution depended, was overcoming the resistance of Old Bolshevik leaders—particularly Kamenev and Stalin—to a strategic change in Bolshevik policy.

And yet, the importance of this struggle within the Bolshevik Party serves to underscore the far-reaching implications of the earlier disputes within the Russian Social Democratic Labour Party over questions of political perspective. Even if one accepts that Lenin played the critical role in overcoming resistance within the Bolshevik Party to adopting an orientation toward the seizure of power and the establishment of a proletarian dictatorship, the fact is that Lenin was waging a struggle against those who adhered to the political line that he himself had upheld for many years in opposition to the perspective of Leon Trotsky.

When Lenin returned to Russia in April 1917 and repudiated the perspective of the "democratic dictatorship of the proletariat and the peasantry," it was widely understood that he was adopting—even if he failed to acknowledge this openly—the political line with which Trotsky had been associated for more than a decade—that of Permanent Revolution.

The Theory of Permanent Revolution

I will review briefly the basic issues that confronted the Russian revolutionary movement in the final decades of the tsarist regime. In its efforts to plot the trajectory of Russian socio-political development, Russian socialist thought advanced three possible and conflicting variants. Plekhanov, the father of Russian Marxism, conceived of Russian social development in terms of a formal logical progression, in which historical stages of development were determined by a given level of economic development. As feudalism was replaced by capitalism, the latter in turn, when all the required conditions of

---

[10] Leon Trotsky, *Trotsky's Diary in Exile, 1935* (New York: Atheneum, 1963), pp. 46-47.

economic development had been attained, would give way to socialism. The theoretical model with which Plekhanov worked assumed that Russian development would follow the historical pattern of Western Europe's bourgeois-democratic evolution. There existed no possibility that Russia might move in a socialist direction before the more advanced countries to its west. At the turn of the twentieth century, Plekhanov maintained, Russia still had before it the task of achieving its bourgeois democratic revolution—by which he meant the overthrow of the tsarist regime and the creation of the political and economic preconditions for a future, distant, social revolution. In all probability, Russia had before it many decades of bourgeois democratic parliamentary development before its economic and social structure could sustain a socialist transformation. This formal conception of Russia's development constituted the accepted wisdom that prevailed among broad layers of the Russian social democratic movement during the first years of the twentieth century. However, there was an unresolved contradiction in Plekhanov's position, which reflected the peculiar character of Russia's social development. As early as 1889, Plekhanov had foreseen that the Russian working class would play the leading role in the impending revolution. He declared at the founding congress of the Second International that the Russian revolution could succeed only as a workers' revolution. But how was this insight to be reconciled with a perspective that insisted that political power, in the aftermath of the revolution, would be wielded by the Russian bourgeoisie? Plekhanov was never able to provide a convincing answer to this question.

The events of 1905—that is, the eruption of the first Russian Revolution—generated serious questions about the viability of Plekhanov's theoretical model. The most significant aspect of the Russian Revolution was the dominant political role played by the proletariat in the struggle against tsarism. Against the background of general strikes and insurrection, the maneuverings of the political leaders of the Russian bourgeoisie appeared petty and treacherous. No Robespierre or Danton was to be found among the bourgeoisie. The Cadet Party (Constitutional Democrats) bore no resemblance to the Jacobins.

Lenin's analysis went further and deeper than Plekhanov's. The former accepted that the Russian Revolution was of a bourgeois-democratic character. But this definition did not adequately exhaust the problem of the relation of class forces and balance of power in the revolution. Lenin insisted that the task of the working class was to strive, through its independent organization and efforts, for the most expansive and radical development of the bourgeois democratic revolution—that is, for an utterly uncompromising struggle to demolish all economic, political and social vestiges of tsarist feudalism; and thereby to create the most favorable conditions for the establishment of a genuinely progressive constitutional-democratic framework for the flowering of the Russian workers' movement. For Lenin, at the very heart of this democratic revolution was the resolution of the "agrarian question"—by which he meant the destruction of all the economic and juridical remnants of feudalism. The vast landholdings of the nobility constituted an immense barrier to the democratization of Russian life, as well as to the development of a modern capitalist economy.

Lenin's conception of the bourgeois revolution—in contrast to that of Plekhanov—was not limited by formalistic political prejudices. He approached the bourgeois-democratic revolution from within, so to speak. Rather than beginning with a formal political schema—that a parliamentary democracy would be the unavoidable outcome of the bourgeois revolution—Lenin sought to deduce the political form from the essential and internal social content of the revolution.

Recognizing the immense social tasks implicit in Russia's impending democratic revolution, Lenin—in contrast to Plekhanov—insisted that their achievement was not possible under the political leadership of the Russian bourgeoisie. The triumph of the bourgeois democratic revolution in Russia was possible only if the working class waged the struggle for democracy independently of and, in fact, in opposition to the bourgeoisie. But due to its numerical weakness, the mass basis of the democratic revolution could not be provided by the working class alone. The Russian proletariat, by advancing an uncompromisingly radical democratic resolution of the agrarian issues, had to mobilize behind it the multi-millioned Russian peasantry.

What then, would be the state form of the regime arising from this revolutionary alliance of the two great popular classes? Lenin proposed that the new regime would be a "democratic dictatorship of the proletariat and peasantry." In effect, the two classes would share state power and jointly preside over the fullest possible realization of the democratic revolution. Lenin offered no specifics as to the precise nature of the power-sharing arrangements that would prevail in such a regime, nor did he define or describe the state forms through which this two-class dictatorship would be exercised.

Notwithstanding the political radicalism of the democratic dictatorship, Lenin insisted that its aim was not the economic reorganization of society along socialist lines. Rather, the revolution would of necessity remain, in terms of its economic program, capitalist. Indeed, even in his advocacy of a radical settlement of the land question, Lenin stressed that the nationalization of land—directed against the Russian latifundia—was a bourgeois-democratic, rather than socialist measure.

In his polemics, Lenin was unwavering on this critical point. He wrote in 1905:

> Marxists are absolutely convinced of the bourgeois character of the Russian revolution. What does this mean? This means that those democratic transformations ... which have become indispensable for Russia do not, in and of themselves, signify the undermining of capitalism, the undermining of bourgeois rule, but on the contrary they clear the soil, for the first time and in a real way, for a broad and swift, for a European and not an Asiatic, development of capitalism. They make possible for the first time the rule of the bourgeoisie as a class.[11]

The position of Trotsky differed radically from that of the Mensheviks and Lenin. Notwithstanding their different conclusions, both Plekhanov and Lenin based their perspectives on an estimate of the given level of Russian economic development and the existing relations of social forces within the country. But Trotsky's real point of departure was not the existing economic level of Russia or its internal relation of class forces, but rather the *world-historical* context within which Russia's belated democratic revolution was destined to unfold.

Trotsky traced the historical trajectory of the bourgeois revolution, from its classical manifestation in the eighteenth century, through the vicissitudes of the nineteenth century and finally, in the modern context of 1905. He explained how the change in historical conditions—especially the development of world economy and the emergence of the international working class—had altered the social and political dynamics of the bourgeois democratic revolution. Traditional political equations based on the conditions that prevailed in the middle of the nineteenth century were of little value in the new situation.

Trotsky detected the political limitation of Lenin's formula. It was politically unrealistic: it evaded the problem of state power. Trotsky did not accept that the Russian proletariat would limit itself to measures of a formally democratic character. The reality of class relations would compel the working

---

[11] Cited in: *Writings of Leon Trotsky [1939-40]*, p. 65.

class to exercise its political dictatorship against the economic interests of the bourgeoisie. In other words, the struggle of the working class would of necessity assume a socialist character. But how was this possible, given the backwardness of Russia, which, considering the limitations of its own economic development, was clearly not ready for socialism?

Looking at the Russian Revolution from within, there did not seem to be any solution to this problem. But examining the Russian Revolution from the vantage point of both world history and the international development of the capitalist economy, an unexpected solution presented itself. As early as June 1905, Trotsky noted that "capitalism has converted the whole world into a single economic and political organism." Trotsky grasped the implications of this change in the structure of world economy:

> This immediately gives the events now unfolding an international character, and opens up a wide horizon. The political emancipation of Russia led by the working class will raise that class to a height as yet unknown in history, will transfer to it colossal power and resources, and will make it the initiator of the liquidation of world capitalism, for which history has created all the objective conditions.[12]

Trotsky's approach was a critical theoretical breakthrough. It shifted the analytical perspective from which revolutionary processes were viewed. Prior to 1905, the development of revolutions was seen as a progression of national events, whose outcome was determined by the logic of its internal socio-economic structure and relations. Trotsky proposed another approach: to understand revolution in the modern epoch as essentially a world-historic process of social transition from class society, which is rooted politically in nation-states, to a classless society developing on the basis of a globally-integrated economy and internationally-unified mankind.

Trotsky developed this conception of the revolutionary process at the point at which the socialist movement was being confronted with a flood of socio-economic and political data that could not be adequately processed within the existing theoretical framework. The sheer complexity of the modern world economy defied the old formal definitions. The impact of world economic development influenced, to a heretofore unprecedented extent, the contours of each national economy. Within even backward economies there could be found—as a result of international foreign investment—certain

---

[12] Leon Trotsky, *Permanent Revolution* (London: New Park, 1971), p. 240.

highly advanced features. There existed feudalist or semi-feudalist regimes, whose political structures were encrusted with the remnants of the Middle Ages, that presided over a capitalist economy in which heavy industry played a major role. Nor was it unusual to find in countries with a belated capitalist development a bourgeoisie that showed less interest in the success of "its" democratic revolution than did the indigenous working class. Such anomalies could not be reconciled with formal strategical precepts whose calculations assumed the existence of social phenomena less riven by internal contradictions.

Trotsky's great achievement consisted in elaborating a theoretical structure that was equal to modern social, economic and political complexities. There was nothing utopian in Trotsky's approach. It represented, rather, a profound insight into the impact of world economy on social and political life. A realistic approach to politics and the elaboration of effective revolutionary strategy was possible only to the extent that socialist parties took as their objective starting point the primacy of the international over the national. This did not simply mean the promotion of international proletarian solidarity. Without understanding its essential objective foundation in world economy, and without making the reality of world economy the basis of strategical thought, proletarian internationalism would remain a utopian ideal, essentially unrelated to the program and practice of nationally-based socialist parties.

Proceeding from the analysis of the historical development of world capitalism and the objective dependence of Russia on the international economic and political environment, Trotsky foresaw the socialist development of Russia's revolution. The Russian working class would be compelled to take power and adopt measures of a socialist character. Yet in proceeding along socialist lines, the working class in Russia would inevitably come up against the limitations of the national environment. How would it find a way out of its dilemma? By linking its fate to the European and world revolution of which its own struggle was, in the final analysis, a manifestation.

Trotsky's theory of Permanent Revolution made possible a realistic conception of world revolution. The age of national revolutions had come to an end—or, to put it more precisely, national revolutions could only be understood within the framework of the international socialist revolution.

Trotsky and the Bolsheviks

When one considers the implications of Trotsky's analysis, one can better appreciate his differences with both the Bolsheviks and the Mensheviks. It is not my intention here to minimize in any way the significance of Lenin's great achievement, which was to understand more profoundly than anyone else the political significance of the struggle against political opportunism in the revolutionary movement and to extend that struggle to every level of party work and organization. And yet, as crucial and critical as questions of revolutionary organization are, the experience of the twentieth century has taught the working class, or should teach the working class, that even the firmest organization, unless directed by a correct revolutionary perspective, can and will become, in the final analysis, an obstacle to revolution.

For Trotsky, what determined his attitude to all tendencies within the Russian social democratic labor movement was their perspective and program. To what extent, Trotsky asked, was their political program based on a correct assessment of the world forces that would determine the evolution and fate of the Russian Revolution? Trotsky, from this standpoint, was justifiably critical of the program and orientation of the Bolshevik Party. Let me read from an article written in 1909 in which he surveyed the different positions held by the varying factions in the Russian Social Democratic Labor Party. Trotsky wrote:

> Lenin believes that the contradictions between the proletariat's class interests and objective conditions will be resolved by the proletariat imposing a political limitation upon itself, and that this self-limitation will be the result of the proletariat's theoretical awareness that the revolution in which it is playing a leading role is a bourgeois revolution. Lenin transfers the objective contradiction into the proletariat's consciousness and resolves it by means of a class asceticism which is rooted, not in religious faith, but in a "scientific" schema. It is enough to see this intellectual construct clearly, to realize how hopelessly idealistic it is.
>
> ... The snag is that the Bolsheviks visualize the class struggle of the proletariat only until the moment of the revolution's triumph, after which they see it as temporarily dissolved in the "democratic" coalition, reappearing in its pure form—this time as a direct struggle for socialism—only after the definitive establishment of a republican system. Whereas the Mensheviks, proceeding from the abstract notion that "our revolution is a bourgeois revolution," arrive at the idea that the proletariat must adapt all its tactics to the behavior of the liberal bourgeoisie in order to ensure the

transfer of state power to that bourgeoisie, the Bolsheviks proceed from an equally abstract notion—'democratic dictatorship, not socialist dictatorship'—and arrive at the idea of a proletariat in possession of state power imposing a bourgeois-democratic limitation upon itself. It is true that the difference between them in this matter is very considerable: while the anti-revolutionary aspects of Menshevism have already become fully apparent, those of Bolshevism are likely to become a serious threat only in the event of victory.[13]

This was a prescient insight into what was actually to occur in the Russian Revolution. Once the tsarist regime was overthrown, the limitations of Lenin's perspective of the democratic dictatorship became immediately clear. Trotsky went on to say that the Russian working class would be forced to take power and "will be confronted with the objective problems of socialism, but the solution of these problems will, at a certain stage, be prevented by the country's economic backwardness. There is no way out from this contradiction from the framework of a national revolution." So Trotsky recognized that the limitations of Lenin's perspective were not merely in its political calculations, but that those political calculations proceeded from a national, rather than an international, appreciation of the framework in which the Russian Revolution would unfold.

Trotsky continued:

> The workers' government will from the start be faced with the task of uniting its forces with those of the socialist proletariat of Western Europe. Only in this way will its temporary revolutionary hegemony become the prologue to a socialist dictatorship. Thus permanent revolution will become, for the Russian proletariat, a matter of class self-preservation. If the workers' party cannot show sufficient initiative for aggressive revolutionary tactics, if it limits itself to the frugal diet of a dictatorship that is merely national and merely democratic, the united reactionary forces of Europe will waste no time in making it clear that a working class, if it happens to be in power, must throw the whole of its strength into the struggle for a socialist revolution.[14]

---

[13] Leon Trotsky, "Our Differences," in: *1905* (New York: Random House, 1971), pp. 314-317.

[14] Ibid., pp. 317-318.

This was the central question. The political evaluation of the form of state power flowed from the differing appraisals of the significance of the international as the determining factor in the political outcome of the revolutionary movement. The following point must be made in assessing the development of the Bolshevik Party. Every program reflects the influence and interests of social forces. In countries with a belated bourgeois development, in which the bourgeoisie is incapable of defending consistently the national and democratic tasks of the revolution, elements of those tasks become part of the program of the working class. The working class must take up those democratic and national demands that retain a progressive significance. There have been many occasions in the course of the twentieth century when the socialist movement has been compelled to advance democratic and national responsibilities, and draw into its own ranks elements for whom those tasks are of primary significance—and for whom the socialistic and internationalist aspirations of the working class are less important. The intermingling of national-democratic and socialist tendencies significantly influenced the development of the Bolshevik Party. Lenin certainly represented, within the framework of the Bolshevik Party, the most consistent opposition to such nationalist and petty bourgeois democratic prejudices. He was aware of their presence and could not ignore them.

Lenin wrote in December 1914 after the outbreak of the First World War:

> Is a sense of national pride alien to us, Great-Russian class conscious proletarians? Certainly not! We love our language and our country, and we are doing our very utmost to raise *her* toiling masses (i.e., nine-tenths of *her* population) to the level of a democratic and socialist consciousness. To us it is most painful to see and feel the outrages, the oppression and the humiliation our fair country suffers at the hands of the tsar's butchers, the nobles and the capitalists. We take pride in the resistance to these outrages put up from our midst, from the Great-Russians; in *that* midst having produced Radishchev, the Decembrists and the revolutionary commoners of the seventies; in the Great-Russian working class having created, in 1905, a mighty revolutionary party of the masses; and the Great-Russian peasantry having begun to turn towards democracy and set about overthrowing the clergy and the landed proprietors ...
>
> ... We are full of national pride because the Great-Russian nation,

too, has created a revolutionary class, because it, *too*, has proved capable of providing mankind with great models of the struggle for freedom and socialism, and not only with great pogroms, rows of gallows, dungeons, great famines and great servility to priests, tsars, landowners and capitalists.[15]

Lenin was the author of these lines. It would be unjust to read this article as a political concession by Lenin to Great Russian chauvinism. His entire biography testifies to his unyielding opposition to Great Russian nationalism. Yet the article, an attempt by Lenin to exert a revolutionary influence on these deep-rooted nationalist sentiments among the working masses and to utilize these sentiments for revolutionary ends, reflected the sensitivity he felt towards the strong nationalist sentiments not only in the working class as a whole, but also within his own party. There is a fine line between utilizing nationalist sentiments for revolutionary purposes and adapting revolutionary aims to nationalism. There is not an exact correspondence between the message that an author intends to convey and how the message is interpreted. There is, all but inevitably, a degradation in the political quality of the message as it makes its way across an ever broader audience. What Lenin had probably intended to be a tribute to the revolutionary traditions of the Great Russian working class might well have been interpreted by the more backward sections of party workers as an elevation of the revolutionary capacities of Great Russians. Trotsky was justifiably critical of Lenin's formulation. As he wrote in 1915:

> To approach the prospects of a social revolution within national boundaries is to fall victim to the same national narrowness which constitutes the substance of social-patriotism. ... In general, it should not be forgotten that in social-patriotism there is, alongside of the most vulgar reformism, a national revolutionary Messianism which deems that its own national state, whether because of its industrial level or because of its "democratic" form and revolutionary conquests, is called upon to lead humanity towards socialism or towards "democracy". If the victorious revolution were really conceivable within the boundaries of a single more developed nation, this Messianism, together with the programme of national defence would have some relative historical justification. But as a matter of fact this is inconceivable.

---

[15] V. I. Lenin, *Collected Works*, Volume 21 (Moscow: Progress Publishers, 1964), pp. 103-104.

To fight for the preservation of a national basis of revolution by such methods as undermine the international ties of the proletariat, actually means to undermine the revolution itself, which can begin on a national basis but which cannot be completed on that basis under the present economic, military, and political interdependence of the European states, which was never before revealed so forcefully as during the present war.[16]

It would be worthwhile to study the conditions under which Lenin re-evaluated his political perspective. His study of world economy under the impact of the First World War gave him a deeper insight into the dynamics of the Russian Revolution and led him to adopt, in essence, the perspective that had been associated with Trotsky for so many years.

When Lenin read his *April Theses* in 1917, it was understood by those in the hall that he was arguing along the lines of Trotsky. The charge of "Trotskyism" was immediately raised and, in this very fact, we can understand the extent of Trotsky's intellectual contribution to the success of the revolution that year. Trotsky had already provided an intellectual and political framework within which the debate inside the Bolshevik Party could go forward. It did not come as a bolt from the blue. If Lenin's personality and his unchallenged stature within the Bolshevik Party made possible a relatively rapid victory of the new perspective, Trotsky's championing of the perspective of the theory of Permanent Revolution facilitated Lenin's fight within the Bolshevik Party, particularly under conditions where the masses in Russia in 1917 were moving to the left.

In a certain sense, what occurred in the spring, summer and autumn of 1917 was a form of what had occurred 12 years before. I would like to read an interesting passage from the book called *The Origins of Bolshevism* by the Menshevik Theodore Dan. He makes the following observation about 1905:

This background of the "days of liberty" [the climax of the 1905 revolution] was such, as we have seen, that practically speaking both Mensheviks and Bolsheviks were pushed towards "Trotskyism". For a short time "Trotskyism" (which at that time, to be sure, still lacked a name), for the first and last time in the history of the Russian Social-Democracy, became its unifying platform.[17]

---

[16] Cited in: Leon Trotsky, *The Third International After Lenin* (London: New Park Publications, 1974), p. 53.

[17] Theodore Dan, *The Origins of Bolshevism* (New York: Schocken Books, 1970), p. 345.

That is to say that in 1905, under conditions of the most explosive movement of the Russian working class to the left, the perspective of Trotsky acquired immense prestige and stature. This process was repeated in 1917. The triumph of 1917 was a vindication of Trotsky's perspective of Permanent Revolution. But the beginning of the political reaction in 1922–1923 against the October Revolution and the resurgence of Russian nationalism was also expressed politically in the resurfacing of the old anti-Trotskyist tendencies within the Bolshevik Party. It is not possible to treat the tendencies of that time as if they were unrelated to the political divisions that had existed in 1917 within the Bolshevik Party. This does not mean that they were precisely the same.

The growth of Bolshevism in 1917 was based on an explosive radicalization of the working class in the major urban centers. The social forces which underlay the growth of the party in 1922 and 1923, and which were the source of great concern to Lenin, were to a great extent non-proletarian elements, specifically from the lower middle classes in the urban areas for whom the revolution had opened up innumerable career opportunities, not to mention from remnants of the old tsarist bureaucracy. For such elements, the Russian Revolution was seen, more or less, as a national rather than international event. As early as 1922, Lenin began to warn of the growth of a type of national Bolshevism, and he became increasingly strident in his denunciation of chauvinistic tendencies. In late 1922 and early 1923 those warnings were directed specifically against Stalin, who had come to personify in Lenin's mind an odious social type, the "Great Russian chauvinist bully."

The struggle against Trotskyism was, in essence, a reemergence of the political opposition to the theory of Permanent Revolution within the party. What prevented Trotsky from stating this explicitly? I think the answer is to be found in the extraordinarily difficult circumstances created by Lenin's final illness and his death. Trotsky found it virtually impossible to speak as frankly as I suspect he would have liked about the differences that had previously separated him from Lenin. It was left to Adolf Joffe to write, in the famous letter composed hours before committing suicide in November 1927 to protest Trotsky's expulsion from the Communist Party, that he had often heard Lenin state that on basic questions of perspective it had been Trotsky, rather than himself, who had been correct, including on the question of Permanent Revolution.

Trotsky was hardly unaware of the nationalist subtext of the political tensions developing within the party leadership. Near the end of his life, Trotsky stated explicitly that the struggle against Trotskyism in the Soviet Union was rooted in the pre-1917 differences within the Bolshevik Party. He wrote in 1939: "It may be said that the whole of Stalinism, taken on the theoretical plane, grew out of the criticism of the theory of permanent revolution as it was formulated in 1905."[18]

Trotsky will be remembered and will continue to occupy a vast place in the consciousness of the revolutionary movement as the theoretician of world revolution. Of course, he lived longer than Lenin and was faced with new problems. But there is a basic continuity in all of Trotsky's works from 1905 until his death in 1940. The struggle for the perspective of world revolution is the decisive and essential theme of all his work. All of Lenin is contained in the Russian Revolution. But for Trotsky, it was an episode in his life—a very great episode to be sure, but only an episode in the greater drama of world socialist revolution.

A review of Trotsky's work in the aftermath of his fall from political power is beyond the scope of a single lecture. But in bringing this lecture to a conclusion, I wish to place emphasis on one critical element of Trotsky's theoretical legacy—that is, his role as the last great representative of classical Marxism.

In speaking of classical Marxism, we have two fundamental conceptions in mind: first, that the basic revolutionary force in society is the working class; and second, that the fundamental task of Marxists is to work indefatigably, theoretically and practically, to establish its political independence. The socialist revolution is the end product of this sustained and uncompromising work. The political independence of the working class is not achieved through clever tactics, but in the most fundamental sense, through education—first and foremost, of its political vanguard. There exist no shortcuts. As Trotsky frequently warned, the greatest enemy of revolutionary strategy is impatience.

The twentieth century witnessed the greatest victories and the most tragic defeats of the working class. The lessons of the past 100 years must be assimilated, and it is only our movement that has begun that task. In history, nothing is wasted and forgotten. The next great upsurge of the international working class—and the international scope of that upsurge is guaranteed by the global integration of capitalist production—will witness the intellectual resurgence of Trotskyism, i.e., classical Marxism.

---

[18] *Writings of Leon Trotsky [1939-1940]*, p. 64.

Conté drawing of Trotsky made in 1923 by Sergei Pichugin. Following Trotsky's down-fall, the artist glued a card over the drawing, which was discovered seventy-five years later by his family, in the late 1990s. From the David King Collection.

Leon Trotsky, Soviet Historiography & the Fate of Classical Marxism[1]

Forty-five years have passed since the publication of the last volume of Isaac Deutscher's extraordinary biographical triptych of Leon Trotsky, *The Prophet Armed, Unarmed* and *Outcast*. It would be difficult to think of another biography that had so profound and far-reaching intellectual and political influence. When Deutscher began his project in the early 1950s, Trotsky had been dead for more than a decade. But his murderer, Joseph Stalin, remained very much alive in the Kremlin—the object of a worldwide campaign of public veneration, as disgusting as it was absurd, in which virtually every Communist party participated. Deutscher compared his task as a biographer to that of Thomas Carlyle, who had complained that his study of Cromwell had required that he "drag out the Lord Protector from under a mountain of dead dogs, a huge load of calumny and oblivion."[2]

By the time Deutscher completed his third volume in 1963, the political environment had changed dramatically. Stalin died in March 1953. In February 1956, at the 20th Congress of the CPSU, Khrushchev delivered his so-called "secret speech." He all but denounced Stalin as a political criminal, responsible for the imprisonment, torture and murder of countless thousands of Old Bolsheviks and loyal communists during the purges of the 1930s. Of course, Khrushchev hardly acknowledged the full extent of Stalin's crimes. The indictment was as evasive as it was incomplete. But the impact of

---

[1] Lecture given at the National Convention of the American Association for the Advancement of Slavic Studies (AAASS) in Philadelphia on November 21, 2008.

[2] Isaac Deutscher, *The Prophet Unarmed* (London: Verso, 2003), p. vii.

Khrushchev's speech was politically devastating. The unstated but inescapable conclusion that flowed from the exposure of Stalin's crimes was that the Moscow Trials of 1936-1938 were a frame-up and that the Old Bolshevik defendants had been murdered. The thought that "Trotsky was right" haunted countless leaders and members of the CPSU and associated Stalinist parties throughout the world. And if Trotsky was right about the trials, what else had he been right about?

Amidst the turmoil that erupted inside the Stalinist parties—initiating a process of internal decomposition that led, within 30 years, to their political disintegration—Deutscher's trilogy assumed immense political significance. The discrediting of Stalin was, to a great extent, a vindication of Trotsky. In the climate of the time, the heroic image of Trotsky evoked by the metaphoric title of Deutscher's biography did not seem at all hyperbolic. Notwithstanding its significant limitations—especially in the final volume, in which Deutscher pursued rather obtrusively his own past political disputes with Trotsky—the three volumes introduced the heroic personality of the great revolutionary to a new generation of politically radicalized intellectuals and youth. And what a personality it was! What other figure in modern history exhibited such a vast repertoire of intellectual, political, literary, and martial skills? Deutscher succeeded in imparting to his narrative an immense dramatic tension. But the drama of Trotsky's life did not have to be invented, nor did it require artistic exaggeration. His life was, after all, the concentrated expression of the vast historical drama and tragedy of the Russian Revolution.

By the 1960s, the Soviet Union had lost its claim on the imagination of intellectuals and students. Deutscher's biography served as an introduction to the old disputes of the 1920s, in which the work of Trotsky had loomed so large. So many of Deutscher's readers then made their way to a study of Trotsky's writings, which gradually became more widely available.

Throughout the 1960s and into the 1970s, interest in the life and work of Trotsky was intense. In 1978, on the eve of Trotsky's centenary, Professor Baruch Knei-Paz published *The Social and Political Thought of Leon Trotsky*. Knei-Paz's approach to his subject, however critical, reflected the predominant sentiment among Soviet scholars that Trotsky was an important political and *intellectual* presence. Knei-Paz noted that Trotsky "is, even now, and perhaps not unjustly, considered to be the quintessential revolutionary in an age which has not lacked in revolutionary figures." He described Trotsky's achievements "in the realm of theory and ideas" as "prodigious." Trotsky, he wrote, "was among the first to analyse the emergence, in the twentieth century, of social change in backward societies, and among the first, as well, to attempt to explain the political consequences which would almost invariably grow out of such change."[3] As a Marxist and an adherent of Trotsky's political conceptions, I respectfully disagree with many elements of Professor Knei-Paz's analysis and interpretation. But his meticulous scholarship certainly demonstrated that Trotsky's life provides fertile ground for serious research. Though Trotsky was a man of action *par excellence*, he was also an outstanding thinker. Knei-Paz estimated that Trotsky's writings, if brought together in a single edition, would "easily fill ... sixty to seventy thick volumes—without including the vast material contained in the Trotsky Archives at Harvard University."[4]

Professor Knei-Paz set himself definite limits—a necessity for any scholar attempting to tackle a subject as vast and complex as Trotsky's life and times. He explained that his work was "a study of Trotsky's own thought, not that of his opponents or followers, nor of the ideological and political movement which came to be identified with his name."[5] Even with this disciplined focus, Professor Knei-Paz required 598 pages of the Clarendon Press's compact typography to complete his assignment. But he still left the scholarly community with not only a great deal to argue about, but also a great deal to do.

And yet, Knei-Paz's book turned out to be almost the last really significant academic contribution to the field of Trotsky studies. That this would be the case would have been hard to foresee in 1978. Knei-Paz's book was, after all, published on the very eve of an event that should have encouraged Trotsky scholarship—the opening on January 2, 1980 of the previously closed section of the Trotsky Archive at the Houghton Library at Harvard University. Until then, Isaac Deutscher, with the special permission of Trotsky's widow Natalia Sedova, had been the only writer to gain access to this vast collection of the revolutionary's private papers. But as it turned out, the opening of this archive had only marginal impact on American and British researchers in the field of Soviet history. During the past 28 years, very little material from this vast archive has found its way into published academic work.

This drying up of Trotsky scholarship after 1978 is a curious phenomenon. After all, the deepening crisis of the Soviet Union and Eastern Europe throughout the 1980s certainly justified a more intensive review of the work

---

[3] Baruch Knei-Paz, *The Social and Political Thought of Leon Trotsky* (Oxford: Oxford University Press, 1978), p. viii.

[4] Ibid., p. xi.

[5] Ibid., p. xiii.

of Trotsky, who had been the foremost critic of Stalin and Stalinism, and who had foreseen the demise of the USSR. As a matter of fact, Trotsky's depiction, in *The Revolution Betrayed* (published in 1936), of the process of capitalist restoration anticipated, with astonishing accuracy, the economic transformation of the former USSR under the auspices of Yeltsin in the early 1990s. However, in most English-language works dealing with the history, economics, politics and social structure of the Soviet Union, Trotsky appears as a minor, and even marginal figure. The only notable and original contribution to Trotsky studies that appeared in the 1980s—such a tumultuous decade in Soviet history—was a small monograph, entitled *Leon Trotsky and the Art of Insurrection*, that focused on Trotsky's achievements as a military strategist. Surprisingly, this highly favorable assessment of Trotsky's contributions in the art and science of war, insurrection and military command was authored by an officer and professor at the US Army War College, Colonel Harold W. Nelson.

The situation in Trotsky studies deteriorated in the 1990s. American and British scholarship produced nothing substantial in this field during the entire decade. The only published work that perhaps stands out as an exception, though a minor one, is a single volume of essays, produced by the Edinburgh University Press in 1992 under the title *The Trotsky Reappraisal*. During this decade, a disturbing trend emerged in Britain, which consisted of recycling and legitimizing old anti-Trotsky slanders. This trend was exemplified by the so-called *Journal of Trotsky Studies*, which was produced at the University of Glasgow. The favorite theme of this journal was that Trotsky's writings were full of self-serving distortions. This claim was repeatedly made without any respect for the factual record. Among its more absurd contributions was an article that set out to prove that Trotsky, in his *History of the Russian Revolution,* had vastly exaggerated his own role in the October insurrection. It informed us that while serious revolutionaries like Stalin went out into the streets to do the heavy lifting, a somewhat befuddled Trotsky was left behind in the Smolny Institute to answer the phones. Mercifully, this journal expired after four issues.

The current decade has seen no improvement. Two new Trotsky biographies were published, the first in 2003 and the second in 2006, by Professors Ian Thatcher and Geoffrey Swain. These works contained no new research. I have already provided a detailed analysis of their work in an extended review, entitled *Leon Trotsky and the Post-Soviet School of Historical Falsification.*[6]

---

[6] David North, *Leon Trotsky and the Post-Soviet School of Historical Falsification,* (Oak Park, MI:

It is worth contrasting the prevailing treatment of Trotsky to the massive volume of material on Stalin. He seems to exert a never-ending fascination on historians. Of course, Stalin, no less than Hitler, is a legitimate subject of scholarly research. There are no appropriate or inappropriate subjects for historical study. But, as Wilde might have suggested, the one unconditional requirement for the writing of history, like for the writing of novels, is that it should be done well. The problem is that much of the writing on Stalin is done badly. Many of the works are crassly journalistic, exploiting in a sensationalist manner material acquired from the Soviet archives. Works by Radzinsky and Sebag-Montefiore provide examples of this genre. More troubling, however, are studies by scholars who seem genuinely anxious to rehabilitate Stalin and Stalinism. At times, the conclusions arrived at by such historians are truly bizarre. For example, Professor Stephen Kotkin, in his book *Magnetic Mountain*, argues that Stalinism was the culmination of the Enlightenment project. Stalinism, he writes:

> ... constituted a quintessential Enlightenment utopia, an attempt, via the instrumentality of the state, to impose a rational ordering on society, while at the same time overcoming the wrenching class divisions brought about by nineteenth-century industrialization. That attempt, in turn, was rooted in a tradition of urban-modeled, socially oriented utopias that helped make the Enlightenment possible. Magnitogorsk had very deep roots.[7]

At its worst, this tendency, in the guise of providing more "nuanced" appreciations of historical events, advances strange justifications of Stalin and his crimes. Along these lines, in Robert W. Thurston's *Life and Terror in Stalin's Russia 1934-1941*, published by the Yale University Press in 1996, we are offered this appraisal of Stalin's prosecutor, Andrei Vyshinsky:

> Thus, in 1935-36, despite his appalling role in the show trials that began in August 1936, Vyshinskii advocated major improvements in legal procedures. Simultaneously he scorned key NKVD practices and urged much greater tolerance of ordinary citizens' criticisms, so long as they did not touch fundamental policy.[8]

Mehring Books, 2007). See also Part II.

[7] Stephen Kotkin, *Magnetic Mountain* (Berkeley: University of California Press, 1995), p. 364.

[8] Robert W. Thurston, *Life and Terror in Stalin's Russia 1934–1941* (New Haven: Yale University Press, 1996), p. 9.

And, referring to Kamenev, Zinoviev and other defendants in the 1936 trial, Thurston offers this thinly-concealed legitimization of their condemnation by Stalin:

> Probably guilty of nothing more than talking about political changes, these men, according to Western standards of justice, did not deserve punishment. But they had engaged in opposition, had had contacts with Trotsky and leaked secret documents to the West, and had wanted to remove Stalin, all of which they had lied about, while proclaiming their complete loyalty. These points provided material for Stalin's suspicious mind. Why were such people lying? How many more like them existed, and what were their real intentions? Given the Trotsky bloc and the language of the Riutin Memorandum, it might have been easy for people less morbid than Stalin to visualize terrorism at work in some of the many industrial accidents of the period. He embellished matters considerably and told massive lies of his own—but the evidence just given suggests that at this point he took steps to eliminate people who had misled him and conspired with an archenemy, Trotsky. This decision, though unjust, was not part of a plan to create political terror.[9]

While the Stalin industry is a going concern in the field of Soviet scholarship, the protracted depression in Trotsky studies continues. This finds expression not only in the very limited and generally poor quality of research into Trotsky's life, but also in the absence of significant work on his political comrades in the Left Opposition. How many of the leaders of the Left Opposition, beginning with Christian Rakovsky and Adolf Joffe, have been the subject of full-length English-language biographies? What work has been done on Smirnov, Smilga, Boguslavsky, Ter-Vaganian, and Voronsky? There has not been, as yet, any comprehensive study of the Left Opposition and its activities. A persistent theme of many contemporary works on the Great Terror is that it had little to do with Trotsky, who by the 1930s, it is claimed, was without any influence within the Soviet Union. But is this really true? What research has been conducted into the activities of Oppositionists? And even if Stalin's repression made systematic agitation impossible, is it really the case that the Trotskyist *Bulletin of the Opposition* exercised no influence on the thinking of disaffected elements within the Soviet state and party appa-

[9] Ibid., pp. 26-27.

ratus? Moreover, had all recollection of Trotsky among Civil War veterans of the Red Army, within the officer corps and among rank-and-file soldiers, vanished by 1936? Was Victor Serge simply exercising his artistic license when he wrote in 1937 of Trotsky that within the Soviet Union, "Everyone thinks of him, since it is forbidden to think of him ... As long as the Old Man lives, there will be no security for the triumphant bureaucracy."[10] These questions cannot be answered until the necessary research is carried out.

But why has this work not been done? This is a complex question which, I suspect, will itself at some point become a subject for students of intellectual history. I will not claim to have the definitive answer, but I would like to point to several factors that may have affected the perception and reception of Trotsky in the academic and scholarly community. Let me state from the outset that references to Trotsky's political "irrelevance" are neither credible nor serious. Trotsky quite clearly played a decisive role in the Russian Revolution, one of the key events of the twentieth century. He was also, as it so happens, one of this century's most brilliant literary figures. Walter Benjamin noted in his diary that Bertolt Brecht in 1931 "maintained that there were good reasons for thinking that Trotsky was the greatest living European writer."[11] With these qualifications it should hardly be necessary to justify "another book" about Trotsky. One might also, for good measure, add that Trotsky's political and intellectual legacy, however controversial and contested, continues to exert influence on contemporary politics. Trotsky is quite obviously not irrelevant for history. Why then has he become irrelevant for historians?

The conservative political and intellectual climate that has prevailed for nearly three decades has been a substantial factor in determining the reception of Trotsky in the scholarly community. Supreme Court justices take note of the election returns and historians read the newspapers. As Trotsky aptly observed in 1938, the force of political reaction not only conquers, it also convinces. The dissolution of the USSR in 1991 brought in its wake a flood of embittered denunciations of the entire Soviet experience. The works of right-wing opponents of the socialist project like Martin Malia, Robert Conquest, the indefatigable Richard Pipes and former Stalinist François Furet promoted an intellectually-stultifying environment that discouraged a serious, let alone sympathetic, investigation of the political heritage of Russian and European

---

[10] Victor Serge, *From Lenin to Stalin* (New York: Pathfinder, 1973), p. 133.

[11] Walter Benjamin, *Selected Writings, Volume 2: 1927-1934* (Cambridge, MA: Belknap Press, 1999), p. 477.

Marxism. It is difficult to imagine the classics of Soviet studies that date from
the 1950s and 1960s—works like Leopold Haimson's *Origins of Bolshevism*,
Samuel Baron's *Plekhanov,* or for that matter, E. H. Carr's encyclopedic study
of early Soviet history—being written in the 1990s. The prevailing intellectual
climate was not congenial for those, like the Russian scholar Vadim Rogovin,
who sought to explore, within the context of the Marxist and Bolshevik tradition, revolutionary socialist alternatives to Stalinism.

However, not all the problems relating to the academic reception of
Trotsky flow directly from the political environment of the last 30 years.
There are other long-term intellectual tendencies at work, which substantially predate the elections of Margaret Thatcher in Britain and Ronald Reagan
in the United States. I am referring to a protracted process, spanning many
decades, of a steadily deepening alienation of substantial sections of left intellectuals from the theoretical framework and political outlook associated with
the "classical Marxism" of which Leon Trotsky was among the most outstanding and, certainly, the last great representative.

It is not possible at this time to offer an exposition of Trotsky's philosophical world view and his conception of politics and human culture. But it
must be said, for the sake of the argument being presented here, that crucial
elements of this world view included an irreconcilable commitment to philosophical materialism, belief in the law-governed character of the historical
process, confidence in the power of human reason (to the extent that this faculty is understood materialistically) and its ability to discover *objective* truth,
and, associated with this, belief in the progressive role of science. Trotsky
was a determinist, an optimist, and an internationalist, convinced that the
socialist revolution arose necessarily out of the insoluble contradictions of the
world capitalist system. Above all, he insisted that there existed a revolutionary force within society, the working class, that would overthrow the capitalist system and lay the foundations for world socialism.

None of these elements of the outlook of classical Marxism—least of all
its optimism—has survived within any significant section of the left intelligentsia. Even by the 1920s, the shattering impact of World War I, the collapse of the Second International, and, somewhat later, in the aftermath of
the October Revolution, the political defeats suffered by the working class
in Central and Western Europe, undermined confidence in the Marxist outlook and perspective among substantial sections of the left petty-bourgeois
intelligentsia. As early as 1926, Hendrik de Man's frontal assault on Marxism,
The Psychology of Socialism, gave voice to the growing skepticism among left

intellectuals in the materialist explanation of the development of political consciousness and in the efficacy of Marxist political practice. Marxism's confidence in the revolutionary effect of objective socio-economic processes on mass working-class consciousness, de Man argued, was misplaced. The rationally grounded appeals of Marxists to objective class interests were inadequate as a means of winning the working class to socialism. Many of the arguments advanced by de Man subsequently found their way into the writings of the theoreticians of the Frankfurt School.

The victory of Hitler in 1933, the Moscow Trials, the defeat of the Spanish Revolution and, finally, the Stalin-Hitler Pact completed the political demoralization of the left intelligentsia. The basic perspective of socialism, they believed, had been discredited. The working class had failed. There existed no revolutionary subject in contemporary society. Trotsky, in one of his last major essays, grasped the implications of such arguments: "If we grant as true that the cause of the defeats is rooted in the social qualities of the proletariat itself then the position of modern society will have to be acknowledged as hopeless."[12] Just seven years later, in their *Dialectic of the Enlightenment*, Max Horkheimer and Theodor Adorno arrived at precisely this conclusion.

It does not seem an exaggeration to state that the intelligentsia was overwhelmed and exhausted by the tragedies of the twentieth century: the two world wars, fascism, the Stalinist betrayal of socialism, and the protracted paralysis of the workers' movement beneath the weight of bureaucracy. Pessimism gave way to cynicism and complacency. Paradoxically, overcoming the intellectual demoralization would have required systematic research into the causes of past defeats, and this demanded, in turn, engagement with the ideas of Trotsky and the great school of classical Marxism. But objective conditions, embedded in the long post-World War II economic expansion of capitalism, worked against such an engagement.

What then are the prospects for a re-engagement with Trotsky's ideas? In formulating an answer to this question, I think it best to employ the same approach taken by Trotsky himself. He insisted on understanding the vicissitudes of his own life within the context of the development of the socialist revolution: within Russia, Europe and the world as a whole. In assessing the shifts in his own fortunes, Trotsky stated that he did not see personal tragedy, but rather different stages in the contradictory unfolding of the world

---

[12] Leon Trotsky, "The USSR in War," in: *In Defence of Marxism* (London: New Park, 1971), p. 15.

socialist revolution. The rise of the revolutionary wave carried Trotsky into power. Its ebb drove him into exile.

It has been many decades since Marxism, as Trotsky would have understood that term, has played any significant role in the life of the working class. Those were decades of capitalist economic stability and substantial growth. The class struggle, to the extent that it manifested itself at all, was kept within traditional channels, under the police supervision of the labor bureaucracies. Now, however, it appears that history has quite suddenly taken one of its surprising turns. The world in which we are meeting today already appears very different from that which existed when the AAASS met last year in New Orleans. Over the past few weeks, references to the Great Depression of the 1930s have become commonplace. It has been acknowledged, even by the president of the United States, that the unfolding crisis has brought American and world capitalism to the brink of collapse.

It is not difficult to imagine that this is a crisis that Leon Trotsky, who coined the phrase "The Death Agony of Capitalism," would have understood very well. The old "catastrophe" theory which so many anti-Marxists have had a good laugh over no longer seems so funny, let alone outlandish.

Social being does, in the final analysis, determine social consciousness. If, as seems very likely, the deepening crisis compels on the part of historians a re-examination of long-standing and discredited assumptions, and with it, a more critical attitude toward the existing forms of society, then I suspect that we will soon be witnessing a renewal of intense scholarly interest in the life and work of Leon Trotsky.

Trotsky as leader of the Red Army in the Civil War

Part II

The Post-Soviet School of Historical Falsification:
A Review of Two Biographies of Leon Trotsky
by Professors Geoffrey Swain & Ian Thatcher

Police mug-shot of Trotsky, under house arrest in Norway,
just before his departure for Mexico in December 1936

The Post-Soviet School of Historical Falsification[1]

A Review of Two Biographies of Leon Trotsky by Professors Geoffrey Swain and Ian Thatcher

Trotsky, by Geoffrey Swain. 237 pages, Pearson Longman, 2006
Trotsky, by Ian D. Thatcher. 240 pages, Routledge, 2003

1. Stalin's Terror & the Political Lie

The year 2007 marks the 70th anniversary of the most terrible event in the history of the Soviet Union. Having staged in August 1936 a political show trial in Moscow that provided a pseudo-judicial cover for the murder of Lev Kamenev, Grigory Zinoviev, Ivan Smirnov and other leaders of the October Revolution, Stalin launched in 1937 a campaign of terror whose goal was the destruction of all remnants of Marxist political thought and culture in the Soviet Union. The terror targeted for extermination virtually everyone who had played a significant role in the October Revolution of 1917, or who had at any point in their careers been identified with any form of Marxian and socialist opposition to the Stalinist regime, or were associated—either personally or through their comrades, friends and family—with a Marxian political, intellectual and cultural milieu.

Even after the passage of 70 years, the number of those murdered by

[1] Published on the *World Socialist Web Site* (www.wsws.org) on May 9, 10, 11 & 12, 2007. [www.wsws.org/articles/2007/may2007/lectlett-m22.pdf]

the Stalinist regime in 1937–1938 has not been conclusively established. According to a recent analysis by Professor Michael Ellman of the University of Amsterdam, the "best estimate that can currently be made of the number of repression deaths in 1937–1938 is the range of 950,000–1.2 million, i.e., about a million. This is the estimate which should be used by historians, teachers and journalists concerned with twentieth century Russian—and world—history."[2] Ellman notes that the discovery of new evidence may at some point require a revision of this figure.

There exists substantial archival evidence that provides a detailed picture of how Stalin and his henchmen in the Politburo and NKVD organized and carried out their campaign of mass murder. The Military Collegium of the USSR Supreme Court played a central role in the process of judicially-sanctioned mass murder. A total of 54 defendants were sentenced at the three public show trials in Moscow. But there were tens of thousands of people who were tried behind closed doors by the Military Collegium and sentenced to death after "trials" that usually were completed within ten to fifteen minutes.[3] The victims were drawn from lists of individuals that had been prepared by the NKVD, along with a proposed sentence. These were submitted for review by Stalin and the Politburo. The names were those of "leading Party, Soviet, Komsomol, Trade Union, Red Army and NKVD officials, as well as writers, artists and prominent representatives of economic institutions, who had been arrested by the same NKVD."[4] Stalin and his Politburo reviewed these lists and, in almost all cases, approved the recommended sentences—mostly death by shooting. There are 383 lists in the Presidential Archive in Moscow submitted to Stalin between February 27, 1937, and September 29, 1938, which contain the typed names of 44,500 people. The signatures of Stalin and his colleagues, along with their penciled-in comments, are on these lists.[5]

The Military Collegium handed down 14,732 sentences in 1937 and another 24,435 in 1938. Stalin was the principal director of the terror and was deeply involved in its daily operations. On just one day, September 12, 1938, Stalin

[2] "Soviet Repression Statistics: Some Comments," *Europe-Asia Studies*, Vol. 54, No. 7 (November 2002), p. 1162.

[3] Material relating to the work of the Collegium is based on Marc Jansen and Nikita Petrov, "Mass Terror and the Court: The Military Collegium of the USSR," *Europe-Asia Studies*, Vol. 58, No. 4 (June 2006), pp. 589-602.

[4] Ibid., p. 591.

[5] Ibid.

approved 3,167 death sentences for action by the Military Collegium.[6] There exists a substantial amount of information on how the Military Collegium conducted its work. Its secret trials were usually conducted at Moscow's Lefortovo prison. The official mainly in charge of the process was the Collegium's president, Vasily Ulrikh. On a busy day, the Collegium could handle 30 or more cases. It was often necessary to set up additional Collegium courts to deal with the crush of prisoners. The usual procedure was to bring prisoners before the Collegium. The charge was read to the accused, who was generally asked only to acknowledge the testimony that he had given during his earlier "investigation." Whether the defendant answered in the affirmative or negative, the trial was then declared to be over. After hearing five such cases, the Collegium retired to consider its verdicts, which had already been decided and written down. The defendants were then recalled to hear their fate—almost always death. The sentences were generally carried out the same day.[7]

This was hard work for the Collegium members and they required substantial nourishment to keep them going. They retired to the deliberation room for their meals, which, according to the account of a Lefortovo prison official, consisted of "various cold snacks, including different kinds of sausages, cheese, butter, black caviar, pastries, chocolate, fruits and fruit juice." Ulrikh washed the food down with brandy.[8]

The Collegium members did not only hand down verdicts. Frequently they attended and even carried out the executions that they had ordered. Ulrikh occasionally returned home from work with the blood of his victims on his greatcoat.

Moscow was not the only city in which the secret trials were held. Parallel processes were conducted in cities throughout the USSR. The terror did not subside until the Stalinist regime had murdered virtually all the representatives of the Marxist and socialist culture that had laid the intellectual foundations for the October Revolution and the formation of the Soviet Union. Soviet society was traumatized by the massive killing. As the Russian Marxist historian Vadim Z. Rogovin wrote:

> A wasteland of scorched earth was formed around the murdered leaders of Bolshevism, insofar as their wives, children and

---

[6] Ibid., p. 593.

[7] Ibid., p. 595.

[8] Ibid., p. 596.

closest comrades were eliminated after them. The fear evoked by the Stalinist terror left its mark on the consciousness and behavior of several generations of Soviet people; for many it eradicated the readiness, desire and ability to engage in honest ideological thought. At the same time, the executioners and informers from Stalin's time continued to thrive; they had secured their own well-being and the prosperity of their children through active participation in frame-ups, expulsion, torture, and so forth.[9]

Stalin's crimes were justified on the basis of grotesque lies, which portrayed the Marxist opponents and victims of the bureaucratic-totalitarian regime—above all, Leon Trotsky—as saboteurs, terrorists and agents of various imperialist and fascist powers. But the lies that formed the basis of the show trial indictments of Trotsky and other Old Bolsheviks had been prepared over the previous 15 years, that is, dating back to the anti-Trotsky campaign initiated in 1922 by Stalin and his self-destructive allies, Kamenev and Zinoviev.

As Trotsky explained in the aftermath of the first two Moscow Trials (the proceeding of August 1936 was followed by the second show trial in January 1937), the origins of the judicial frame-up were to be found in the falsification of the historical record that had been required by the political struggle against "Trotskyism"—that is, against the political opposition to the bureaucratic regime headed by Stalin. "It remains an incontestable historical fact," Trotsky wrote in March 1937, "that the preparation of the bloody judicial frame-ups had its inception in the 'minor' historical distortions and 'innocent' falsification of citations."[10]

No one who has studied the origins of the Stalinist terror and grappled seriously with its consequences is inclined to underestimate the politically reactionary and socially destructive implications of historical falsification. We know from the example of the Soviet Union that the political process that first manifested itself as the falsification of the history of the Russian Revolution eventually metastasized into the mass extermination of Russian revolutionaries. Before Stalin entered into history as one of its worst murderers, he had already burnished his reputation as its greatest liar.

Trotsky not only exposed the lies of Stalin; he also explained the objective roots and function of the regime's vast system of political and social duplicity:

---

[9] Vadim Z. Rogovin, *1937: Stalin's Year of Terror* (Oak Park, MI: Mehring Books, 1998), pp. xxii-xxiii.

[10] Leon Trotsky, *The Stalin School of Falsification* (London: New Park Publications, 1974), p. ix.

Thousands of writers, historians and economists in the USSR write by command what they do not believe. Professors in universities and school teachers are compelled to change written textbooks in a hurry in order to accommodate themselves to the successive stage of the official lie. The spirit of the Inquisition thoroughly impregnating the atmosphere of the country feeds ... from profound social sources. To justify their privileges the ruling caste perverts the theory which has as its aim the elimination of all privileges. The lie serves, therefore, as the fundamental ideological cement of the bureaucracy. The more irreconcilable becomes the contradiction between the bureaucracy and the people, all the ruder becomes the lie, all the more brazenly is it converted into criminal falsification and judicial frame-up. Whoever has not understood this inner dialectic of the Stalinist régime will likewise fail to understand the Moscow trials.[11]

It may appear astonishing in retrospect that so many people who considered themselves on the left were prepared to justify, and even actually believe, the accusations hurled by Vyshinsky, the Stalinist prosecutor, against the Old Bolshevik defendants at the Moscow Trials. A substantial section of liberal and leftist public opinion accepted the legitimacy of the Moscow Trials and in this way lent its support to the terror that was raging in the USSR. The Stalinist regime—whatever its crimes within the USSR—was seen, at least until the Non-Aggression Pact with Hitler in August 1939, as a political ally against Nazi Germany. Pragmatic considerations, rooted in the social outlook of the petty-bourgeois "friends of the USSR," underlay the pro-Stalin apologetics of large sections of "left" public opinion. Even the refutation of key elements of the indictments was ignored by Stalin's apologists.[12] The work of

---

[11] Ibid., p. xiii.

[12] For example, at the first Moscow Trial, the defendant Holtzman testified that he had been sent as a courier to Copenhagen in 1932, where he supposedly met Trotsky's son Leon Sedov at the Hotel Bristol and received from him seditious anti-Soviet instructions. It soon emerged that Copenhagen's Hotel Bristol had burned down in a fire fifteen years earlier, in 1917. The crucial conspiratorial meeting could not have taken place. At the second trial, the Old Bolshevik and former Left Oppositionist Yuri Pyatakov testified that while in Berlin in December 1935 on Soviet business, he had secretly flown to Oslo. Pyatakov claimed to have been driven to Trotsky's home. Once there, Pyatakov—reciting a script that had been written by the NKVD interrogators—testified that Trotsky informed him of his [Trotsky's] links to the intelligence agencies of Nazi Germany. Pyatakov then confessed that he agreed to join Trotsky's anti-Soviet and pro-Nazi conspiracy. But even before the trial was over, Pyatakov's testimony

the Dewey Commission, which took its name from the American liberal philosopher who served as chairman of the 1937 Inquiry into the Soviet charges against Leon Trotsky, stood in noble opposition to the cynical, dishonest and reactionary attitudes that prevailed in the circles of left public opinion, especially in Britain, France and the United States.

The Work of E. H. Carr and Isaac Deutscher

Nearly two decades were to pass before the edifice of Stalinist lies erected at the Moscow trials began to crumble. The decisive event in this process was the "secret speech" given by Khrushchev in February 1956, before the 20th Congress of the Communist Party of the Soviet Union, in which the criminal character of Stalin's terror was acknowledged for the first time. But this exposure was preceded by significant developments in the field of historical research that contributed immeasurably to a factually accurate and more profound understanding of the history of the Soviet Union and to the role of Leon Trotsky.

The first major event in the historical rehabilitation of Trotsky was the publication of E. H. Carr's monumental history of Soviet Russia, and especially its fourth volume, entitled *The Interregnum*. This volume, making extensive use of official Soviet documents available in the West, provided a detailed account of the political struggles that erupted inside the leadership of the Soviet Communist Party in 1923-1924. Carr was not politically sympathetic to Trotsky. But he brilliantly summarized and analyzed the complex issues of program, policy and principle with which Trotsky grappled in a difficult and critical period of Soviet history. Carr's account made clear that Trotsky became the target of an unprincipled attack that was, in its initial stages, motivated by his rivals' subjective considerations of personal power. While Carr found much to criticize in Trotsky's response to the provocations of Stalin, Zinoviev and Kamenev, the historian left no doubt that he viewed Trotsky as, alongside of Lenin, the towering figure of the Bolshevik Revolution. In "many spheres" of revolutionary political activity, Carr maintained in a later volume, Trotsky "outshone" even Lenin. As for Stalin, Carr wrote that Trotsky "eclipsed" him "in almost all." But the decline in revolutionary fervor inside

---

was blown to pieces. The Norwegian press reported that no foreign plane had landed in Oslo's airport between September 1935 and May 1936! Pyatakov's story, which was absolutely central to the entire Stalinist frame-up, was exposed as a brazen concoction.

the USSR, ever more noticeable after 1922, affected Trotsky's political fortunes. "Trotsky was a hero of the revolution," wrote Carr. "He fell when the heroic age was over."[13]

The second major event in the study of Soviet history was the publication of Isaac Deutscher's magisterial biographical trilogy: *The Prophet Armed*, *The Prophet Unarmed* and *The Prophet Outcast*. April 2007 marked the centenary of Deutscher's birth; and it is appropriate to pay tribute to his achievement as a historian and biographer. Even though I speak as one who disagrees profoundly with many of Deutscher's political judgments—particularly as they relate to Trotsky's decision to found the Fourth International, which Deutscher opposed—it is difficult to overestimate the impact of Deutscher's *Prophet* trilogy. He was not being immodest when he compared his own work to that of Thomas Carlyle who, as the biographer of another revolutionary, Oliver Cromwell, "had to drag out the Lord Protector from under a mountain of dead dogs, a huge load of calumny and oblivion."[14] Deutscher proudly cited a British critic who wrote that the first volume of the trilogy, *The Prophet Armed*, "undoes three decades of Stalinist denigration."[15]

In addition to the work of Carr and Deutscher, in the 1950s, 1960s and 1970s, a new generation of historians made significant contributions to our understanding of the Russian Revolution, the origins and development of the Soviet Union and its leading personalities. Leopold Haimson, Samuel Baron, Robert Daniels, Alexander Rabinowitch, Robert Tucker, Moshe Lewin, Marcel Liebman, Richard Day and Baruch Knei-Paz come immediately to mind. To recognize the value of their work and to appreciate their scholarship does not, and need not, imply agreement with their judgments and conclusions. The enduring significance of their collective efforts, and those of others whom I have not named, is that they contributed to the refutation of the lies, distortions and half-truths in which the history of the Russian Revolution and the Soviet Union had been enshrouded for so many decades. And not only falsifications of the Soviet government, but also the stultifying anti-Marxist propaganda of the US government in the era of the Cold War.

To have some sense of the impact of these historians' work on the intellectual climate of their times, permit me to cite several passages from the text of a study of Trotsky's life that was published in 1973 as part of the well-known

---

[13] E. H. Carr, *Socialism in One Country*, Vol. 1 (Baltimore, MD: Pelican Books, 1970), p. 167.

[14] *The Prophet Unarmed* (London & New York: Verso, 2003), p. vii.

[15] Ibid.

"Great Lives Observed" series. This series—published by Prentice-Hall, the long-established distributor of academic textbooks—was a mainstay of university history courses in the 1960s and 1970s. Thousands of students taking courses in Russian or modern European history would have been introduced to the figure of Leon Trotsky through this volume, and this is what they would have read in its very first paragraph:

> With the passage of time historical figures either shrink or grow in stature. In the case of Leon Trotsky time, after a brief eclipse, has increased his image so that he appears today, for good or evil, as one of the giants of the first half of the twentieth century. The renewed interest in Trotsky's life is reflected by the numerous studies which are beginning to appear, and by the sudden availability of almost all his writings. For many of the New Left generation he has reclaimed both the prestige and the mantle of *the* revolutionary leader.[16]

The introduction provided, on the basis of the findings of contemporary scholars, a concise assessment of Trotsky's revolutionary career. "The argument supporting Trotsky's claim to importance," it stated, "rests on his contribution to political theory, his literary legacy, and above all his role as man of action." As a theorist, Trotsky's analysis of Russian social forces and his elaboration of the theory of Permanent Revolution "suggests that as a Marxist thinker he could, on the power of his creativity, go beyond the formulations of Marx and Engels." Trotsky, therefore, deserved to be placed within the "brilliant coterie of Marxist theorists such as Plekhanov, Kautsky, Luxemburg and, for that matter Lenin himself." As a literary figure, Trotsky stood above even these great Marxists. "Magnificent word play, scathing sarcasm, and brilliant character sketches are the hallmarks of his writing. To read Trotsky is to observe the literary artist at work." And then there were Trotsky's achievements as a man of action. The introduction noted that "Trotsky's role in Russian revolutionary history is second only to that of Lenin's," and underscored his "decisive leadership in the Military Revolutionary Committee that paved the way for the October insurrection ..." It also called attention to Trotsky's "determined efforts to build the Red Army in the face of enormous obstacles ..."[17]

---

[16] *Trotsky*, edited by Irving H. Smith (Englewood Cliffs, N.J.: Prentice-Hall, 1973), p. 1.

[17] Ibid.

None of these achievements was known to the mass of Soviet citizens. There existed no honest account of Trotsky's life and work within the USSR, because Soviet historians "have long since abandoned the responsibility of objective historical writing and have busied themselves with the grotesque efforts to create a new demonology." Within the Soviet Union, Trotsky remained "an abstraction of evil—a militating force against the future destiny of the Soviet people."[18] But outside the USSR, the situation was different:

> Soviet demonology, absurd from its inception, has been largely vanquished, at least in the Western world. Part Three of this book contains selections of relatively recent writers on the problem of Trotsky. The best examples of this more objective scholarship are Edward Hallett Carr's multi-volume study, *The Bolshevik Revolution*, and Isaac Deutscher's painstaking three-volume study of Trotsky. The historical debate may be never ending, but in the light of these more recent studies Trotsky's role in the Russian experience can be seen in a new and positive perspective. In the West, the miasmic cloud has disappeared; the demonic hierarchy has been exorcized. We can now come to grips with the material forces and issues which motivated and inspired the action and deeds of Leon Trotsky.[19]

I have quoted extensively from this text because it provides a clear summary of what the general student studying history at the college level would have been told about Leon Trotsky some 35 years ago.[20] When one turns to

---

[18] Ibid., pp. 1-2.

[19] Ibid.

[20] A review of this volume by an academic journal, *The History Teacher*, substantiates this appraisal of its target audience:

> In regard to teaching and classroom use, this edition should find considerable acceptance. Unlike others in the series, this work does not promise to lose its readers in a host of overquotations from its figure's philosophical or political expositions. It succinctly describes Trotsky's achievements and provides the reader with the varying historical interpretations of his career.
> A worthy instructor of any modern Russian course should be able to make effective use of the text by utilizing the relatively short selections as jumping off points for further examination of their author's full theses. The casual student will undoubtedly enjoy it for its brevity—only 170 pages. More importantly, however, will be the use that the real student of Russian history can obtain from it. Stimulated by its content but disappointed by its brevity, he will hopefully delve

the texts that are now being presented to students, it becomes immediately apparent that we are living in a very different—and far less healthy—intellectual environment. But before I may do so, it is necessary to examine, if only briefly, the treatment of Trotsky in Soviet historical literature in the aftermath of the Twentieth Congress and Khrushchev's "secret speech."

Soviet History After the 20th Congress

The official exposure of Stalin's crimes in 1956 placed the Kremlin bureaucracy and its many apologists on the defensive. The party-line version of history had been for nearly two decades Stalin's own *Short Course of the History of the CPSU*. From the moment Khrushchev ascended the podium of the Twentieth Party Congress, this compendium of incredible lies, soaked in human blood, lost all credibility. But with what could it be replaced? To this question the Stalinist bureaucracy never found a viable answer.

Every important question relating to the history of the Russian revolutionary movement—the events of 1917, the Civil War, the early years of the Soviet state, the inner-party conflicts of the 1920s, the growth of the Soviet bureaucracy, the relation of the Soviet Union to international revolutionary movements and struggles, industrialization, collectivization, Soviet cultural policy and the Stalinist terror—posed unavoidably the issue of Lev Davidovich Trotsky. Every criticism of Stalin raised the question: Was Trotsky right? The historical, political, theoretical and moral issues that flowed from the exposure of Stalin's crimes and the catastrophic impact of his policies and personality on every aspect of Soviet society could not be dealt with by simply removing Stalin from his glass-encased mausoleum alongside Lenin and reburying his corpse under the wall of the Kremlin.

Isaac Deutscher had nourished the hope—a hope that reflected the limitations of his political outlook—that the Stalinist bureaucracy would finally, at long last, find some way to come to terms with history and make its peace with Leon Trotsky. It proved a vain hope. To deal honestly with Trotsky would have required that at some point his writings be made available. But notwithstanding the passage of decades, Trotsky's exposure and denunciations of the

more deeply into the actual diaries, autobiographies, and biographies that exist concerning Leon Trotsky. The success of any edited text in this series ought to be measured by the number of students who do just that. (Vol. 7, No. 2 [February 1974], pp. 291-292).

Stalinist regime remained as explosive in their revolutionary potential as they had been during his own lifetime.

After Gorbachev came to power in 1985 and unveiled his policy of *glasnost*, there was a great deal of public discussion about the official rehabilitation of Trotsky. As the 70th anniversary of the October Revolution approached, it was widely anticipated that Gorbachev would take this opportunity to acknowledge Trotsky's role in the leadership of the October Revolution and his struggle against Stalin. But the very opposite occurred. On November 2, 1987, speaking in a televised address to a national audience, Gorbachev again denounced Trotsky in traditional Stalinist terms. Trotsky, he said, was "an excessively self-assured politician who always vacillated and cheated."[21]

By the time Gorbachev delivered his shameful speech, interest in Trotsky and the struggle of the Left Opposition against Stalinism was developing rapidly in the Soviet Union. Soviet journals such as *Argumenty i fakty* that published, for the first time since the 1920s, documents relating to Trotsky, enjoyed a massive increase in their circulation. Trotskyists from Europe,

---

[21] That was not all. Gorbachev continued:

> Trotsky and the Trotskyites negated the possibility of building socialism in conditions of capitalist encirclement. In foreign policy they gave priority to export of revolution, and in home policy to tightening the screws on the peasants, to the city exploiting the countryside, and to administrative and military fiat in running society.
>
> Trotskyism was a political current whose ideologists took cover behind leftist pseudo-revolutionary rhetoric, and who in effect assumed a defeatist posture. This was essentially an attack on Leninism all down the line. The matter practically concerned the future of socialism in our country, the fate of the revolution.
>
> In the circumstances, it was essential to disprove Trotskyism before the whole people, and denude its antisocialist essence. The situation was complicated by the fact that the Trotskyites were acting in common with the new opposition headed by Grigory Zinoviev and Lev Kamenev. Being aware that they constituted a minority, the opposition leaders had again and again saddled the party with discussions, counting on a split in its ranks.
>
> But in the final analysis, the party spoke out for the line of the Central Committee and against the opposition, which was soon ideologically and organizationally crushed.
>
> In short, the party's leading nucleus, headed by Josef Stalin, had safeguarded Leninism in an ideological struggle. It defined the strategy and tactics in the initial stage of socialist construction, with its political course being approved by most members of the party and most working people. An important part in defeating Trotskyism ideologically was played by Nikolai Bukharin, Feliks Dzerzhinsky, Sergei Kirov, Grigory Ordzhonikidze, Jan Rudzutak and others. (*New York Times*, November 3, 1987).

Australia and the United States traveled to the Soviet Union and delivered lectures that were widely attended. Gorbachev's speech was clearly an attempt to respond to this changed situation, but it proved utterly unsuccessful. The old Stalinist lies—denying Trotsky's role in the October Revolution, portraying him as an enemy of the Soviet Union—had lost all credibility.

Within little more than four years of Gorbachev's speech, the Soviet Union had ceased to exist. Trotsky's warning that the Stalinist bureaucracy, unless overthrown by the working class, would ultimately destroy the Soviet Union and clear the way for the restoration of capitalism was vindicated.

2. Swain, Thatcher & the "Myth" of Trotsky

The collapse of the Soviet Union in December 1991 raised with new urgency the issue of the historical role of Leon Trotsky. After all, the Soviet implosion demanded an explanation. Amidst the bourgeois triumphalism that attended the dissolution of the USSR—which by the way not a single major bourgeois political leader had foreseen—the answer seemed obvious. The Soviet collapse of December 1991 flowed organically from the October 1917 Revolution. This theory, based on the assumption that a non-capitalist form of human society was simply impossible, found its way into several books published in the aftermath of the Soviet collapse, of which the late Professor Martin Malia's *The Soviet Tragedy* was the most significant example.

However, books of this sort evaded the problem of historical alternatives; that is, were the policies pursued by Stalin and his successors the only options available to the USSR? Had the Soviet Union pursued different policies at various points in its 74-year history, might that have produced a significantly different historical outcome? To put the matter as succinctly as possible: Was there an alternative to Stalinism? I am not posing this as an abstract hypothetical counterfactual. Did there exist a socialist opposition to Stalinism? Did this opposition propose serious and substantial alternatives in terms of policy and program?

The answers to such crucial questions demand a serious reengagement with the ideas of Leon Trotsky and the oppositional movement that he led within the USSR and internationally. This, however, has not happened. Rather than building upon the achievements of earlier generations of scholars and drawing upon the vast new archival resources that have become available over the past 15 years, the dominant tendency in the historiography of the Soviet Union has been in a very different direction.

The years since the fall of the USSR have seen the emergence of what can best be described as the Post-Soviet School of Historical Falsification. The principal objective of this school is to discredit Leon Trotsky as a significant historical figure and to deny that he represented an alternative to Stalinism or that his political legacy contains anything relevant in the present and valuable for the future. Every historian is entitled to his or her viewpoint. But their interpretation of history must be grounded in a serious, honest and principled attitude toward the assembling of facts and the presentation of evidence. It is this essential quality that is deplorably absent in two new biographies of Leon Trotsky, one by Professor Geoffrey Swain of the University of Glasgow and the other by Professor Ian D. Thatcher of Brunel University in West London. These works have been brought out by large and influential publishing houses. Swain's biography has been published by Pearson Longman; Thatcher's by Routledge. Their treatment of the life of Leon Trotsky is without the slightest scholarly merit. Both works make limited use of Trotsky's own writings, offering few substantial citations and even ignoring major books, essays and political statements.

Despite their publishers' claims that the biographies are based on significant original research, there is no indication that either Swain or Thatcher made use of the major archival collections of Trotsky's papers held at Harvard and Stanford Universities. Well-established facts relating to Trotsky's life are, without credible evidentiary foundation, "called into question" or dismissed as "myths," to use the authors' favorite phrases. While belittling and even mocking Trotsky, Swain and Thatcher repeatedly attempt to lend credibility and legitimacy to Stalin, frequently defending the latter against Trotsky's criticism and finding grounds to justify the attacks on Trotsky and the Left Opposition. In many cases, their own criticisms of Trotsky are recycled versions of old Stalinist falsifications.

The formats of the Swain and Thatcher biographies are similar in design and page length, and are clearly directed toward a student audience. The authors know of course that the books will be the first acquaintance with Trotsky for most of their readers, and they have crafted these two books in a manner calculated to disabuse readers of any further interest in their subject. As Professor Swain proclaims with evident satisfaction in the first paragraph of his volume, "Readers of this biography will not find their way to Trotskyism."[22] Nor, he might have added, will they derive any understanding

---

[22] Geoffrey Swain, *Trotsky* (London: Pearson Longman, 2006), p. 1. Hereafter referred to as Swain.

of Trotsky's ideas, the principles for which he fought and his place in the history of the twentieth century.

The "Myth" of Trotsky

Both biographies proclaim that they challenge, undermine and even disprove "myths" about Trotsky's life and work. In a brief foreword to the Thatcher biography, the publisher asserts that "Key myths about Trotsky's heroic work as a revolutionary, especially in Russia's first revolution in 1905 and the Russian Civil War, are thrown into question."[23] Swain asserts that in his book "a rather different picture of Trotsky emerges to that traditionally drawn, more of the man and less of the myth."[24] What "myths " are they setting out to dispel? Significantly, both authors denounce the work of Isaac Deutscher, whom they hold responsible for creating the heroic historical persona that prevails to this day. Thatcher asserts condescendingly that Deutscher's trilogy reads like "a boy's own adventure story," a characteristic which "gives an indication of the attractions, as well as the weaknesses, of Deutscher's tomes." Thatcher implies that Deutscher's biography is a dubious exercise in hero-worship, which "abounds with instances in which Trotsky saw further and deeper than those around him." With evident sarcasm, Thatcher suggests that Deutscher credited Trotsky with an improbably long list of political, practical and intellectual achievements. He accuses Deutscher of indulging in improper "invention" and of "diversions into fiction." These flaws, writes Thatcher, "do detract from the work's status as a history, and as historians we must approach Deutscher both critically and with caution."[25]

In fact, all historical works—even masterpieces of the genre—must be read critically. But Thatcher denigrates Deutscher's work not for its weaknesses, but for its greatest strength—its masterly restoration of Trotsky's revolutionary persona. As for the specific example used by Thatcher to support his claim of invention and diversions into fiction, he provides what turns out to be an incomplete citation from *The Prophet Armed*. When read in its entirety, Deutscher's use of analogy to recreate the mood that prevailed within the Bolshevik leadership at a time of intense crisis—the con-

---

[23] Ian D. Thatcher, *Trotsky* (London and New York: Routledge, 2003). Hereafter referred to as Thatcher.

[24] Swain, p. 2.

[25] Thatcher, pp. 14-17.

flict over the Brest-Litovsk treaty in February 1918—may be appreciated as an example of the author's extraordinary literary skills and psychological insight.[26]

---

[26] Thatcher claims that "Deutscher simply puts thoughts into his subjects' heads for which there is no evidence." Thatcher cites a passage from Deutscher "which compares the disputes amongst the Bolsheviks over the peace with Germany with a dilemma faced by the Paris Commune over whether to wage a revolutionary war, and if so against whom ..." Thatcher then presents the passage to which he objects:

> Trotsky, who so often looked at the Russian Revolution through the prism of the French, must have been aware of this analogy. ...He must have seen himself as acting a role potentially reminiscent of Danton's, while Lenin's part was similar to Robespierre's. It was as if the shadow of the guillotine had for a moment interposed itself between him and Lenin. ... This consideration was decisive in Trotsky's eyes. In order to banish the shadow of the guillotine he made an extraordinary sacrifice of principle and personal ambition. (Thatcher, p. 16).

When one contrasts Thatcher's citation to the original passage as it appears in Deutscher's biography, it is immediately clear that the accusation of fictionalizing is entirely inappropriate. As Deutscher made very clear, he was using an analogy to clarify a complex political dispute. His recreation of what Trotsky might have been thinking in that situation—his conflict with Lenin over whether Soviet Russia should accept German terms at Brest-Litovsk—is well within the bounds of historical writing, particularly as Deutscher has made clear that there is an element of speculation on his part. Those passages left out by Thatcher are presented in italics:

> *Some analogy to the situation which was likely to arise if Trotsky had acted otherwise may be found in the three-cornered struggle which developed between the Commune of Paris, Danton and Robespierre during the French Revolution. In 1793 the Commune (and Anacharsis Cloots) stood, as Bukharin and the Left Communists were to do, for war against all the anti-revolutionary governments of Europe. Danton advocated war against Prussia and agreement with England, where he hoped that Fox would replace Pitt in office. Robespierre urged the Convention to wage war against England; and he strove for an agreement with Prussia. Danton and Robespierre joined hands against the Commune, but, after they suppressed it they fell out. The guillotine settled their controversy.*
>
> Trotsky, who so often looked at the Russian Revolution through the prism of the French, must have been aware of this analogy. *He may have remembered Engels's remarkable letter to Victor Adler, explaining all the "pulsations" of the French Revolution by the fortunes of war and the disagreements engendered by it.* He must have seen himself as acting a role potentially reminiscent of Danton's, while Lenin's part was similar to Robespierre's. It was as if the shadow of the guillotine had for a moment interposed itself between him and Lenin. *This is not to say that, if the conflict had developed, Trotsky, like Danton, would necessarily have played a losing game; or that Lenin was, like Robespierre, inclined to settle by the guillotine an inner party controversy. Here the analogy ceases to apply. It was evident that the war party, if it won, would be driven to suppress its opponents—otherwise it could not cope with its task. A peaceable solution of the crisis in the party was possible only under the rule of the*

The significance of the two authors' antipathy toward Deutscher's trilogy emerges quite clearly in Swain's biography. He writes accusingly that "Deutscher went along with, and indeed helped to foster the Trotsky myth, the idea that he was 'the best Bolshevik': together Lenin and Trotsky carried out the October Revolution and, with Lenin's support, Trotsky consistently challenged Stalin from the end of 1922 onwards to save the revolution from its bureaucratic degeneration; in this version of events Trotsky was Lenin's heir."[27]

A "myth," as defined by Webster, is "an unfounded or false notion." But all the items listed by Swain as elements of the Deutscher-propagated "Trotsky myth" are grounded in facts supported by documentary evidence that has been cited by numerous historians over the past half-century. While Swain implies that Deutscher was involved in a conspiracy against historical truth (he "went along with, and indeed helped foster the Trotsky myth"), his real aim is to discredit historical work—that of Deutscher and many others—that shattered decades of Stalinist falsification. Well-established historical facts relating to Trotsky's life are subjected to the literary equivalent of a drumhead court-martial and declared to be mere "myths." No evidence of a factual character capable of withstanding serious scrutiny is produced to support the summary verdict pronounced by Swain and Thatcher. The aim of their exercise in pseudo-biography is to restore the historical position of Trotsky to where it stood before the works of Deutscher and, for that matter, E. H. Carr were published—that is, to the darkest period of the Stalin School of Falsification.

The appeal to authority

Let us now examine the method the two professors employ to discredit well-established historical facts. One of Swain's and Thatcher's favorite techniques is to make an outrageous and provocative statement about Trotsky, which flies in the face of what is known to be factually true, and then support it by citing the work of another author. Their readers are not provided

---

adherents of peace, who could better afford to tolerate opposition. This consideration was decisive in Trotsky's eyes. In order to banish the shadow of the guillotine he made an extraordinary sacrifice of principle and personal ambition. (*The Prophet Armed* [New York: Vintage Books, 1965], pp. 390-91).

[27] Swain, p. 1.

with new facts that support Swain's and Thatcher's assertion. Rather, they are simply told that the statement is based on the work of some other historian.

Thus, Swain announces that he has

> drawn heavily on the work of other scholars. Ian Thatcher has rediscovered the pre-1917 Trotsky as well as showing clearly how unreliable Trotsky's own writings can be. James White has completely reassessed the Lenin and Trotsky relationship in 1917, showing that the two men's visions of insurrection were entirely different. Eric van Ree demolished the notion that Trotsky was Lenin's heir. Richard Day, writing more than 30 years ago, argued convincingly that Trotsky, far from being an internationalist, firmly believed in the possibility of building socialism in one country. More controversially, Nikolai Valentinov suggested nearly 50 years ago that in 1925, far from opposing Stalin, Trotsky was in alliance with him; although Valentinov's suggestion of a pact sealed at a secret meeting has not stood the test of time, other evidence confirms a period of testy collaboration.[28]

Presented here is what is known in logic as an appeal to authority. However, such an appeal is valid only to the extent of the authority's credibility. In this particular instance, the argument is not settled simply by citing Thatcher, White, van Ree, Day and Valentinov. We must know more about them, their work, and the evidence upon which they based their conclusions. And we must also know whether they actually held the position being attributed to them. As we shall see, the last question is particularly important, for when dealing with the work of Professors Swain and Thatcher, absolutely nothing can be taken for granted.

In regard to Swain's reference to Professor James White of the University of Glasgow, for anyone familiar with his work the latter hardly qualifies as a historian whose judgments on the subject of Trotsky can be accepted as authoritative, or, for that matter, even credible.[29]

---

[28] Swain, pp. 1-2.

[29] Professor James White has taught for many years at the University of Glasgow and has been a major influence on Thatcher. White has devoted considerable effort to rehabilitating Stalin and discrediting Trotsky. In his zeal to belittle Trotsky, White has at times appeared to play the clown—as with his claim, in a notorious article published in his short-lived *Journal of Trotsky Studies* (co-edited with Ian Thatcher), that on the deciding night of the October 1917 insurrection, Trotsky did nothing of importance. "Thus

As for van Ree, who is also one of Thatcher's favorite sources, his work as a historian must certainly be approached with caution, if not a face mask. As an ex-Maoist who is now a passionate anti-Communist, he recently offered, in a book entitled *World Revolution: The Communist Movement from Marx to Kim il-Jong*, the following assessment of Lenin and Trotsky:

> Yet all things considered they too were rogues, leaders of gangs of political thugs. They enjoyed prosecuting civil war. They proclaimed the Red Terror because they imagined themselves to be actors in a fantastic historical drama. They had the privilege of being allowed to repeat the performance at which Maximilien de Robespierre had failed, and they were determined that this time round no one would be left alive who could possibly turn their fortunes against them. Lenin and Trotsky took pride in the fact that they did not care a jot about democracy or human rights. They enjoyed the exercise of their own brutality.[30]

Aside from their overheated character, none of these statements could be cited as an example of sober historical judgment. Professor van Ree is evidently a very angry man with quite a few political chips on his shoulder. He is not qualified to render decisive judgment on the nature of the Lenin-Trotsky relationship. However, I should note that according to the account given by van Ree in the above cited work, Lenin and Trotsky were partners in crime who shared the same criminal world view. Holding that view, how could van Ree "demolish the notion that Trotsky was Lenin's heir"? Moreover, in a discussion of the relationship between Lenin and Trotsky, the word "heir" has a political rather than legal connotation. Whether or not Trotsky should be considered Lenin's "heir" is precisely the sort of question over which historians will probably argue for decades to come. It is not likely to be settled in one essay, even one written by a

---

while other members of the Military Revolutionary Committee went off to engage in some kind of revolutionary action, Trotsky was left behind with Kamenev—who had opposed the insurrection—to answer the telephone." [Vol. 1, 1993, p. 18]. That is how Professor White described the work of the principal strategist and leader of the insurrection. White has also insisted, in defiance of well-established historical fact, that Stalin's political line toward the Provisional Government in March 1917 more or less coincided with that fought for by Lenin upon his return to Russia in April. As for the specific matter of the Lenin-Trotsky relationship in 1917, it has long been known—indeed Trotsky wrote about it in his autobiography in 1929—that there were differences between the two principal leaders of the Bolshevik Party on the execution of the insurrection. The differences related to tactics, not "vision."

[30] http://www.nlpvf.nl/docs/VanRee_WorldRevolution_screen.pdf, p. 25.

scholar of substantially greater skill, knowledge, insight and judgment than Mr. van Ree. For Swain to assert that van Ree "demolished the notion that Trotsky was Lenin's heir" proves only that Swain has not thought through with sufficient care the complex historical, political, social and theoretical issues that arise in any serious study of the Lenin-Trotsky relationship.

Let us now consider Swain's invocation of Professor Richard B. Day to substantiate his own provocative thesis that Trotsky, "far from being an internationalist, firmly believed in the possibility of building socialism in one country." I must confess that I rubbed my eyes in amazement upon seeing Professor Day cited as an authority for such an outlandish statement. In contrast to the gentlemen to whom I have already referred, Professor Day is an outstanding and respected historian who for many decades has carried out serious work on the struggles within the Soviet government during the 1920s over economic policy. In particular, he has subjected the work of E. A. Preobrazhensky to serious analysis and shed light on significant differences that existed within the Left Opposition on important problems of economic theory and policy.

Swain's reference to Day contains both distortion and falsification. In the work cited by Swain, *Leon Trotsky and the Politics of Economic Isolation*, Day employs certain formulations suggesting that Trotsky did not reject the possibility of socialism in one country, but opposed the conception that this could be achieved, as Stalin proposed, on an autarchic basis. Moreover, Day's discussion of Trotsky's position on "socialism in one country" must be read in the context of the book's presentation of the debate over Soviet economic policy. Swain, however, seizes on several ambiguous phrases employed by Day in the opening pages of his book, and proceeds to misrepresent the central analytical line of *Leon Trotsky and the Politics of Economic Isolation*. Whatever the limitations of Day's argument, there is absolutely nothing in his book to support Swain's claim that Trotsky was not an internationalist.[31] This is a bla-

---

[31] To deal appropriately with Day's argument would require a detailed examination. His thesis does not lend itself to a careless one-line summary. At no time does Day suggest that there existed any similarity between "socialism in one country" as that term found expression in Stalin's program, and Trotsky's acceptance of the possibility of initiating socialist *construction* within the USSR, as long as that construction recognized the necessity of contact with the world market and a correct international revolutionary policy. Day describes Stalin's efforts to present his arguments in defense of economic nationalism as "utter nonsense" that found acceptance in a demoralized political environment in which "the party wished to be deceived." Day observes that Stalin's "clever marshalling of quotations allowed him to impart a degree of forensic sophistication to an argument which otherwise would have been dismissed as a contemptible fraud." (*Leon Trotsky and the Politics of Economic Isolation* [Cambridge: Cambridge

tant falsification of the argument presented in *Leon Trotsky and the Politics of Economic Isolation*.[32]

I will not waste my time refuting the reference to Valentinov, an old Menshevik and bitter opponent of Trotsky. Swain does not even bother to provide us with an actual quote from Valentinov. No evidence whatever is offered to substantiate this claim. As for Valentinov's tale of "a pact sealed at a secret meeting," Swain himself acknowledges that it "has not stood the test of time." In other words, it was a fabrication. But why then does Swain even bring it up?

"Rhetorical Internationalism"

Swain's use of sources whom he acknowledges to be unreliable is characteristic of his cynical attitude to the historical record. He has no compunction about making statements that contradict everything that is known and documented about Trotsky's life. He tells us that "Trotsky believed in world revolution, but no more and no less than every other Bolshevik, and like all other Bolsheviks this belief was largely rhetorical."[33] In other words, there was, according to Swain, no difference in the place that the perspective of world revolution played in the lifework of Leon Trotsky from that which it played in the thoughts and activities of Molotov, Voroshilov and Stalin! How does one even begin to answer an absurdity of this magnitude?

Readers are to believe that the political conceptions that governed Trotsky's political activity over a period of nearly 40 years, and which found

---

University Press, 1973], pp. 100-101). This last sentence might serve as a fair description of Swain's procedure.

[32] This is not merely my subjective opinion. After reading Swain's false presentation of the matter, I contacted Professor Day in Canada and brought this matter to his attention. In an e-mail letter written on March 13, 2007, I cited the relevant passage from Swain's biography, and asked Professor Day whether he was aware of it. I added that the citation from Swain "strikes me as a rather crass misrepresentation of your argument in *Leon Trotsky and the Politics of Economic Isolation*. As I understand, you considered the decisive question in the inner-party struggle over economic policy to be whether socialism could be built in an isolated country. On this critical point, the position held by Trotsky—as you have consistently argued—was fundamentally opposed to the conceptions advanced by Preobrazhensky, not to mention Stalin." I received on the same day a response from Professor Day, stating that "you are absolutely correct concerning my point of view." He then added, "There really has been so much interminable garbage written about Trotsky, and I am distressed to hear of another addition to the pile from Professor Swain. I truly cannot imagine how anyone could possibly say that Trotsky was not an 'internationalist' from beginning to end. It is a stunning misreading of the historical record."

[33] Swain, p. 2.

expression in countless speeches and thousands of pages of written documents, represented nothing more than external posturing devoid of serious intellectual, emotional and moral substance. Everything was merely a political subterfuge, a cover for what were essentially nationalist preoccupations related to the factional power struggle that Trotsky was conducting in the Soviet Union. As Swain writes:

> His critique of the failed German Revolution in 1923 was simply camouflage for an attack on his then domestic opponents Zinoviev and Kamenev. It was the same with his writings on the British General Strike, although here his opponents were Bukharin and Stalin. As to his enthusiasm for China in 1927, that too was essentially domestic in focus... It was only in emigration, in 1933, when he had buried the concept of Thermidor, that Trotsky explored the idea of how the revival of the working class movement in Europe might have a beneficial impact on the Soviet Union and halt the degeneration of the workers' state. Then internationalism became central to his ideas.[34]

Swain evidently assumes that his student readership will be totally ignorant of the events and issues under discussion. He produces no evidence of a factual character to back his conclusion. Nor does he attempt to support his argument on the basis of an analysis of Trotsky's writings. This glaring omission reflects his general disinterest in Trotsky as a writer. Swain makes a point of telling his readers that his biography makes no reference to the "great" work by Professor Baruch Knei-Paz, *The Social and Political Thought of Leon Trotsky*. Swain acknowledges that this may come as a surprise to Trotsky scholars. But he defends his omission by arguing that Knei-Paz attributed greater importance to Trotsky's writings than they merit:

> Knei-Paz collects together Trotsky's writing under certain themes, bringing together early and later essays into a coherent exposition; this approach makes Trotsky a far greater thinker than he was in reality. Trotsky wrote an enormous amount and, as a journalist, he was always happy to write on subjects about which he knew very little.[35]

---

[34] Swain, p. 3.

[35] Ibid. His exclusion of Knei-Paz reflects his work's essentially dishonest intentions. Swain can find no useful purpose in the work of Knei-Paz, whose point of departure is the explicit

When a historian delivers such an unqualified judgment, it is to be expected that he will proceed to substantiate his claim. Swain should have supported it by pointing to specific essays or articles in which Trotsky showed himself to be ignorant of the subject matter with which he was dealing. Swain fails to present a single citation to support his argument. Instead, he continues in the same vein: "Trotsky could write beautifully, but he was no philosopher."[36] In fact, Trotsky never claimed to be one. But this did not prevent him from grasping more profoundly and precisely the social, political and economic realities of the age in which he lived than the philosophers of his generation. Who better understood the nature of twentieth century imperialism and fascism: Martin Heidegger, who ostentatiously proclaimed his allegiance to Hitler, or Trotsky? Who had deeper and clearer insights into the bankruptcy of Fabian reformism in Britain: Bertrand Russell or Trotsky?[37]

A more honest and capable historian might have included in an analysis of Trotsky's stature as a writer the following extract from the diaries of the great German literary critic, Walter Benjamin: "June 3, 1931 ... The previous evening, a conversation with Brecht, Brentano, and Hesse in the Café du Centre. The conversation turned to Trotsky; Brecht maintained there were good reasons for thinking that Trotsky was the greatest living European writer."[38] One can only imagine what Swain might have contributed to this conversation had he been present at the Café du Centre. "Well perhaps, Bertolt. But Trotsky is no philosopher!"

acknowledgement that Trotsky was an important political thinker and a major figure in twentieth century European culture. For Knei-Paz, Trotsky was not only a "quintessential revolutionary in an age which has not lacked in revolutionary figures." Trotsky's "achievements in the realm of theory and ideas is in many ways no less prodigious: he was among the first to analyze the emergence, in the twentieth century, of social change in backward societies, and among the first, as well, to attempt to explain the political consequences which would almost inevitably grow out of such change. He wrote voluminously throughout his life, and the political thinker in him was no less an intrinsic part of his personality than the better-known man of action." (Baruch Knei-Paz, *The Social and Political Thought of Leon Trotsky* [London: Oxford University Press, 1978] pp. viii-ix).

[36] Swain, p. 3.

[37] Trotsky did write many brilliant essays on the subject of dialectical materialist philosophy. But Swain says nothing about these works, nor does he evince the slightest interest in the philosophical method employed by Trotsky in his writings.

[38] Walter Benjamin, *Selected Writings, Volume 2: 1927-1934* (Cambridge, MA: Harvard University Press, 1999), p. 477.

As one works through the entire biography, one cannot help but be amazed by the indifference that Swain displays toward Trotsky's writings. Many of his most important works are barely mentioned, or even totally ignored. Though he acknowledges Trotsky's decisive role in the victory of the Red Army in the Civil War, Swain ignores his important writings on military theory. This is a significant omission, because many of the political and theoretical differences that arose between Trotsky and the Stalinist faction in later years were anticipated in the earlier conflicts over military policy.[39] There is no reference to Trotsky's extraordinary manifestos and speeches prepared for the first four Congresses of the Communist International (1919-1922). He makes no mention of Trotsky's far-sighted analysis of the emergence of American imperialism to a position of world domination and its evolving relationship with a declining and dependent Europe. This does not prevent Swain from proclaiming pompously that Trotsky "had absolutely no understanding of European politics."[40] One might just as well write that Einstein had no understanding of physics! Such ludicrous statements are written for only one purpose: to fill the minds of students who are unfamiliar with Trotsky's life and the historical period in which he lived with intellectually disorienting absurdities.

Swain's effort to convert Trotsky into an enthusiastic partisan of the Stalinist program of "socialism in one country" amounts to a grotesque distortion and outright falsification of his actual views. Swain attributes to Lenin the authorship of this conception, noting that Stalin's lecture in which the new program was introduced invoked a quotation from an article Lenin had written in 1915. He fails to explain that Stalin ripped this quote out of context,

---

[39] While Swain at least credits Trotsky for the victory of the Red Army in the Civil War, his account fails to identify or analyze the elements of his military leadership that were critical to the victory of the revolutionary forces. For a serious study of Trotsky's development as a military theorist and revolutionary general, the interested reader would be well-advised to consult the perceptive work of Col. Harold Walter Nelson, *Leon Trotsky and the Art of Insurrection* (London: F. Cass, 1988). Writing as a military expert, Col. Nelson (who taught at the US Army War College) provides a thoroughly objective and professional account of Trotsky's maturation as a significant figure in military history. Nelson concentrates on the period between 1905 and 1917, and Trotsky emerges in his account "as a genuine revolutionary general—one who can lead and coordinate decisive revolutionary action. He comes to understand the problems of armed conflict which the revolution must solve, he gains an appreciation of the resources which the revolution can call upon to solve these problems, he develops schemes for organizing these resources for maximum effectiveness, and he discerns the factors which motivate the men who must fight to gain the revolutionary victory." (p. 4).

[40] Swain, p. 195.

and conveniently ignored the innumerable statements by Lenin emphatically linking the fate of socialism in Russia to the world revolution. More seriously, whether from ignorance, sheer incomprehension or design, Swain falsifies the views of Leon Trotsky. Referring to the 1925 series of articles by Trotsky published under the title *Towards Socialism or Capitalism?*, Swain asserts that its logic "was clear. Socialism in one country could work if the correct economic policy was followed and state industrial investment gradually accelerated."[41]

If one identifies the possibility of initiating socialist construction within the USSR (which Trotsky advocated and encouraged) with the long-term viability of a Soviet form of nationalism (which Trotsky emphatically rejected), the theoretical content and political implications of the debate over economic policy are rendered incomprehensible. Even in *Towards Socialism or Capitalism?*, written in 1925 when he was still working through the implications of the nationalist shift in the theoretical basis of Soviet economic policy, Trotsky explicitly warned that the long-term survival of world capitalism meant that "socialism in a backward country would be confronted with great dangers."[42] In September 1926 he declared that "The Opposition is profoundly convinced of the victory of socialism in our country not because our country can be torn free of the world economy and of world revolution but because the victory of the proletarian revolution is guaranteed the world over."[43] In other words, socialism could be built in Russia if the working class conquered power in revolutionary struggles beyond its borders. Trotsky's speech to the Fifteenth Conference on November 1, 1926, was a comprehensive attack on the perspective of national socialism.[44] Swain, of course, ignores this and other crucial texts that must be examined in order to deal correctly with the issue of "socialism in one country."

Swain on 1923

Swain's treatment of the crucial opening round of Trotsky's struggle against the degeneration of the Soviet Communist Party is little more than a defense of

---

[41] Swain, p. 160.

[42] Leon Trotsky, *Towards Socialism or Capitalism?* (London: New Park Publications, 1976), p. 60.

[43] Leon Trotsky, *The Challenge of the Left Opposition* 1926-27 (New York: Pathfinder Press, 1980), p. 106.

[44] Ibid., pp. 130-164.

the emerging Stalinist faction against Trotsky's criticisms. Especially significant is Swain's condemnation of a letter and series of articles written by Trotsky in early December 1923 under the title, *The New Course*. Swain writes:

> In the programmatic essay *The New Course*, written on 8 December and published after some haggling in *Pravda* on 11 December 1923, Trotsky denounced the increasingly bureaucratic leadership of the Party, asserting that the old, established leadership was in conflict with a younger generation. In one of those exaggerated parallels he loved, he compared the situation among the Bolshevik leaders with the time in the history of the German Social Democratic Party when the once radical allies of Marx and Engels slipped almost imperceptibly into a new role as the fathers of reformism. It was a nice image, but Kamenev, Stalin and Zinoviev were hardly going to relish the implication that only Trotsky was the true revolutionary and that they were mere reformists.
>
> In writing *The New Course*, Trotsky not only insulted his Politburo colleagues but, in Bolshevik terms, he gave them the moral high ground. He had reached an agreement and then broken it. He had done the same with Lenin at the height of the Brest-Litovsk crisis. During the Trade Union Debate he had joined the Zinoviev Commission only to declare he would take no part in its work. The resolution against factionalism adopted at the Tenth Party Congress had been aimed specifically at preventing this sort of behavior. Whether or not Trotsky's behavior had verged on factionalism in autumn 1923 could be open to interpretation, but *The New Course* was factionalist beyond doubt. He had signed up to a compromise, and then broken with it, challenging the revolutionary credentials of his Politburo comrades in the process.[45]

What Swain offers here is not an objective account of the political origins, issues and events related to the conflict that erupted inside the Soviet Communist Party, but rather his own highly partisan defense of those who were the objects of Trotsky's criticisms. Swain's angry references to Trotsky's behavior during the Brest-Litovsk crisis in 1918 and the trade union conflict in 1920 read as if they were copied from the texts of Stalin's own speeches. Swain tells us that Kamenev, Zinoviev and Stalin "were hardly going to relish"

---

[45] Swain, p. 152.

Trotsky's criticisms, as if that somehow invalidates what Trotsky wrote in *The New Course*.

It is peculiar, to say the least, for a historian writing in 2006 to upbraid Trotsky for having engaged in "factionalist" behavior in launching what was to become one of the epochal political conflicts of the twentieth century. Swain, enjoying the benefit of hindsight, knows how all of this was to eventually turn out. The suppression of inner-party democracy, against which Trotsky raised his protest, was ultimately to grow into a brutal totalitarian dictatorship that carried out mass murder. And while Trotsky's criticisms may have bruised the egos of Kamenev and Zinoviev, the two Old Bolsheviks suffered a far more terrible fate at the hands of Stalin thirteen years later. Moreover, for Swain to chastise Trotsky's warning of the danger of political degeneration of the older generation of Bolshevik leaders as "exaggerated" is nothing less than incredible. As history was to demonstrate all too tragically, Trotsky's invocation of the example of the German Social Democratic leaders was, if anything, an underestimation of the dimensions of the tragedy that awaited the Bolshevik Party.

As for the specific charge that the writing of *The New Course* was inappropriate and factional behavior, it is not based on an honest reading of the historical record. Swain conveniently fails to note that the Politburo was dominated by a secret faction formed by Stalin, Zinoviev and Kamenev, which was grounded not on programmatic agreement, but rather on a shared determination to undermine Trotsky's political influence. Trotsky was working inside a Politburo whose deliberations were tainted by *ex parte* agreements worked out behind the scenes by Stalin, Zinoviev and Kamenev. Moreover, as E. H. Carr explained quite cogently in 1954, Trotsky's letter of December 8, 1923—part of the set of documents known as *The New Course*—was of an entirely principled character.

Carr also explains that the triumvirate and Trotsky had approached the drafting of the December 5, 1923, resolution on party reform with very different aims and criteria. For Stalin, Kamenev and Zinoviev, the actual content of the resolution was of secondary or even tertiary significance. Their interest in arriving at an agreement with Trotsky was based on purely tactical considerations, related to the struggle for power. With opposition to the increasingly bureaucratic and high-handed methods of the leadership spreading, the triumvirs were seeking to prevent, or at least delay, Trotsky's open break with the Central Committee leadership. For Trotsky, in contrast, the resolution raised matters of high principle. Carr noted the difference between Trotsky and his opponents. "Trotsky, accustomed to see differences within the party fought out and settled through the drafting of party resolutions, attached to a victory on paper a practical value which, in the new conditions of party leadership, it no longer possessed."[46]

Carr's assessment is endorsed by historian Robert V. Daniels in his influential *The Conscience of the Revolution*. Explaining the sequence of events that led to the writing of *The New Course*, Daniels writes: "Trotsky, aware of the hostility toward him that was barely concealed behind the resolution, undertook to stress its reform implications in an open letter to a party meeting on December 8. This New Course letter was an enthusiastic endorsement and explanation of the resolution of December 5, with emphasis on the role of the party rank-and-file in its execution..."[47]

Entirely absent from Swain's account is an analysis of the objective processes that underlay the deepening political conflict. Swain offers virtually no assessment of the changes that were taking place under the impact of the New Economic Policy (NEP) within the Soviet Union and their reflection within the Party. He provides no political or intellectual portraits of Trotsky's opponents. He does not examine the changing composition of the Bolshevik Party, or examine the phenomenon of bureaucratism that was to have such catastrophic consequences for the fate of the Bolshevik Party and Soviet society.

Swain's dismissal of Trotsky's final exile

Swain devotes just 25 pages to the last twelve years of Trotsky's life. To describe his treatment of those years as superficial would be a compliment. The most catastrophic event in post-World War I European history, the accession of Hitler and his Nazi party to power in Germany, barely receives a mention. Swain takes no note of the relationship between this event and the most important political decisions made by Trotsky during his final exile: his call for a political revolution in the USSR and for the founding of the Fourth International. After briefly noting that Trotsky, arriving in Prinkipo in 1929 following his expulsion from the USSR, called on his supporters to remain inside the Communist International, Swain writes: "By 1933 he had changed his mind..."[48] No reference is made to the cataclysmic event that produced this

---

[46] E.H. Carr, *The Interregnum* (New York: MacMillan, 1968) p. 305.

[47] Robert V. Daniels, *The Conscience of the Revolution: Communist Opposition in Soviet Russia* (New York: Simon & Schuster, 1960), p. 223.

[48] Swain, p. 194.

change in policy—the accession of Hitler to power as a result of the betrayal of the Communist International and its German party. Swain makes no assessment of Trotsky's writings on the German crisis. One has only to compare Swain's near silence on the subject to E. H. Carr's treatment of Trotsky's efforts to rouse the German working class against the fascist threat. In his last work, *The Twilight of the Comintern*, Carr considered Trotsky's writings on the German crisis of 1931-33 to be of such importance that he included an appendix devoted to this subject. "Trotsky," he wrote, "maintained during the period of Hitler's rise to power so persistent and, for the most part, so prescient a commentary on the course of events in Germany as to deserve record."[49]

Similarly the Moscow Trials and the ensuing purges are assigned a few sentences, substantially less than Swain devotes to Trotsky's brief personal relationship with Frida Kahlo in Mexico. The writing of Trotsky's most important political treatise *The Revolution Betrayed* is noted in one sentence. Trotsky's passionate essays on the Spanish Revolution, warning that the popular front policies of the Stalinists were clearing the path for a Franco victory, go unmentioned. The *Transitional Program*, the founding document of the Fourth International, is not referred to. Swain also ignores the last great polemical documents written by Trotsky on the nature of the USSR. Finally, Swain concludes his biography with the observation that Trotsky might have done better had he quit politics after the 1917 October Revolution and devoted himself entirely to journalism, in which, presumably, Trotsky would have been able—as Swain has already told us—"to write on subjects about which he knew very little."

3. Thatcher's Method of Historical Falsification

I have already made brief reference to the method of Ian Thatcher. Let us return to this subject by reviewing three paragraphs that appear in the introduction to Thatcher's biography of Trotsky.

> From Trotsky's account of 1917 only he emerges with honour. If in 1924 one accepted the arguments of "Lessons of October," then only one man could replace the now dead Lenin, namely Leon Trotsky. It is perfectly understandable, then, that having

---

[49] E. H. Carr, *Twilight of the Comintern, 1930-1935* (New York: Pantheon Books, 1982), p. 433.

been accused of the sins of Menshevism in 1917, Trotsky's colleagues sought to refute his "Lessons of October." This they did in a series of speeches and articles, which were then gathered together and published in Russian and in translations in book form.

Leading Bolsheviks (including Kamenev, Stalin, Zinoviev and Bukharin) and key representatives from the Communist International (the Comintern) and the Communist Youth League (the Komsomol) argued that Trotsky's essay was not a genuine history of the October Revolution. If one consulted the key documents of the time and a growing supply of memoir literature, for example, Trotsky's detractors claimed that one would discover how far his memory had painted a distorted picture. Most notably, Trotsky had minimized the roles played by Lenin and the Bolshevik Party and had exaggerated his own contribution. It was, for example, wrong to claim that in 1917 there was a long and sustained battle between a Lenin seeking to rearm the party with Trotsky's theory of permanent revolution and a right-Menshevik faction within Bolshevik ranks. In actual fact Lenin's analysis of the events of 1917 grew out of a long-held theory of the Russian Revolution. Once Lenin had convinced colleagues of the correctness of his developing strategy, the party acted in a unified way to guarantee victory. In this process, neither Lenin nor the party was in any way influenced by Trotsky or Trotskyism.

Indeed, the anti-Trotsky case continues, the whole history of Leninism and Bolshevism before and after 1917 was one of opposition to Trotskyism. Unfortunately, Trotsky had failed to realize that he was only effective in 1917 because he acted under the guidance of the Bolshevik Party. Indeed, Trotsky had never fully understood the implications of joining the Bolshevik Party. He had not made a full commitment to becoming a Bolshevik. If he had, then he would have produced a very different history. Trotsky would, for example, have admitted his past and recent theoretical, as well as organisational, errors. Only in this way would youth understand the proper relationship between Leninism and Trotskyism, and how to avoid the sins of the latter. "Lessons of October" was an attempt by Trotsky to replace Leninism with Trotskyism. This, however, the Bolshevik Party would not allow him to achieve. The leadership understood the dangers of Trotskyism, revealed in Trotsky's underestimation of the importance of the peasantry, and in his mistaken policies during the peace negotiations with Germany, in the debate over the trade unions and on the issue of currency reform.[50]

The significance of these paragraphs is that they exemplify a highly-contrived stylistic technique repeatedly employed by Thatcher in order to mask his falsification of history—that is, his construction of a seemingly objective historical narrative out of the factional statements of Trotsky's mortal political enemies. Virtually everything written in the above-cited three paragraphs is a lie. The "criticisms" of Trotsky have been drawn together by Thatcher from a series of mendacious attacks written by Stalin, Zinoviev and Kamenev in November and December 1924 in order to discredit Trotsky's brilliant analysis of the political differences and struggles within the Bolshevik Party during the critical year of the revolution.

Trotsky's *Lessons of October* explored events and controversies that Zinoviev, Kamenev and Stalin—whose right-wing and conciliatory policies had placed them in opposition to Lenin at various points in 1917—did not wish to have aired. Stalin and Kamenev had allied themselves with the Mensheviks in March 1917, prior to Lenin's return to Russia. In October 1917, Kamenev and Zinoviev had opposed the insurrection. Furthermore, the role of Trotsky in securing the victory of the Bolsheviks in October 1917 was rivaled only by that played by Lenin himself. The arguments presented in the above-cited paragraphs were fabricated in order to deflect the impact of Trotsky's criticisms in *Lessons of October* as well as to destroy his reputation as a revolutionary leader. As historian Robert V. Daniels has written, the charges made against Trotsky in response to *Lessons of October* "were either entirely fabricated or exaggerated beyond all measure—it was the man that the offended leaders were bent on destroying, not doctrinal error."[51]

Thatcher neither explains the context of the attack on Trotsky nor challenges its factual validity. He adopts a pose of studied even-handedness in his presentation of lies and fabrications. The "anti-Trotsky case"—Thatcher's euphemism for the bureaucracy's gigantic slander campaign—is endowed with reasonableness, dignity and legitimacy. In effect, Thatcher offers the pages of his biography as a dumping ground for the political and historical

---

[50] Thatcher, pp. 6-8.

[51] Robert V. Daniels, *The Conscience of the Revolution* (New York: Simon and Schuster, 1969), p. 244. Another excellent source for an objective presentation of the controversy sparked by *Lessons of October* is E. H. Carr's *Socialism in One Country*, Vol. 2 (Baltimore, MD: Pelican Books, 1970), pp. 11-44.

falsifications upon which the emerging Soviet bureaucracy built its struggle against Trotsky. This insidious and dishonest technique, in which old lies are repackaged as objective historical narrative, is employed repeatedly by Thatcher.

The "myth" of 1905

Like Swain, Thatcher promises to expose "key myths" about Trotsky's life, such as his role in the 1905 Revolution. Let us examine how Professor Thatcher goes about his work. Given the fact that Trotsky's crucial role in the 1905 Revolution has been universally accepted by scholars throughout the world, one would imagine that Thatcher would recognize that a challenge to this scholarly consensus required a careful marshalling of new facts and arguments. As it turns out, despite the attention called to this very issue by the publisher's introduction (which is also cited on the back cover of the volume), Thatcher's "demythologizing" of Trotsky's role in 1905 takes up no more than one relatively brief *paragraph*.

He begins by writing that "It is difficult to gauge the exact influence that Trotsky had upon the course of the 1905 Revolution."[52] Yes, it may be difficult to determine the exact influence, but there exists a substantial body of information that permits certain informed judgments about the degree and scale of his influence. Numerous memoirs from the period testify to his commanding political presence. Trotsky became the chairman of the Petersburg Soviet, and edited two newspapers, *Russkaya gazeta* and *Nachalo*, which enjoyed large circulations. As if anticipating the latter objection, Thatcher claims that "We have no way of knowing how many people were affected by his journalism."[53] Again, this is not true. In an article that appeared under his byline in *History Review* in September 2005, Thatcher himself acknowledges that the circulation of these two newspapers may have been as high as 100,000, which was at least 20,000 higher than those of their rivals.[54] In his Trotsky biography, Thatcher abruptly introduces a new line of argument, which is irrelevant to

[52] Thatcher, p. 35.

[53] Ibid.

[54] Thatcher tries to downplay the significance of the circulation figures by suggesting that the press run may have been greater than the actual readership. That is of course possible. But it is also possible that the readership, when copies that were passed around are considered, may have been greater than the press run.

the issue of Trotsky's political influence in the 1905 Revolution. "It is unlikely," writes Thatcher, "that his words reached many peasants. He simply
lacked connections with the villages, and there was not a mass distribution of
his appeals to the peasantry."[55]

This is really beside the point. The influence of Trotsky and the Russian
Social Democratic movement as a whole in 1905 arose on the basis of the
mass urban proletarian constituency. The St. Petersburg Soviet was a political
organ of the working class. It arose on a wave of revolutionary working class
activity that included the mass general strike of October 1905. The peasantry
joined the unrest *en masse* only in 1906, in the aftermath of the physical suppression of the socialist-led working class movement.

Thatcher continues: "Even in the capital, his main stomping-ground, he
did not create or found any specific institution or faction. He was not, for
example, the guiding force behind the emergence of the Soviet of Workers'
Deputies, *even though he may subsequently have been, as one participant re-
cords, 'the unchallenged leader of the Mensheviks in the Petersburg Soviet'* [em-
phasis added]."[56] Like the issue of the peasantry, the question of Trotsky's
factional affiliations is tossed in by Thatcher for no other reason than to try
to build a case against the established historical record. At that point in the
history of the Russian Social Democratic movement, factional identities were
far more fluid than they were to become by 1917. Indeed, Trotsky's political position was actually strengthened by his relative independence from the
main political factions. Let us note Thatcher's awkward formulation: Trotsky
"may subsequently have been" the unchallenged leader of the Mensheviks in
the Soviet. Only "may have been"? Thatcher presents no evidence to the contrary, even though one can safely assume he would have trumpeted it had he
been able to find it. However, he proceeds to make a novel argument. "In the
memoirs of the prime minister of the day, Count Witte, Trotsky does not
merit a mention ... this only confirms the limited impression Trotsky made at
the time on the popular consciousness."[57]

This is the argument of a sly trickster, not of a conscientious scholar.
Count Witte, the tsar's prime minister, failed to mention Trotsky in his memoirs! This single detail is endowed by Thatcher with extraordinary historical
significance. From the failure of Witte to mention Trotsky, Thatcher claims

[55] Thatcher, p. 35.

[56] Ibid.

[57] Ibid.

we can draw far-ranging conclusions about Trotsky's place in popular con-sciousness in the autumn of 1905. One must ask why Thatcher has made no reference to other memoirs, written by individuals who were more familiar than Count Witte—an aged aristocrat who was most at home in palaces and vast leafy estates—with what was happening in the workers' districts of St. Petersburg? It is characteristic of unscrupulous and bad scholarship to conceal or disregard historical evidence that runs counter to one's argument. But this is precisely what Thatcher has done. For example, he should have brought to the attention of his student readers the recollections of Anatoly Lunacharsky, who was a participant in the 1905 Revolution as a member of the Bolshevik faction. In his renowned *Revolutionary Silhouettes*, Lunacharsky provided this estimate of Trotsky's role in 1905:

> His popularity among the Petersburg proletariat at the time of his arrest was tremendous and increased still more as a result of his picturesque and heroic behaviour in court. I must say that of all the social-democratic leaders of 1905-06 Trotsky undoubtedly showed himself, despite his youth, to be the best prepared. Less than any of them did he bear the stamp of a certain kind of émigré narrowness of outlook which, as I have said, even affected Lenin at that time. Trotsky understood better than all the others what it meant to conduct the political struggle on a broad, national scale. He emerged from the revolution having acquired an enormous degree of popularity, whereas neither Lenin nor Martov had ef-fectively gained any at all. Plekhanov had lost a great deal, thanks to his display of quasi-Kadet tendencies. Trotsky stood then in the very front rank.[58]

Lunacharsky also recalled an incident during which Trotsky was praised, in the presence of Lenin, as the strong man of the St. Petersburg Soviet. This was a time of factional conflict between Lenin and Trotsky, and so the former did not necessarily enjoy hearing of his rival's political triumph. According to Lunacharsky, "Lenin's face darkened for a moment, then he said: 'Well, Trotsky has earned it by his brilliant and unflagging work."[59]

Thatcher also chose not to mention another contemporary memoir—that of the Menshevik leader Theodore Dan—which leaves no question

---

[58] Anatoly Lunacharsky, *Revolutionary Silhouettes* (London: Penguin Press, 1967), pp. 60-61.

[59] Ibid., p. 60.

about the immense political influence of Leon Trotsky in 1905. The political perspective with which Trotsky was now associated—the recognition of the proletarian and socialist character of the revolution—captured the imagination of substantial forces among both the Bolshevik and Menshevik tendencies.

Dan recalled "that practically speaking both Mensheviks and Bolsheviks were pushed toward 'Trotskyism.' For a short time 'Trotskyism' (which at that time, to be sure, still lacked a name), for the first and last time in the history of the Russian Social-Democracy, became its unifying platform. Hence it was no accident also that after the arrest (in November) of Khrustalyov, the chairman of the Petersburg Soviet of Workers' Deputies, it was precisely Trotsky ... who became his natural heir, challenged by no one—for the few short days the Soviet itself still had to live."[60]

Thatcher's failure to cite important eyewitness sources that contradict and disprove his attempt to call into question Trotsky's role in the 1905 Revolution, discredits not only his biography but places his integrity as a historian under a shadow. I must stress that his improper handling of this particular issue, i.e., Trotsky's role in 1905, is not an isolated episode. It is emblematic of the method he employs throughout his biography to discredit Trotsky.

Thatcher's falsification of the inner-party struggle

Thatcher's treatment of the political struggle that arose within the Russian Communist Party in the early 1920s is a travesty of scholarly writing. As in the introduction, Thatcher incorporates the arguments of Trotsky's factional opponents into what he attempts to palm off as an objective presentation of historical events. For example, in a crucial section of the biography that deals with the eruption of the inner-party struggle in October 1923, Thatcher writes that Trotsky "took up his anti-bureaucracy programme with his usual sense of urgency and passion, believing that the party was entering a new epoch through which *only his methods* would ensure a safe passage [emphasis added]."[61]

Thatcher continues:

---

[60] Theodore Dan, *The Origins of Bolshevism* (New York: Schocken Books, 1970), p. 345.

[61] Thatcher, p. 125. In reality, Trotsky never made such subjective claims of personal infallibility. And Thatcher does not produce a single citation in which Trotsky argued that "only his methods" would work.

His colleagues on the party's leading bodies were, however, not convinced. They doubted whether matters were really as bad as Trotsky depicted. Yes, there were economic problems, but these were quite expected. In any case there was no imminent danger of collapse. The party anticipated several years of hard and steady work before it could claim to have fully rectified the economy. Looking at the party, Trotsky's comrades claimed that they could congratulate themselves on educating a new generation of cadres. The influx of this fresh blood would no doubt expedite the resolution of important tasks. Having rejected Trotsky's analysis of imagined ills besetting the regime, a majority of the old Bolsheviks wondered whether he could be trusted to develop sound and sensible policies. If Trotsky was prone to exaggeration of difficulties, he was, they argued, remarkably vague in his solutions. For a majority of the Politburo, Trotsky was part of a problem, not an answer. For example, if he was concerned by an absence of systematic leadership why did he not attend important meetings of the Council of Labour and Defense and of the Cabinet? There was little evidence of conscientiousness in Trotsky's work habits. Furthermore, there was a marked absence of concrete proposals from Trotsky. This was hardly surprising, since his policy record was far from promising. In recent times Trotsky had suffered a series of defeats as he opposed Lenin over, amongst other matters, the Brest-Litovsk peace and the trade unions. For his colleagues, Trotsky's discontents were not rooted in reality, but in a hurt sense of pride stemming from personal disappointments. Thus, Trotsky could not have been pleased when, in April 1923, the Twelfth Congress shelved his more militant approach to religious affairs. In September 1923 Trotsky was certainly upset by personnel changes to the Military-Revolutionary Committee. Finally, and most annoying of all for Trotsky, came the Central Committee's refusal to grant him dictatorial powers. Trotsky was warned that his unfounded criticisms were encouraging anti-party platforms, sowing unnecessary disruption to important party work, and threatening a war between the older and younger generations.[62]

This passage, as written by Thatcher, creates the impression that the majority on the Politburo—euphemistically referred to as "Trotsky's

---

[62] Ibid., pp. 125-126.

comrades"—was responding to Trotsky's criticism in a manner that was both restrained and reasonable. It was confronted, in the person of Trotsky, with something of a loose cannon, with whom it was hard, if not impossible, to work. He pestered his "colleagues" with exaggerated warnings and unreasonable demands, while failing to carry out the assignments for which he was responsible. Moreover, Trotsky had a poor grasp of reality and a history of stirring up trouble, even with Lenin, was motivated by subjective bitterness, and, worst of all, was demanding dictatorial powers. Thatcher's presentation clearly invites his students to form a negative opinion of Trotsky and his political work.

What Thatcher has not communicated to his readers is that the above-quoted passage is his own tendentious rephrasing of an unscrupulous and dishonest factional document produced by Trotsky's bitter political opponents—soporifically referred to by Thatcher as "comrades" and "colleagues"—on October 19, 1923, in response to Trotsky's important letter of October 8, 1923, and the famous oppositional "Letter of the 46" of October 15, 1923. There are no quotation marks and no footnotes. There is no clear indication given by Thatcher that the arguments he so benignly summarizes were, in fact, a pack of factionally-motivated lies and half-truths.[63]

Nor does Thatcher inform his readers that Trotsky prepared a withering response to this letter, which he dispatched on October 23, 1923, to refute the accusations of Zinoviev, Kamenev and Stalin, who had formed an unprincipled anti-Trotsky faction known as the Triumvirs.

One has only to consult E. H. Carr's *The Interregnum*, in which this material is reviewed (or at least that part of it that had come to light by the early 1950s), to recognize the deliberately misleading character of Thatcher's approach. Carr cites passages from Trotsky's "stinging retort" to the Triumvirs, and leaves no doubt as to where truth lay in this exchange.[64]

---

[63] The October 19, 1923 letter is included in the collection of documents published in *The Struggle for Power: Russia in 1923*, edited and translated by Valentina Vilkova. Although Thatcher frequently cites Vilkova, he does not list her work as a source for the Oct. 19 letter, nor does he refer to her assessment of this document. Vilkova writes that the Oct. 19 letter "is a vivid illustration of the methods used by the majority when carrying out the discussion. Most probably that document has been written by Stalin, since the argumentation and the style of presentation almost coincided with that of the speech of the General Secretary at the October Plenary Meeting of the Central Committee. The letter contained seriously strained interpretations, sheer lies, and the falsification of both the historical facts and the appraisal of the situation in the Party and in the country as a whole." (New York: Prometheus Press, 1996) p. 28.

[64] E. H. Carr, *The Interregnum* p. 299.

Trotsky's speech at the 13th Congress

One of Deutscher's great achievements as a biographer was his portrayal of the heroism and pathos of Trotsky's struggle, under increasingly difficult circumstances, versus the immense and reactionary bureaucracy arrayed against him. Thatcher, determined to erase the historical record, employs rhetorical tricks, incompatible with serious scholarship, to belittle Trotsky's struggle and portray it in a demeaning and unflattering light. Once again I must call attention to his deceptive use of citations. Thatcher refers to Trotsky's main speech at the Thirteenth Party Congress in May 1924, and writes, "It was, it has been argued, 'the most inept speech of his career.'"[65]

Who, one wonders, was the original author of this damning judgment? Was it written, perhaps, by a participant at the Congress, either an opponent or supporter of Trotsky? As it turns out, the source is to be found in a volume, published by the University of Toronto Press in 1974, of *Resolutions and Decisions of the Communist Party of the Soviet Union*. This volume includes a set of documents from the Thirteenth Congress, which is briefly introduced by Professor Richard Gregor, the volume's editor. Gregor writes that Trotsky "made what may well be the most inept speech of his career."[66] He offers no argument in support of this appraisal, and the speech itself is not reproduced. Furthermore, Gregor is hardly a historian to whom one turns for a well-considered and unbiased judgment of Soviet politics.[67] Other than serving the utilitarian purpose of belittling Trotsky, there is no compelling reason why Gregor's passing remark about the speech to the Thirteenth Congress should have been cited as if it were an authoritative judgment.

---

[65] Thatcher, p. 127.

[66] Gregor, p. 221.

[67] In his general introduction to the entire volume, Gregor bitterly denounces Lenin in terms redolent of Cold War anti-communist ideologues. He argues that Stalinism was the logical outcome of Lenin's personal intolerance and political doctrine.

> Lenin was the mentor and Stalin the pupil who carried his master's legacy to its logical conclusion. The pages of history are full of accounts of atrocities committed in the name of high principles. The two bolshevik leaders were no exception. As difficult as it may be to accept it, both, in their own ways, wished to serve what they regarded as the most worthy cause; and there lies one of the ironies of history, for there are no men more dangerous and more ruthless than those who "know" how to save mankind (p. 38).

Let us further examine Thatcher's use of Trotsky's Thirteenth Congress speech, which concluded with the well-known and oft-cited phrase, "Right or wrong this is my party, and I will take responsibility for its decision to the end." Thatcher himself quotes several sentences from Trotsky's speech, including the sentence cited above. He then writes, "Trotsky could thus have no grounds for complaint when the Thirteenth Congress affirmed the anti-Trotsky resolution of the Thirteenth Conference."[68] It all seems rather straightforward. Trotsky said, my party right or wrong, so how could he object when it passes a resolution directed against him? But Thatcher has withheld from his readers those passages that show Trotsky's speech to be far more subtle and combative than the citation provided in Thatcher's text indicates. Trotsky states emphatically his disagreement with the resolution, and asserts his responsibility to argue against those policies he considers incorrect.[69] By presenting a bowdlerized citation, Thatcher misrepresents Trotsky's position and legitimizes the actions taken against him by his opponents.

Thatcher falsifies the Lenin-Trotsky relationship

Thatcher asserts that "Lenin's relationship with Trotsky was highly problematic." He contends that in Lenin's political Testament of December 1922, "Trotsky was not given a recommendation higher than any other comrade." This is not true. While expressing reservations over Trotsky's "excessive self-assurance" and "excessive preoccupation with the purely administrative side of work," Lenin said he was "distinguished by his outstanding ability" and "personally perhaps the most capable man in the present C.C. [Central Committee]..."[70] The same Testament warned against Stalin's accumulation of "unlimited authority concentrated in his hands..."[71] Lenin's famous

---

[68] Thatcher, p. 128.

[69] In a relevant passage, Trotsky stated, "The English have a proverb: My country right or wrong. We can say with much greater historical justification: Whether it is right or wrong in any particular, specific question at any particular moment, this is my party. And although some comrades may think I was wrong in raising this or that point; although some comrades may think I have incorrectly described this or that danger; I for my part believe that I am only fulfilling my duty as a party member who warns his party about what he considers to be a danger." For the full text of Trotsky's speech see *The Challenge of the Left Opposition 1923-25* (New York: Pathfinder Press, 1975 [fifth printing of 2002]), pp. 161-180. The citation presented here appears on page 179.

[70] Lenin, *Collected Works*, Vol. 36 (Moscow: Progress Publishers, 1966), p. 595.

[71] Ibid., pp. 594.

addendum to his Testament, which Thatcher fails to mention, urged the Central Committee to remove Stalin from the position of general secretary.[72] Thatcher then writes: "Lenin was unlikely to have given his stamp of approval to Trotsky for the post of leader because, even in 1922-3 when he relied upon the Commissar of War to present some of his views, he remained suspicious of him. *Lenin's biographer has emphasised that he would have dropped Trotsky at the next available opportunity* [emphasis added]."[73]

This is a deliberately misleading and false presentation. Numerous historical studies have established, based on a well-documented record, that the last months of Lenin's life were dominated by his growing suspicion of and hostility to Stalin. Lenin's increasing distrust of Stalin was expressed in several documents written in the months and weeks before his career-ending stroke in March 1923. During the same period, Lenin drew ever closer to Trotsky, whom he viewed as his most important ally in the developing struggle against Stalin. But let us concede that the political developments in the critical period between December 1922 and March 1923 allow for varied interpretations. That still leaves us with Thatcher's reference to the alleged finding of "Lenin's biographer" that Lenin, had he lived, "would have dropped Trotsky at the next available opportunity."

The biographer cited in the relevant footnote is Robert Service, author of a three-volume study of Lenin. This is not the place for an evaluation of the qualities of Mr. Service's biography, of which I do not have a high opinion. But the issue here concerns Thatcher's use of citations. Turning to pages 273-274 of the Service biography (as indicated in Thatcher's footnote), there is no reference to a plan by Lenin to get rid of Trotsky. In fact, Service offers an entirely different assessment of Lenin's plans. While in the past, according to Service, Lenin had used Stalin to control Trotsky, "the disputes with Stalin over policies on foreign trade and on other matters reversed the situation: Trotski was needed in order to control the ever more rampant Stalin." Despite his past conflicts with Trotsky, "The October Revolution and the Civil War had brought them together, and Lenin was inviting Trotski to resume close collaboration."[74] A few pages later, Service comments further on Lenin's view of Trotsky and Stalin: "Of the two men, he had come to prefer

---

[72] Ibid., p. 596.

[73] Thatcher, p. 131.

[74] Robert Service, *Lenin: A Political Life*, Vol. 3 (Bloomington and Indianapolis: Indiana University Press, 1995), pp. 273-274.

Trotski despite his reservations. This was obvious in Lenin's recent letters seeking an alliance with him on questions of the day where Stalin stood in his way. In late December [1922], too, Lenin asked Krupskaya to confide the message to Trotski that his feelings towards him since Trotski had escaped from Siberia to London in 1902 had not changed and would not change 'until death itself.'"[75] Once again, we see that Thatcher, in the interest of his own campaign to discredit Trotsky, has attributed to another historian a statement he has not made.

Historians, like everyone else, are fallible. They make mistakes. Not every incorrect citation is proof of professional incompetence, let alone of a secret plan to distort and falsify. When one comes across such errors it is necessary to maintain a sense of proportion. But the problem that presents itself in the Thatcher biography is not a series of isolated mistakes but a system of distortion and falsification. Thatcher's presentation is designed to create among readers—especially students—not only a false image of Trotsky, but also a disoriented and distorted conception of an entire historical epoch.

What finds expression in the biographies written by Thatcher and Swain is a process that may be legitimately described as the erosion of historical truth. The historical image of Trotsky as a great revolutionary fighter and thinker that emerged out of the exposure of Stalin's lies and crimes—that is, out of the discrediting of the pervasive anti-Trotsky demonology that was pumped out of the Soviet Union (and for that matter all of Eastern Europe and China) and sustained by countless academics affiliated with Stalinist parties all over the world—is once again under attack. A sort of anti-historical intellectual counterrevolution is in progress, to which Thatcher and Swain are making their own disreputable contributions. Only in this way can we understand their zeal in attempting to belittle Trotsky, in even making him appear ridiculous.

Problems of Everyday Life

Let us examine Thatcher's treatment of Trotsky's remarkable essays published under the title *Problems of Everyday Life*. Thatcher strains to present Trotsky as an effete snob, who "was far from impressed with the general mores of Russian society. He viewed the mass of Russians as uncultured. He described them as illiterate, inefficient, dirty, unpunctual, prone to swearing

[75] Ibid., p. 285.

and abusive language, and under the sway of superstition."[76] Presented in this way, the reader is clearly encouraged to view Trotsky as an elitist, distant and remote from the great mass of the Russian people. This intended image is reinforced by Thatcher's sarcastic remark that "one cannot help thinking that his ideal human type consisted of his own habits writ large. His advice is littered with its own brand of simplifications …"[77]

Thatcher's summary is a spiteful and dishonest caricature of Trotsky's writings on *Problems of Everyday Life*. What is portrayed by Thatcher as an example of Trotsky's self-aggrandizing conceit, an immodest tribute to his own special qualities, is, when properly and knowledgeably viewed in the context of the history of the Russian revolutionary movement, one of the finest and most deeply felt elucidations of the relationship between culture, the development of proletarian class consciousness and the struggle for socialism. Presented by Thatcher as an irritating laundry list of Trotsky's personal objections to the Russian workers, the characteristics cited—illiteracy, inefficiency, propensity to swearing, etc.—were all manifestations of the terrible oppression suffered by the masses in tsarist Russia. They were part of what generations of the best elements in the democratic and socialist intelligentsia often described as "our terrible Russian reality." Their struggle against the shameful expressions of human degradation eventually found a profound response in the working class.[78]

---

[76] Thatcher, p. 135.

[77] Ibid., p. 137.

[78] As explained very well by Professor S. A. Smith of the University of Essex, "From the 1880s a stratum of 'conscious' workers emerged, who rebelled against the poverty and degradation which surrounded them and who struggled to advance themselves through education. Modelling themselves on the radical intelligentsia, they identified with the ideal of *kul'turnost'* which the intelligentsia represented. This concept of 'culturedness' connected ideas of growth of the individual to reflections on the evolution of society at large. On the one hand, it denoted inner cultivation, in the sense of intellectual development, refinement of manners and moral development: in short, the forging of a self worthy of man's innate dignity and capable of commanding respect in others. On the other hand, *kul'turnost'* was a sociological category used to evaluate the level of civilization achieved by a particular society along an evolutionary spectrum. In this respect, Russia was characterized precisely by its lack of *kul'turnost'*, perceived as lying closer to '*Asiatic*' barbarism than to western-European civilization." Smith continues, "For 'conscious' workers, a crucial element in the acquisition of *kul'turnost'* was the repudiation of swearing. Like the intelligentsia, these workers saw the ubiquity of swearing as a symptom of lack of culture that enslaved Russian society. At the individual level, swearing was a sign of the underdevelopment of *lichnost'*, that inner sense of personal dignity and worth as a human being, and a sign of lack of respect for others. And learning to regulate

When these writings are read as contributions to the development of class consciousness and *kul'turnost*, it is possible to appreciate the broader dimensions and ramifications of the issues raised by Trotsky in his *Problems of Everyday Life*, and of the significance of his essays such as "The Struggle for Cultured Speech" and "Civility and politeness as a necessary lubricant in daily relations." Interestingly, as Professor S. A. Smith points out, "the struggle for cultured speech faded from the political agenda" in the late 1920s, after Stalin secured his grip on power.[79] It is only necessary to add that much of what Trotsky writes in these articles is not only of historical interest, let alone merely relevant to a Russian audience. As we today confront our own terrible reality, where culture is under relentless attack and every form of social backwardness spawned and encouraged, *Problems of Everyday Life* remains a book for our times.

At certain points in his biography, Thatcher descends to levels that can only be described as utterly absurd. He declares that, "One can even claim that Trotsky was as dismissive of his female compatriots as any other egocentric man."[80] He offers as proof a passage from a librarian's memoir, which recalled that Trotsky's wife apparently went to borrow a journal on his behalf. And so, writes Thatcher, "we discover Trotsky using his wife as a (unpaid?) secretary..."[81] Thatcher also berates Trotsky for failing, as he had advised in one of his essays, "to view reality through women's eyes very seriously." What evidence does Thatcher present to support this reprimand? "Certainly he did not advocate a female candidate to replace Lenin; nor did he produce the promised fuller account of what he thought a woman's perspective on the world might be."[82] How does one begin to reply to such criticisms?[83]

---

speech (and emotions) was seen as vital to achieving the intellectual and moral self-activity that was at the heart of *kul'turnost'*. By extension, the capacity to control speech indicated an individual's potential to exercise control over wider aspects of working life and, ultimately, over society as a whole. At the social level, the widespread use of *mat* [swearing] among workers was, for the conscious minority, a depressing reminder of the political backwardness of the working class." ("The Social Meanings of Swearing: Workers and Bad Language in Late Imperial and Early Soviet Russia," *Past and Present*, No. 160 [August 1998], pp. 177-179).

[79] Professor Smith writes that "during the Stalin era, it became acceptable for the new breed of official to use *mat*." (Ibid., p. 200).

[80] Thatcher, p. 137.

[81] Ibid.

[82] Ibid., p. 138.

[83] Thatcher fails to indicate who that female candidate might have been. So as not to permit

4. When Lies are Told Against History

Thatcher on the impossibility of revolution

There are two interrelated arguments Thatcher makes repeatedly in his biography: 1) There is no reason to believe that either Russian or European history would have developed any differently had Trotsky defeated Stalin; and 2) Trotsky's criticisms of Stalin were, on the whole, unfair. Dealing with economic policy, Thatcher states, "Of course, even if by some miracle Trotsky had been able to grasp the reins of power, there are many reasons to doubt whether he would have enjoyed the sorts of policy successes his programme promised. One can question, for example, whether a Soviet economy managed by Trotsky could have provided industrial expansion and improved living standards."[84]

Yes, "one can question" anything. But the issue is not whether one can determine, to the point of certainty, the likelihood of the success of the program of the Left Opposition. Certainty is not attainable, nor is that the issue. The real question is: did the Left Opposition demonstrate significantly greater understanding of the problems of the Soviet economy than the Stalinist leadership, and did the Left Opposition exhibit far greater foresight than the bureaucracy in anticipating problems and proposing ameliorative action before disaster struck? To these two critical questions, we can reply unambiguously in the affirmative. On this basis, we can then ask whether—based on a more timely response to looming dangers and the avoidance of their worst consequences—it is reasonable to believe that the Soviet economy would have achieved greater successes and with far fewer human sacrifices. Here, too, the answer is clearly yes. Thatcher never

---

this point to go entirely unanswered, I will cite a brief passage from *The Autobiography of a Sexually Emancipated Communist Woman*, by Alexandra Kollontai, a leading female member of the Bolshevik Party. After the revolution she assumed the leadership of the Coordinating Office for Work Among Women. In relation to this assignment, Kollontai wrote, "The law liberalizing abortion was put through and a number of regulations of benefit to women were introduced by our Coordinating Office and legally confirmed. ... Our work received the wholehearted support from Lenin. And Trotsky, although he was overburdened with military tasks, unfailingly and gladly appeared at our conferences" ([New York: Herder and Herder, 1971], p. 42). This comment was written in 1926. By that time, it was no longer politic to praise Trotsky. This fact invests Kollontai's words with probative value.

[84] Thatcher, pp. 151-152.

explores the issues in this way. He makes no reference to the detailed program produced by the Left Opposition in 1927. Instead, we are left with a peculiar form of fatalism that translates into a historical apology for Stalin and Stalinism. Thatcher takes this same approach to every important issue of international revolutionary policy.

Turning to the disastrous defeat of the Chinese Revolution in 1927, in which Stalin's subordination of the Chinese Communist Party to the bourgeois Kuomintang of Chiang Kai-shek played a major role, Thatcher asserts that "even had the CCP abandoned the Kuomintang in 1926, there is no evidence to suggest that it could have enjoyed any greater success in 1927."[85] What "evidence" has Thatcher assessed? Where did he conduct research into the events of 1925-1927? There is a rich body of political and historical literature, a significant amount of which was produced by Chinese revolutionaries, analyzing the catastrophic consequences of Stalin's policies in the period of 1925-1927.

There is no evidence that Thatcher is in the least familiar with this literature. It is a historical fact that Chiang Kai-shek's massacre of Shanghai workers in April 1927 was facilitated by the failure of the Communist Party to take defensive measures that might have either forestalled the attack, or at least allowed the cadre to beat it back. The passivity of the CCP was dictated by Stalin's insistence that the Chinese Communists avoid antagonizing Chiang and the bourgeois Kuomintang. For nearly a year, Trotsky and the Left Opposition warned of the suicidal dangers arising from such a policy. To claim that it would have made no difference, even had their warnings been acted upon in a timely manner, is to elevate hopelessness to the status of an immutable historical condition, at least as far as socialist revolution is concerned.

On the question of Germany, Thatcher argues along the same lines. "There is a certain attraction to Trotsky's account of KPD blunders and the possibility that had the German communists adopted a different course Hitler's triumph could have been avoided," Thatcher writes. "The support such a case has received in subsequent studies is hardly surprising. After all, who does not wish that the National Socialist German Workers Party (NSDAP) had never taken power? One can still question, however, whether history would have been so different had Trotsky had a greater influence on events. ... Trotsky overestimated the power of the workers and underestimated the strength of fascism. It is possible that Hitler would have risen to power even over a coalition of communists and social democrats. ... A change in KPD policies as

---

[85] Thatcher, p. 156.

demanded by Trotsky might have been insufficient to keep the NSDAP from government."[86]

The critical role played by the catastrophic policies of the two main working class parties—the SPD and KPD—in facilitating Hitler's victory is not a matter of serious historical controversy. There are, of course, many questions as to why these parties pursued such disastrous and self-destructive policies. But it is as close to a historical certainty as anything can be that the working class parties, despite their millions of members, pursued policies that ultimately reduced themselves to a state of complete political impotence. To state that the action or inaction of two mass parties would, in any event, have had no effect on the outcome of the political struggle in Germany, that Hitler would have conquered *no matter what*, is to render the whole subject of the working class movement and socialist politics politically and historically irrelevant. This is the conclusion that flows inevitably from Thatcher's argument.[87]

While Thatcher repeatedly insists that the adoption of Trotsky's policies would have made no difference whatsoever, he argues time and again against Trotsky's criticisms of Stalin. He is so unshakeable in his hostility toward Trotsky and sympathy for Stalin that one cannot help but think that his work is driven by an unstated political agenda. Long ago, in his justly famous *What Is History?*, E. H. Carr advised us to listen carefully for the buzzing of bees in a historian's bonnet. The bees in a good historian's bonnet emit a pleasing and sophisticated sound that harmonizes beautifully with the factual material that it accompanies. But the bees in Mr. Thatcher's

---

[86] Ibid., pp. 179-181.

[87] The argument that Hitler's victory was in any sense inevitable is not made by any serious contemporary historian. Indeed, emphasis has generally been placed on the extremely contingent character of Hitler's accession to power. As Ian Kershaw, the author of a widely-respected two-volume biography of Hitler, has written, "There was no inevitability about Hitler's accession to power. Had Hindenburg been prepared to grant to Schleicher the dissolution that he had so readily allowed Papen, and to prorogue the Reichstag for a period beyond the constitutional sixty days, a Hitler Chancellorship might have been avoided. With the corner turning of the economic Depression, and with the Nazi movement facing potential break-up if power were not soon attained, the future—even if under an authoritarian government—would have been very different. Even as the cabinet argued outside Hindenburg's door at eleven o'clock on 30 January, keeping the President waiting, there was a possibility that a Hitler Chancellorship might not materialize. Hitler's rise from humble beginnings to 'seize' power by 'triumph of the will' was the stuff of Nazi legend. In fact, political miscalculation by those with regular access to the corridors of power rather than any actions on the part of the Nazi leader played a larger role in placing him in the Chancellor's seat." (*Hitler 1889-1936: Hubris* [New York: W. W. Norton, 1998], p. 424).

bonnet emit a very loud, discordant and tendentious sound, rather like Stalinist hornets. My concern here is not Thatcher's politics—to which he is personally entitled—but his treatment of historical facts. The bees (or even hornets) only become a serious problem when their buzzing is so loud that one cannot hear the history.

Thatcher defends Stalin

Defending Stalin against Trotsky's criticism, Thatcher declares that the latter's "thesis of a Stalinist betrayal of the world revolution is as one-sided as it is unconvincing. It ignores, for example, the positive aspects of the Popular Front tactic, evident in the expansion of the communist parties' support and influence."[88] At this point, as Professor Thatcher approaches the conclusion of his biography, the distinction between history writing and tendency polemics has been obliterated. The pretense of writing a biography is virtually dropped, and the reader is being fed what used to be called the Stalinist party line. Thatcher, extolling the Stalinist "successes" of the Popular Front era, ignores Trotsky's analysis of the Seventh Congress of the Comintern in 1935, which implemented—in the aftermath of the catastrophes of Stalinist "Third Period" ultra-leftism—the shift toward alliances with bourgeois parties. Thatcher makes no mention of Trotsky's assessment that the Seventh Congress and the adoption of Popular Frontism signified the repudiation of any link between the Comintern and the perspective of socialist revolution— a development rooted in the foreign policy interests of the Stalinist regime in the USSR. This assessment, it should be pointed out, was endorsed by E. H. Carr, in *The Twilight of the Comintern*.[89]

Thatcher continues, "There is also no evidence to confirm Trotsky's contention, however, that Comintern tactics were dependent on the demands of

---

[88] Thatcher, p. 203.

[89] Carr wrote that "the seventh congress had brought into the open the deep-seated trend, long apparent to the discerning critic, to identify the aims of Comintern with the policies of the USSR; and, after the paradoxical success of the congress, the institution seemed to have lost its reality. It was significant that no further congress, and no major session of IKKI [the executive body of the Comintern], was ever again summoned. Comintern continued to discharge subordinate functions, while the spotlight of publicity was directed elsewhere. Trotsky's verdict that the seventh congress would 'pass into history as the liquidation congress' of Comintern was not altogether unfair. The seventh congress pointed the way to the *dénouement* of 1943 [the formal dissolution of the Communist International]." (*Twilight of the Comintern, 1930–1935* [New York: Pantheon Books, 1982], p. 427).

Soviet diplomacy."[90] Here, Thatcher is arguing against not only Trotsky, but also the overwhelming weight of historical evidence. An author who makes such a claim surrenders any right to be taken seriously as a historian. How would Thatcher explain the overnight change in the policies of Communist parties all over the world, after the negotiation of the Stalin-Hitler Pact of August 1939? There is also the matter of the physical liquidation of large numbers of leading members of national Communist parties during the Stalinist Terror of 1937–1939. Virtually the entire leadership of the Polish Communist Party was wiped out, because Stalin deemed it susceptible to Trotskyist influences. Large sections of the old leadership of the German Communist Party, which had escaped Hitler by fleeing to the USSR, were executed in Moscow during the Terror. The KPD General Secretary, Ernst Thaelmann, who had been captured by the Nazis, was abandoned by Stalin, who declined an opportunity to have him released to Soviet custody after the signing of the pact with Hitler. Thaelmann perished in a concentration camp. The leadership that emerged from Soviet exile in 1945 to assume control of what was to become the East German state consisted of individuals who had been left alive by Stalin—often at the price of denouncing their KPD comrades. Does not all this constitute a form of subordination of Communist parties to the dictates of the Soviet regime?

An understanding of the pervasive Soviet influence in the policies of the Comintern requires an examination of the activities of the GPU (which became the NKVD), the secret police of the Stalinist regime. Trotsky examined this issue in detail in one of his last articles, "The Comintern and the GPU," which he completed less than two weeks before his own assassination by a Stalinist agent.[91] Citing the testimony of Walter Krivitsky, who defected from the GPU, and Benjamin Gitlow, an ex-member of the leadership of the American Communist Party, Trotsky documented the control exerted by GPU agents over the Stalinist organizations. He included an analysis of financial transactions, demonstrating how the flow of cash was used to direct and control the policies of local Stalinist parties. He also demonstrated the financial dependence of these parties on cash from

---

[90] Thatcher, p. 204.

[91] "The Comintern and the GPU" is published in the volume *Stalin's Gangsters*, by Leon Trotsky, published in London by New Park in 1977. The late Harold Robins (1908-1987), who served as the captain of Trotsky's guard in Coyoacán in 1939-40, advised the publishers that Trotsky had suggested this title for a collection of articles on the activities of the GPU.

Moscow. Thatcher does not examine, analyze and reply to this document—the last major statement written by Trotsky before his death on August 21, 1940. He simply ignores it.

Thatcher also mounts an impassioned defense of Stalin on another front. He writes, "Finally, Trotsky clearly underestimated the capacity of the USSR to withstand a German declaration of war, which eventually occurred in June 1941. Stalin proved himself a capable war leader, standing firm at the helm in the initial confusion surrounding the first moments of the German attack."[92] Two issues are raised here: first, Trotsky's assessment of the resilience of the Soviet Union in the event of war; second, Stalin's role as a war leader. In response to the first, Thatcher again falsifies Trotsky's position. He does not cite from Trotsky's most comprehensive statement on the Soviet Union's powers of resistance in the event of war. "The Red Army," written by Trotsky in March 1934, came to the exact opposite conclusion from the one attributed to him by Thatcher. "He who is able and willing to read the books of history," wrote Trotsky, "will understand beforehand that should the Russian Revolution, which has continued ebbing and flowing for almost thirty years—since 1905—be forced to direct its stream into the channel of war, it will unleash a terrific and overwhelming force."[93] This statement hardly qualifies as an underestimation of the USSR.

As for Thatcher's special tribute to Stalin as a war leader, it is curious that he chooses to cite specifically his activities during the "first moments of the German attack." He certainly knows that there are many questions surrounding Stalin's response to the German invasion of June 22, 1941. In numerous books, including the memoirs of leading Soviet officials, it has been claimed that Stalin was emotionally devastated by the news of the invasion, which exposed the utter bankruptcy of his diplomatic game with Hitler and now confronted the USSR with the possibility of total ruin. Thatcher is not unaware of this, and includes a footnote, which states: "Several textbooks claim that when Germany invaded the USSR Stalin was thrown into a panic and it would have been possible to overthrow him ... These claims are convincingly refuted by S.J. Main, 'Stalin in 1941.'"[94]

To claim that the controversy surrounding Stalin's activities in the aftermath of the German invasion has been "convincingly refuted" by Professor Main's brief

---

[92] Thatcher, p. 206.

[93] *Writings of Leon Trotsky [1933-34]* (New York: Pathfinder Press, 1975), p. 259.

[94] Thatcher, pp. 233-234.

two-page article, which is merely a comment on a much longer article by another historian, is a travesty of scholarly judgment and an exercise in political apologetics.[95] Moreover, the issue of what Stalin did or did not do in the last week of June 1941, after the Nazis invaded, is of secondary significance in assessing his responsibility for the catastrophe that overwhelmed the Soviet Union. The horrifying human losses suffered by the Soviet people were the direct consequence of the policies and actions of Stalin: the murder of the leading Soviet marshals and generals, such as Tukhachevsky, Yakir, Gamarnik, Blucher, Yegorov and Primakov; the extermination of 75 percent of the Red Army officer corps in 1937-1938; the killing of the finest representatives of the socialist intelligentsia and working class; the systematic disorganization and dismantling of Soviet military defenses so as not to provoke Hitler; the refusal to act on intelligence that a German invasion was imminent, etc. All this has been amply documented in innumerable books and scholarly articles. But Thatcher ignores it and proclaims that a two-page comment in one journal settles the question of Stalin's role in World War II.[96]

Why "the Bronsteins"?

Beneath the accumulating weight of the falsification of Trotsky's life and crude apologies for Stalin, the intentions of the author himself appear increasingly dubious, not only in an intellectual sense but in a moral one as well. In this regard, it is necessary to take note of Thatcher's repeated references to Trotsky and his wife Natalia Sedova as "the Bronsteins." I noted no less than nine occasions when Thatcher refers to the couple in this way, usually when describing their private living arrangements or their movement from one place of exile to another. Thatcher tells us that "the Bronsteins were living largely off credit in Vienna" (p. 52); "Finally, the Bronsteins were allowed to go to Barcelona"

---

[95] The article referred to by Thatcher is "Stalin in June 1941: A Comment on Cynthia Roberts," by Steven J. Main, in *Europe-Asia Studies* Vol. 48, No. 5 (July 1996), pp. 837-839. Professor Main's comment was in reply to Cynthia Roberts' "Planning for War: The Red Army and the Catastrophe of 1941," in *Europe-Asia Studies*, Vol. 47, No. 8 (December 1995), pp. 1293-1326.

[96] Declaring an intensely controversial historical issue settled is one of Thatcher's favorite rhetorical tricks. He locates an article that supports his opinion and then proclaims it to be "convincing." Of course, many experts remain unconvinced. For example, on the matter of Stalin's responsibility for the catastrophe of 1941, David E. Murphy writes: "Stalin's personal responsibility for the monumental losses of the war years, particularly those suffered in the first tragic months of the war, cannot be minimized or denied." (*What Stalin Knew: The Enigma of Barbarossa* [New Haven and London: Yale University Press, 2005], p. 247).

(p. 77); "the Bronsteins were taken over the border" (p. 164); Prinkipo "provided a home for the majority of the Bronsteins' stay" (p. 165); "in France, for example, the Bronsteins had no less than a dozen addresses of varying leases" (p. 188); "The move to North America, where the Bronsteins arrived in mid-January 1937..." (p. 189), and so on. Why does Thatcher so persistently identify Trotsky and Sedova as "the Bronsteins"? First of all, there is no factual basis for doing so. The two people he is referring to did not make use of that surname. Trotsky's wife Natalia was known by her own legal family name, Sedova. The two children of Lev Davidovich and Natalia—Lev and Sergei—used Sedov as their surname. Trotsky, aside from the fact that he never referred to himself as Bronstein after 1902, used Sedov as his own legal name.

This is not, as might first seem to those unfamiliar with Trotsky's life, a small matter. Like every other aspect of his life, even the name by which he and his family were identified assumed political significance. In January 1937, Trotsky commented on the fact that the Soviet press, upon reporting the arrest of his youngest son on charges of sabotage, referred to him as Sergei *Bronstein*. Trotsky wrote:

> Since 1902 I have invariably borne the name of Trotsky. In view of my illegality, my children under czarism were recorded under their mother's family name—Sedov. So as not to force them to change the name to which they had become accustomed, under Soviet power I took for "civic purposes" the name Sedov (according to Soviet law, a husband can, as is well known, take the name of the wife). The Soviet passport on which I, my wife, and our elder son were sent into exile was made out in the name of the Sedov family. My sons, thus, have never used the name Bronstein.
>
> Just why is it now necessary to drag out this name? The answer is obvious: because of its Jewish sound. To this it is necessary to add that my son is accused of nothing more or less than an attempt to slaughter workers. Is this really so different from accusing the Jews of ritually using the blood of Christians?[97]

It is impossible to believe that Thatcher is not familiar with this and other occasions where Trotsky denounced and identified the use of his original family name as an anti-Semitic ploy. Knowing that it is factually incorrect to do

---

[97] "Anti-Semitic Devices," January 30, 1937, in: *Writings of Leon Trotsky [1936-37]* (New York: Pathfinder Press, 1978), p. 177.

so, why then does Thatcher refer to the Bronsteins, rather than to the Trotskys or the Sedovs? The moral burden falls upon him to dispel the legitimate suspicion that certain base calculations are in play. I am not stating that Thatcher is an anti-Semite. But it is beyond doubt that he is, for whatever reasons, repeatedly calling to the reader's attention the Jewish origins of Trotsky. He should explain his reasons for doing so.[98]

Thatcher's falsification of the Dewey Commission

Thatcher devotes about two pages to the Moscow Trials and Trotsky's struggle to refute their charges. He discusses the formation of the Dewey Commission, and the hearings that were held in April 1937 in Mexico "where the Bronsteins were lodging."[99] After a brief review of the proceedings and the testimony of Leon Trotsky, Thatcher arrives at the Commission's findings. He writes, "*The Moscow trials were declared an unreliable guide to the truth, the accusations against Trotsky unproven* [emphasis added]."[100]

This is a falsification of the findings of the Dewey Commission. On September 21, 1937, the Commission announced its findings, of which there were 23. The first 21 consisted of refutations of specific allegations against Trotsky that were crucial to the claims of the Soviet prosecutors. The decisive summary conclusions were presented in Findings 22 and 23. They stated, "22. We therefore find the Moscow trials to be frame-ups. 23. We therefore find Trotsky and [his son] Sedov not guilty."[101]

Note the difference between the words used by the Dewey Commission and those selected by Thatcher. There is a profound difference between defining a proceeding as a "frame-up" (the word used by the Dewey Commission) and as "an unreliable guide to the truth" (the words used by Thatcher). A frame-up is a pseudo-legal proceeding in which evidence is contrived and concocted to produce a predetermined verdict of guilty. It is not merely an

---

[98] It would not be illegitimate for a biographer to explore the cultural, psychological and political implications of Trotsky's Jewish origins. Some earlier biographers have already attempted to do so, though not with great success. But Thatcher shows no particular interest in this theme, and this makes his heavy-handed and factually incorrect references to "the Bronsteins" especially odd and suspect.

[99] Thatcher, p. 197.

[100] Ibid.

[101] *John Dewey, Vol. 11: 1935-37*, ed. Jo Ann Boydston (Carbondale: Southern Illinois University Press, 1991), p. 323.

"unreliable guide to truth." Its aim is the suppression of truth and it makes use of lies to facilitate, under a pseudo-legal cover, the imprisonment or execution of a wrongfully accused individual. Thatcher could have simply quoted finding 22 of the Dewey Commission. Instead he used the five words "unreliable guide to the truth" to say something very different from the one word "frame-up" used by the Commission.[102]

There is also a fundamental *legal* difference between a finding of not guilty (handed down by the Dewey Commission) and a verdict of "unproven" (the term used by Thatcher). A verdict of not guilty leaves the presumption of the defendant's innocence undisturbed. A verdict of "unproven" is quite a different matter. It carries the implication that while there existed insufficient evidence to return a verdict of guilty, the jury was not convinced of the innocence of the accused. Thatcher, who lived and taught in Glasgow for many years, knows very well the distinction between "not guilty" and "unproven." One of the peculiarities of Scottish law is that it allows juries to return a verdict of "not proven." This has been a subject of substantial legal controversy for several centuries, precisely because of the lingering moral shadow that the so-called "third verdict" leaves behind on the accused.[103] It requires a high degree of naiveté to believe that Thatcher's substitution of "unproven" for the words "not guilty" is an innocent error. He is unquestionably guilty of deliberately falsifying the findings of the Dewey Commission.

What, the reader may ask, is the purpose of such a falsification? And why should one treat it as such a grave matter? The reader should bear in mind the methods employed by Thatcher and Swain, which we have already examined. As they quote each other and their own works are cited by others, the virus of falsification spreads insidiously via a complacent academic community into the broader public. In this particular example, the immense original force of the Dewey Commission verdict is diluted and falsified. In time, as the denunciation of the Moscow trials as a frame-up and the unambiguous acquittal of Trotsky and Sedov fall from historical memory, Thatcher's

---

[102] In remarks made upon the release of the Summary of Findings, John Dewey stated that "the members of the commission have been without exception appalled by the utterly discreditable character of the whole Moscow trial proceedings, at once flimsy and vicious." (Ibid. p. 324).

[103] The novelist Sir Walter Scott famously denounced it as the "bastard verdict."

formulations—eventually to be recycled by other careless historians—contribute to the erosion of previously-established facts and objective truth.

Thatcher's final comments on Trotsky's historical role

After more than 200 pages of distortions, half-truths and outright falsifications, we arrive at Thatcher's final appraisal of Trotsky. "Trotsky, then," he informs his readers, "was not a great political leader or prophet. He spent the majority of his political life in opposition, the exponent of views commanding minority support."[104] To this remark his readers should respond, "Well, Professor Thatcher, that is simply your opinion." And, indeed, it is an opinion unsupported by credible scholarly work, and therefore the reader has no reason to take it particularly seriously. One is reminded of Hegel's admonition, "What can be more useless than to learn a string of bald opinions, and what more unimportant?"[105] As for the basis of this opinion—that Trotsky spent most of his life in opposition—this tells us more about Thatcher's views and character than it does about the revolutionary leader upon whom he is passing judgment.

Thatcher continues:

> Is there anything of lasting merit in Trotsky's works, or were he and his writing of relevance only to his time and experience? An answer to this question will depend, at least in part, on how one rates Marxism and Trotsky's standing as a Marxist.
>
> To begin with the latter question, it is doubtful whether Trotsky made any lasting contribution to Marxist thought. He may even have been unaware of some of Marx's most basic writings. In *The Revolution Betrayed*, for example, Trotsky *several times insists that Marx had nothing to say about Russia*, that the master expected a socialist revolution to begin in the countries of advanced capitalism. This ignores Marx's interest in the question of whether "backward" Russia could bypass capitalism and undertake a direct transition to socialism on the basis of the peasant commune. Marx's response, of evident relevance to Trotsky's theory of permanent revolution, was given in several of

---

[104] Thatcher, p. 214.

[105] *Hegel's Lectures on the History of Philosophy*, tr. E. S. Haldane and Francis H. Simpson (London and New York: Humanities Press, 1974), Vol. 1, p. 12.

his writings, including the Preface to the (1881) Russian edition of the *Communist Manifesto*. Here Marx answered in the affirmative. A Russian Revolution could aim at a direct transition to socialism, but only if it sparked socialist revolutions in the advanced West. If Trotsky had been aware of this and the other texts in which Marx addressed the problem of building socialism in Russia, he would surely have claimed a stronger link between the theory of permanent revolution and Marx, as well as less originality for his conception of the revolutionary process in Russia. If we assume that Trotsky did not know of Marx's concern with Russia, then this points to the conclusion that Trotsky's Marxism was a product of the Russian environment [emphasis added].[106]

In this passage the author combines, in equal measure, ignorance and insolence. This is the sort of writing that could have appeared in scores of Stalinist journals prior to the collapse of the USSR. The specific claim that Trotsky "insisted that Marx had nothing to say about Russia," is a crass misrepresentation of what Trotsky wrote. He explained precisely why it was impossible to derive an analysis of Soviet society from a mechanical application of Marx's historical conceptions.[107] In this, Trotsky demonstrated not his ignorance of Marx's work, but his creative approach to Marxism. Moreover, he based key arguments in *The Revolution Betrayed* on observations of Marx. Trotsky, to cite just one example, employed the concept of "generalized want," suggested by Marx in *The German Ideology*, to explain the origins and social function of the bureaucracy in the USSR as the "gendarme"—the police enforcer of social inequality.

Thatcher's claim that Trotsky was not aware of Marx's writings in 1881 on the prospects for socialism in Russia, and, moreover, that the former did not recognize the link between his own theory of Permanent Revolution and Marx's work is easily contradicted. Thatcher apparently has not read the essay,

---

[106] Thatcher, p. 215.

[107] What Trotsky actually wrote, in a relevant passage, is the following:

> Moreover, Marx expected that the Frenchman would begin the social revolution, the German continue it, the Englishman finish it; and as to the Russian, Marx left him far in the rear. But this conceptual order was upset by the facts. Whoever tries now mechanically to apply the universal historic conception of Marx to the particular case of the Soviet Union at the given stage of its development will be entangled at once in hopeless contradictions. (*The Revolution Betrayed* [Detroit: Labor Publications, 1991], pp. 40-41).

"Marxism and the Relation between Proletarian and Peasant Revolution," written in December 1928. Trotsky specifically reviewed the 1881 correspondence between Marx and the old Russian revolutionist Vera Zasulich, in which Marx worked through the theoretical issues that were concisely summed up in the January 1882 (not 1881 as Thatcher writes) preface to the Russian edition of the *Communist Manifesto*. As for his own intellectual debt to Marx, Trotsky wrote in this essay that "the idea of permanent revolution was one of the most important ideas of Marx and Engels."[108] So here we have Thatcher arguing in his conclusion that Trotsky was unfamiliar with key writings of Marx on the subject of Russia, and it turns out that this fantastic hypothesis is merely the product of Thatcher's failure to do his basic intellectual homework![109]

Having sarcastically posed the question of Trotsky's relevance, Thatcher should tell us why he has written a 240-page book to proclaim his irrelevance. Why did he establish, with his former colleague from the University of Glasgow, James D. White, the short-lived *Journal of Trotsky Studies*, whose publication represented Thatcher's first major anti-Trotsky project? Why has Swain written his 237-page biography?

It is worth noting that Thatcher has no doubts about the relevance of Stalin. In a review of several studies of Stalin that appeared around the time of the fiftieth anniversary of the dictator's death, Thatcher, revealing the bees in his bonnet, confessed a certain nostalgia for "a benign version of Stalinism," adding, "Stalin continues to fascinate and to cause moments of moral uncertainty."[110] What sort of moral uncertainty, one is compelled to wonder, can be caused by the actions of a blood-drenched tyrant who slaughtered an entire generation of socialists, betrayed the principles of the October

---

[108] *The Challenge of the Left Opposition 1928-29* (New York: Pathfinder Press, 1981), p. 349.

[109] Thatcher has also overlooked the speech delivered by Trotsky on November 14, 1922, at the Fourth Congress of the Communist International. Trotsky directly addressed Marx's speculations about the possibility of a transition to socialism based on the peasant communes. He said: "In 1883 Marx, writing to Nicholas Danielson, one of the theoreticians of Russian populism (*Narodnikism*), [said] that should the proletariat assume power in Europe before the Russian *obschina* (communal village agriculture) had been completely abolished by history then even this *obschina* could become one of the starting points for Communist development in Russia. And Marx was absolutely right" ("The NEP and World Revolution," in *The First Five Years of the Communist International*, Vol. 2 [London: New Park Publications, 1974], p. 230).

[110] "Stalin and Stalinism: A Review Article," in *Europe-Asia Studies* (Vol. 56, No. 6, September 2004), p. 918.

Revolution and set into motion the process that led to the destruction of the Soviet Union?

Conclusion

It has been an unpleasant experience to work through the volumes of Mr. Swain and Mr. Thatcher. Despite the length of this essay, I have by no means answered all the distortions and falsifications that appear in their work. Such a comprehensive account would require nothing less than a volume of its own. But I believe that this review has established that neither biography has the slightest scholarly merit. Still the questions remain: Why have these books been written? What is their purpose? The answer, I believe, is to be found in politics. While Thatcher speculates cynically at the conclusion of his book on the relevance of its subject, he hardly believes that Trotsky is so marginal a historical figure. Indeed, Thatcher's obsessive interest in Trotsky suggests he holds privately a very different view. And well he should, for the significance of Trotsky as a historical figure is inextricably linked to the vicissitudes of the international class struggle. To determine the relevance of Trotsky, one must ask several other questions: What is the relevance of socialism? What is the relevance of Marxism? What is the relevance of the class struggle in modern society? Has capitalism attained a new and permanent level of stability? Has the very concept of a "crisis of capitalism" become historically outmoded? These are the questions that must be asked when considering the place of Trotsky in history and the significance of his ideas in the contemporary world.

Leon Trotsky's ideas do not seem all that remote in the light of objective developments. First, the developments in technology and their impact upon the processes of production and exchange have produced a global economy that places tremendous strains on the old national-state structures. Moreover, the precipitous decline in the world economic position of the United States significantly limits the likelihood of a new world order that will regulate inter-state relations and maintain global stability. The world capitalist system is heading toward a systemic breakdown on the scale of the period of 1914–1945.

The fragility of the existing global economic and geo-political order has been intensified by domestic class-based social tensions. During the past quarter century, we have witnessed a collapse of the old mass parties and organizations of the working class. It is hard to think of a political party anywhere in the world that retains any significant degree of credibility among the masses. The old Communist parties, Social Democratic parties, and Labour parties have either collapsed—as is the case with most of the Stalinist organizations—or stagger on as organizations sustained only by a thoroughly corrupt apparatus. To describe them as "working class" is to completely abuse the historical meaning of the term. They are all right-wing bourgeois parties, no less committed to the defense of capitalism and the imperialist interests of the global transnationals than the old traditional bourgeois parties.

But this collapse of every form of Stalinist and Social Democratic reformist-based working class organization proceeds against the backdrop of rising social inequality and intensifying class antagonisms. The old organizations simply lack the political means and credibility to harness the deepening social discontent and channel it into paths that do not threaten the stability of the capitalist system. At some point the intensification of class conflict will find intellectual and political expression. There will be a search for alternatives to the present set-up. This will create an intellectual and social constituency for a revival of interest in the history of the socialist movement, in the revolutionary struggles of the past. It is inevitable that the development of such a climate will lead to a renewed interest in the life and work of Leon Trotsky. That is what happened during the last great wave of radicalization of workers and students. The more politically thoughtful sections of the bourgeoisie recognize this danger and fear it. This is, as we know, the era of preemptive war, and these works represent a sort of preemptive strike against the reemergence of Trotskyist influence. This is why distinguished publishing houses like Routledge and Longman commission biographies such as those produced by Swain and Thatcher.

The political crisis intersects with a profound intellectual crisis. How is one to explain the benign reception of these two miserable books? It is, I believe, bound up with the predominance, for more than a quarter century, of truly reactionary modes of thought, associated with Postmodernism, which repudiate the very concept of objective truth. In the course of this review essay, I have referred several times to E.H. Carr, and I will do so again. Nearly a half-century ago, he warned against the infiltration into history of the Nietzschean principle, formulated in *Beyond Good and Evil*: "The falseness of an opinion is not for us any objection to it..."[111] The contemporary repudiation of objective truth, supported by the claim that the only issue is the

---

[111] Cited in E. H. Carr, *What Is History?* (London: Penguin Books, 1987), p. 27.

internal coherence of a narrative, which is to be judged on its own terms, is inimical to serious scholarly work, or even to rational thought. It encourages a climate where "anything goes," where falsification flourishes, where there is no protest when lies are told about history.

And what does this mean? I began this essay with a review of the Moscow Trials and Stalin's Terror. I explained that what started with historical falsification ended with mass murder. That process is repeating itself in our own time. Whoever wishes to consider the implications and consequences of historical lies has only to consider the lies that were employed to prepare public opinion for the war in Iraq. "Weapons of mass destruction" was a lie that has already led to the deaths of hundreds of thousands.

A new generation now confronts immense and life-threatening problems. Everywhere it faces crisis and decay. The very future of the planet is in question if answers are not found to the crisis of the world capitalist system. The study of history must play a central role in the discovery of those answers required by humanity in the twenty-first century. But how can history be studied if its record is falsified? The working people and youth of the world need truth, and the struggle to discover and defend it is the intellectual driving force of human progress.

Leon Trotsky in Mexico, 1940

Part III

Robert Service's Contribution
to the Falsification of History

Leon Trotsky in exile in Prinkipo, Turkey circa 1930

The "Big Lie" Continues[1]

A Review of *Trotsky: A Biography* by Robert Service

Trotsky: A Biography, by Robert Service, 600 pages,
Harvard University Press, 2009

The Specter of Leon Trotsky

In 1955 James Burnham, the intellectual godfather of modern American neo-conservatism, reviewed *The Prophet Armed,* the first volume of Isaac Deutscher's monumental biography of Leon [Lev Davidovich] Trotsky. Fifteen years had passed since Burnham had resigned from the Fourth International at the climax of a political struggle in which he had crossed polemical swords with Leon Trotsky. It had been a difficult experience for Burnham, who felt somewhat overmatched in this political and literary contest. "I must stop awhile in wonder," Burnham had written in a document addressed to Trotsky, "at the technical perfection of the verbal structure you have created, the dynamic sweep of your rhetoric, the burning expression of your unconquerable devotion to the socialist ideal, the sudden, witty, flashing metaphors that sparkle through your pages."[2]

---

[1] Published on the World Socialist Web Site (www.wsws.org) on November 11, 2009. [www.wsws.org/articles/2009/nov2009/serv-n11.shtml].

[2] James Burnham, "Science and Style: A Reply to Comrade Trotsky," appendix in *In Defense of Marxism,* by Leon Trotsky (London: New Park, 1971), p. 233.

In the aftermath of his repudiation of socialism, Burnham moved rapidly to the extreme right (as Trotsky had predicted). By the mid-1950s he viewed Trotsky's life and work through the prism of his own ideological commitment to a global struggle against Marxism. Deutscher's work filled Burnham with alarm. The problem was not literary in character. Burnham readily acknowledged the author's masterful reconstruction of Trotsky's revolutionary persona.

"Mr. Deutscher has cast his story of Trotsky in the Greek mould, and with sufficient justification," Burnham wrote. "His Trotsky is a protagonist of the most dazzling brilliance, who rises in 1905, 1917 and in the Civil War to successive heights where he fuses with History and becomes her voice." Burnham allowed that the author had succeeded in conveying to his readers Trotsky's extraordinary qualities: "the flaming oratory, which many who heard him believe to have been the greatest of our century; the linguistic facility; the witty and vibrant prose; the quickness with which Trotsky mastered every new subject; the breadth of interest, so rare among the dedicated revolutionaries."

Burnham noted that Deutscher's portrait of Trotsky was not one-sided; that he "conscientiously displays, also, Trotsky's weaknesses..." But despite the many literary virtues of the biography, Burnham denounced it as an "intellectual disaster." Burnham's reason for his condemnation was that "Mr. Deutscher writes from a point of view that accepts and legitimizes the Bolshevik revolution." The biography was "organically warped" and unacceptable. "Not all the scholarly references from all the libraries are enough to wash out the Bolshevik stain."

Burnham confessed his horror that Deutscher had received "all the courtesies of our leading research institutions, the aid of our foundations, the pages of our magazines, publication and promotion by the great Anglo-Saxon Oxford Press." Did the establishment not recognize the danger in allowing, and even encouraging, the details of Trotsky's heroic life and revolutionary ideas to reach the broader public, and especially the youth?

Burnham concluded his review with a cry of despair: "The minds of many of our university students and opinion-makers are being deeply formed, on the supremely important issues with which he [Deutscher] deals, by his ideas. It is surely one more among the many indications of the suicidal mania of the western world."[3] The conclusion that implicitly flowed

---

[3] James Burnham, review of *The Prophet Armed*, by Isaac Deutscher, *Russian Review*, Vol. 14, No. 2 (April 1955), pp. 151-152.

from this review was that Deutscher's book and others like it, which portrayed the October Revolution and its leaders sympathetically, should not be published.

Burnham's fears, at least from his political standpoint, were not without justification. He foresaw the subversive potential of Deutscher's rehabilitation of Trotsky, whose historic role and political ideas had been buried for so many decades beneath the massive heap of Stalinist lies. In February 1956 Khrushchev's "secret speech" at the Twentieth Congress of the Soviet Union's Communist Party more or less admitted that Stalin was a mass murderer and vindicated the indictment issued 20 years earlier by the dictator's implacable opponent. In the years that followed, the political stature of Leon Trotsky rapidly grew throughout the world.

Against the backdrop of growing working class militancy and the radicalization of youth, Deutscher's biographical trilogy—*The Prophet Armed, The Prophet Unarmed* and *The Prophet Outcast*—introduced countless thousands of youth, intellectuals and workers to the deeds and ideas of Leon Trotsky. Organizations that claimed to base themselves on the political heritage of Trotsky grew significantly in the 1960s and 1970s. This was particularly the case in Britain. As early as 1964, the leadership of the Young Socialists, youth movement of the British Labour Party, passed into the hands of the Trotskyist Socialist Labour League. Throughout the 1960s, 1970s, and even into the 1980s, the activities of Trotskyist organizations were a major preoccupation of the principal British Intelligence agency, the MI5.[4]

A New Offensive Against Trotsky

This historical experience is worth recalling as one considers a peculiar literary phenomenon: the publication, within the space of little more than five years, of three biographies of Leon Trotsky by British historians. In 2003 Professor Ian Thatcher of Leicester University (and previously of Glasgow University) produced his *Trotsky*, which was published by Routledge. Three years later Longman published the *Trotsky* of Glasgow University's Geoffrey Swain. And now, as 2009 draws to a close, *Trotsky: A Biography* by Professor Robert Service of St. Antony's College, Oxford, has been brought out with

---

[4] See Christopher Andrew, *Defend the Realm: The Authorized History of MI5* (New York: Alfred A. Knopf, 2009); Peter Wright and Paul Greengrass, *Spycatcher* (New York: Penguin, 1987).

considerable fanfare. The British publisher is Macmillan. In the United States, Service's book has been published by Harvard University Press. What underlies this evident interest of British academics in Leon Trotsky, who has been dead for 70 years?

This reviewer has in another place[5] submitted the works of Thatcher and Swain to an exhaustive analysis, and proved that they are crass exercises in historical falsification, of absolutely no value to anyone interested in learning about the life and ideas of Leon Trotsky. As if heeding Burnham's warning, Thatcher and Swain were determined not to provide Trotsky with a platform, and therefore took care to quote as little as possible from his writings. Both works set out to reverse the popular image of Trotsky that had emerged from Deutscher's great trilogy. Thatcher and Swain belittled Deutscher for creating the "myth" of Trotsky as a great revolutionary, Marxist theoretician, military leader, political analyst and opponent of the totalitarian bureaucracy. The Thatcher-Swain biographies set out to create a new anti-Trotsky narrative, utilizing slanders and fabrications of old Stalinist vintage in the interest of contemporary anti-communism.

Now comes Robert Service's contribution to the ongoing efforts to demolish Leon Trotsky's historical reputation. In its pre-publication promotional material, Harvard University Press proclaims: "Although Trotsky's followers clung to the stubborn view of him as a pure revolutionary and a powerful intellect unjustly hounded into exile by Stalin, the reality is very different. [Service's] illuminating portrait of the man and his legacy sets the record straight."[6] Does it really?

Biography as Character Assassination

Trotsky: A Biography is a crude and offensive book, produced without respect for the most minimal standards of scholarship. Service's "research," if one wishes to call it that, has been conducted in bad faith. His *Trotsky* is not history, but rather an exercise in character assassination. Service is not content to distort and falsify Trotsky's political deeds and ideas. Frequently descending to the level of a grocery store tabloid, Service attempts to splatter filth on Trotsky's personal life. Among his favorite devices is to refer to

---

[5] See Part II of this book.

[6] Harvard University Press, Catalog entry for *Trotsky: A Biography by Robert Service*. http://www.hup.harvard.edu/catalog/SERTRO.html.

"rumors" about Trotsky's intimate relations, without even bothering to identify the rumor's source, let alone substantiate its credibility.

Trotsky once declared, as he defended himself against the slanders of
Stalin's regime: "There is not a single spot on my revolutionary honor."[7]
Service, however, portrays Trotsky as an individual without any honor at all.
He attempts to discredit Trotsky not only as a revolutionary politician, but
also as a man. Service's Trotsky is a heartless and vain individual who used
associates for his own egotistical purposes, a faithless husband who callously
abandoned his wife, and a father who was coldly indifferent to his children
and even responsible for their deaths. "People did not have to wait long before
discovering how vain and self-centred he really was," Service writes of Trotsky
in a typical passage. [56][8]

Service's biography is loaded with such petty insults. Trotsky was "vola-
tile and untrustworthy." "He was an arrogant individual" who "egocentrically
assumed that his opinions, if expressed in vivid language, would win him victory." "His self-absorption was extreme. As a husband he treated his first wife
shabbily. He ignored the needs of his children especially when his political
interests intervened." [4]

Trotsky's intellectual and political life was, Service would have his readers
believe, as shabby as his personal life. Trotsky's "lust for dictatorship and terror
were barely disguised in the Civil War. He trampled on the civil rights of millions of people including the industrial workers." As for his subsequent political
defeat, Service dismisses, without counter-argument, Trotsky's analysis of the
growth of the Soviet bureaucracy and its usurpation of political power. Service
simply asserts, as if he were stating the obvious, that Trotsky "lost to a man
[Stalin] and a clique with a superior understanding of Soviet public life." [4]

According to Service, Trotsky was nothing more than a second- or third-
rate thinker. Trotsky, he writes, "made no claim to intellectual originality:
he would have been ridiculed if he had tried." [109] "Intellectually he flitted
from topic to topic and felt no stimulus to systematize his thinking." [110]
Trotsky wrote quickly and superficially: "He simply loved to be seated at a
desk, fountain pen in hand, scribbling out the latest opus. Nobody dared
disturb him when the flow of words was forming in his head." [319] And
what was the result of this "scribbling"? Service writes: "His thought was a

---

[7] *Writings of Leon Trotsky [1939-40]* (New York: Pathfinder Press, 1973), p. 158.

[8] All references in brackets are to pages in: Robert Service, *Trotsky: A Biography* (Cambridge,
MA: Harvard University Press, 2009).

confused and confusing ragbag." [353] "He spent a lot of his time in disputing, less of it in thinking. Style prevailed over content... This involved an ultimate lack of seriousness as an intellectual." [356] This is Service's verdict on
the literary work of a man who must be counted among the greatest writers
of the twentieth century.[9]

A biographer need not like or even respect his subject. No one would
suggest that Ian Kershaw harbors the slightest sympathy for Adolf Hitler,
to whose life he devoted two extraordinary volumes that were the product
of many years of research. However, whether a biographer admires, despises
or feels a cool and detached ambivalence toward the object of his scholarly
attention, he must respect the factual record and strive to *understand* that
person. The biographer has the responsibility to examine a life in the context
of the conditions of the times in which his subject lived. But this is beyond
Service's intellectual capacities and the boundaries of his knowledge. Instead,
in a manner both pointless and absurd, he assumes from the outset the standpoint of a disapproving career counselor. Trotsky, Service opines in the biography's introduction, "could easily have achieved a great career as a journalist
or essayist if politics had not become his preoccupation." [3] But Trotsky did
choose a career in politics, and revolutionary politics at that, a decision that
Service cannot abide or come to grips with.

Service describes his book as "the first full-length biography of Trotsky
written by someone outside Russia who is not a Trotskyist." [xxi] What is meant
by "full-length"? Service's biography is certainly long, plodding on for 501 pages of actual text. But in terms of content, it is no more than a super-sized version
of the biographies produced by Thatcher and Swain. Like the earlier works, this
is a biography without history. There is not a single historical event that is recounted with anything remotely approaching the necessary level of detail.

---

[9] It should be noted that Service hews closely to the line developed previously by Geoffrey
Swain, who complained that Trotsky has been viewed as "a far greater thinker than he was in
reality. Trotsky wrote an enormous amount and, as a journalist, he was always happy to write
on subjects about which he knew very little." (Geoffrey Swain, *Trotsky* [Pearson, NY: Longman, 2006], p. 3). It must also be noted that Service, in his 2004 biography of Stalin, dealt far
more respectfully with the Soviet dictator and mass murderer. "Stalin was a thoughtful man,"
Service wrote, "and throughout his life tried to make sense of the universe as he found it. He
had studied a lot and forgotten little. ... He was not an original thinker nor even an outstanding
writer. Yet he was an intellectual to the end of his days."(Robert Service, *Stalin: A Biography*
[Cambridge, MA: Harvard University Press, 2005], pp. 569-570). See Fred Williams' review
of Service's biography of Stalin on the *World Socialist Web Site* at http://www.wsws.org/ar-
ticles/2005/jun2005/stal-j02.shtml.

Service reduces the immense and complex drama of the revolutionary epoch in Russia to a series of vacuous tableaux, which serve only as the scenic background for Service's ridicule of Trotsky's alleged political, personal and moral failures. The coming to power of the Nazis in 1933, the eruption of the Spanish Civil War and the formation of the Popular Front in France are dealt with in a few desultory sentences. Even the Moscow Trials and the Terror merit little more than a page. Far more attention is given by Service to Trotsky's brief intimacy with Frida Kahlo!

A Compendium of Errors

Moreover, the biography is full of factual errors that call attention to the author's extremely limited comprehension of the historical material. In the course of a disoriented excursion into Trotsky's pre-1917 views on the subject of revolutionary terror, Service writes that Trotsky "spoke out against 'individual terror' in 1909 when the Socialist-Revolutionaries murdered the police informer Evno Azev, who had penetrated their Central Committee." [113] In fact, *Azef* (the correct transliteration from the Russian spelling) was not murdered in 1909. He was not murdered at all. Azef, who had organized terrorist acts, including assassinations, while working as an agent of the *Okhrana* inside the Socialist Revolutionary Party, survived his exposure and died of natural causes in 1918. Service fails to quote even a single sentence from Trotsky's important article on the Azef affair.

Discussing the events of 1923 in Germany, Service asserts that the revolution failed after "street fighting petered out" in Berlin. [310] In fact, there was no fighting in Berlin. The leadership of the Communist Party called off the uprising before fighting could begin in the capital. The only serious fighting in a major German city occurred in Hamburg.

In a passing reference to the Chinese Revolution, Service states that the Communist International sent instructions for an insurrection against Chiang Kai-shek and the Kuomintang in April 1927. "It was just the excuse that Chiang needed to conduct a bloody suppression of communists in Shanghai and elsewhere." [355] This is wrong. No such plan existed and no such instructions were sent. Service confuses the events in Shanghai in April 1927 with later developments in Canton.

In another passage, Service writes that in June 1928 Trotsky was working on his critique of the programme of the Comintern's Fifth Congress. [371] Actually, the Fifth Congress was held in 1924. The critique to which

Service is referring was addressed to the Sixth Congress, held in the summer of 1928.

Service even manages to get the year of the death of Trotsky's widow, Natalia Sedova, wrong. He states, "She died in 1960, deeply mourned by her network of Mexican, French and American friends." [496] In fact, Sedova died in January 1962 at the age of 79. Several months before her death, in November 1961, as one would expect a biographer of Trotsky to know, Natalia Sedova had written to the Soviet government demanding a review of the Moscow Trials and the rehabilitation of Trotsky. At the end of the book, in yet another gross blunder, Service misidentifies the wife and daughter of Trotsky's youngest son Sergei, as being the wife and daughter of the older son Lev. [500-501] These errors got by not only the editors at Macmillan and Harvard University Press, but also eluded the none-too-watchful eye of Professor Ian Thatcher, who, we are informed by Service, read the entire manuscript.

Following the same procedure as Thatcher and Swain, Service fails to engage himself with Trotsky's writings. With the exception of Trotsky's *My Life,* which Service attempts to discredit, there is no persuasive evidence that the biographer worked systematically through any of Trotsky's published books and pamphlets prior to writing this biography. Aside from the writings of Ian Thatcher, whom he profusely praises, Service has paid little attention to existing scholarly literature on Trotsky. Service affects an attitude of contempt toward biographers, educated in the Marxist tradition, who have taken Trotsky's literary output seriously. The late Pierre Broué, a highly respected historian and the author of a massively researched and authoritative biography of Trotsky, is dismissed as an "idolater." Deutscher is mocked as one who "worshipped at Trotsky's shrine." [xxi]

There is reason to doubt that Service actually read the work of most of the other historians to whom he pays perfunctory tribute in his preface. For example, Service takes note of Professor Alexander Rabinowitch as a historian who subjected Trotsky to "sceptical scrutiny," and lumps him together with James White of Glasgow University, who ridiculously denies that Trotsky played any significant role in the October 1917 seizure of power. [xxi] In fact, Professor Rabinowitch's *The Bolsheviks Come to Power* substantiated Trotsky's role as the principal tactician and practical leader of the Bolshevik victory.

Despite Service's self-satisfied description of his biography as "full-length," there are virtually no extracts from, or adequate summaries of, Trotsky's major political works. Service does not even review the basic concepts and postulates of the theory of Permanent Revolution, which formed the foundation of

Trotsky's political work over a period of 35 years. His voluminous writings on China, Germany, Spain, France and even Britain are barely mentioned.

On the few occasions when Service does refer to one of Trotsky's books, what he has to say is usually wrong. In a thoroughly confused reference to *Literature and Revolution*, Service attributes to Trotsky the view that "It would take many years ... before a 'proletarian culture' would be widely achieved." [317] Trotsky, as anyone who has actually read *Literature and Revolution* knows, emphatically rejected the concept of "proletarian culture."[10] But Service does not know this—either because he did not read the book or because he was not able to understand it.

By now the reader must be wondering how Service, without paying attention to Trotsky's writings, manages to keep himself occupied for 501 pages. How is it possible to write a "full-length biography" of a man who was among the most prolific writers of the twentieth century, without paying the necessary attention to his literary output?

Unearthing Trotsky's "Buried Life"

As if anticipating this question, Service informs his readers at the very outset that his central concern is not with what Trotsky wrote or actually did. "This book's purpose," Service writes, "is to dig up the buried life." He allows that "the evidence starts with the works—his books, articles and speeches—which he published in his lifetime." But that is not sufficient. Even the study of all of Trotsky's writings would "tell us about his big objectives without always elucidating his personal or factional purpose at any given moment. As an active politician he could not always afford to spell out what he was up to." [4-5]

Service continues:

> His written legacy should not be allowed to become the entire story. It is sometimes in the supposedly trivial residues rather than in the grand public statements that the perspective of his career is

---

[10] In opposition to the proponents of "Proletcult" in the early 1920s, Trotsky argued that the proletariat, as an oppressed class, cannot create its own culture. The culture of the future, which will emerge on the basis of a far higher development of the productive forces, when there is no need for a class dictatorship, "will not have a class character. This seems to lead to the conclusion that there is no proletarian culture and that there never will be any and in fact there is no reason to regret this. The proletariat acquires power for the purpose of doing away forever with class culture and to make way for human culture. We frequently seem to forget this." (Leon Trotsky, *Literature and Revolution* [Chicago: Haymarket Books, 2005], p. 155).

most effectively reconstructed: his lifestyle, income, housing, family relationships, mannerisms and everyday assumptions about the rest of humanity. ... As with Lenin and Stalin, moreover, it is as important to pinpoint what Trotsky was silent about as what he chose to speak or write about. *His unuttered basic assumptions were integral to the amalgam of his life* (emphasis added). [5]

This statement is truly one with which Stalin, who was very careful not to tell other people what he really thought, could agree. It is entirely in line with the inquisitorial principle employed by Stalin in the organization of the Moscow trials. Evidence of crimes against the Soviet state was not to be found in the public statements, writings and deeds of the Old Bolshevik defendants. Rather, their terrorist conspiracies flowed from the "unuttered basic assumptions" that had been camouflaged beneath the public record.

And how does Professor Service intend to ferret out Trotsky's "unuttered basic assumptions"? Service announces that Trotsky's "buried life" can be uncovered by examining unpublished early drafts of his writings. "The excisions and amendments tell us about what he did not want others to know. This is particularly true of his autobiography." [5]

This statement forms the basis of Service's major accusation against Trotsky: that his autobiography *My Life*, which he wrote in 1930, is an unreliable and suspect work. Service complains that Trotsky's "account of himself has been accepted uncritically by generations of readers. The reality was different, for whenever inconvenient facts obscured his desired image he removed or distorted them." [11]

Trotsky's "Embarrassments"

And precisely what did Trotsky conceal or falsify in *My Life*? There are two major discrepancies that Service claims to have discovered when he compared the first draft of Trotsky's autobiography, which is deposited at Stanford University's Hoover Institution, with the published version. The first is Trotsky's supposed efforts to conceal the extent of the wealth of his father David Bronstein. The second, to which Service devotes obsessive attention, is Trotsky's supposed attempts to downplay his Jewish origins. Service writes:

As a Marxist he was embarrassed about the wealth of his parents, and he never properly acknowledged their extraordinary qualities and achievements. What is more, the published account of his boyhood in his autobiography tended to drop those passages where he appeared timid or pampered; and without denying his Jewish origin he trimmed back the references to it. By examining the drafts and proofs, we can catch glimpses of aspects of his upbringing that have long lain hidden. Thus he stated publicly only that his father was a prosperous, competent farmer. This hugely understated the reality. David Bronstein, married to Aneta, was among the most dynamic farmers for miles around in Kherson province. By hard work and determination he had dragged himself up the ladder of economic success and had every right to be proud of his achievement." [12]

Before answering Service's allegation that Trotsky downplayed his father's wealth and sought to conceal his ethnic and religious background, let us first draw attention to the dubious character of the underlying claim: that the progression of drafts to their completed form is best understood as a process of concealment and falsification. Service asserts what he must first prove. To support his charge, he would have to show why Trotsky's "excisions and amendments" should not be seen as the proper exercise of artistic discretion by a great master. There are many reasons, which have nothing to do with the intention to conceal, why Trotsky may have removed certain passages and added others.

Service fails to provide a single example in which Trotsky's published account of his childhood differs in any material way from the earlier draft. At any rate, Service's allegations are entirely without substance. That Trotsky "was embarrassed about the wealth of his parents" is a claim for which Service can cite no authority other than his own imagination. Trotsky's account traced his father's rising prosperity, though it must be pointed out that David Bronstein only achieved significant wealth well after Trotsky had left home. The Bronstein family did not move from the mud house in which Trotsky was born into a house built with bricks until the future revolutionary was almost 17 years old. But Trotsky provides in *My Life* a richly detailed and affectionate account of his father's relentless struggle to rise in the world and to accumulate wealth. Writing of his own social position as a child, Trotsky stated: "As son of a prosperous landowner, I belonged to the privileged class rather than to the oppressed."[11]

---

[11] Leon Trotsky, *My Life* (Mineola, NY: Dover Publications, 2007), pp. 86-87.

Max Eastman's 1926 biographical account of Trotsky's early life states that David Bronstein "got rich working and hiring the peasants to work with him. He controlled almost three thousand acres of land around the little Ukrainian village of Ianovka, owned the mill, and was altogether the important man of the place." Eastman knew these facts because Trotsky related them to him. "Trotsky is proud of his father, proud of the fact that he died working and understanding. He loves to talk about him,"[12] Eastman wrote.

Service's own account of the Bronstein family—whom he refers to as "plucky Jews" [14]—is based entirely on what was published in *My Life* and Eastman's *Young Trotsky*. He has conducted no new and independent research that either adds to, or refutes, the information provided by Trotsky and Eastman. There is not a single detail in Service's account of Trotsky's early childhood that cannot be traced back to these two earlier works.

Even more astonishing, in light of his claims to have exposed the untrustworthiness of Trotsky's autobiography, Service relies for his depiction of Trotsky's youth almost entirely on the published version of *My Life*, not on the earlier draft. In the second chapter of his biography, entitled "Upbringing," Service includes nine substantial extracts from Trotsky's autobiographical writing. Eight of them are reproduced from the published version of *My Life*; only one is from the earlier draft. In not one instance is Service able to pinpoint an important discrepancy between the published work and the draft.

That does not mean that Service comes up entirely empty handed in his exploration of the draft version of *My Life*. For example, he discovers that a young school friend whom Trotsky identifies as Karlson in the published edition of the autobiography was identified as "Kreitser" in the draft. [505] This discovery, proudly noted by Service in a footnote, must surely be counted as a major breakthrough in the field of Trotsky studies! If he had accomplished nothing else, Service has, with one mighty footnote, restored young Kreitser's name to its proper place in history.

Trotsky's Origins

Let us now turn to Service's contention that Trotsky sought to downplay his Jewish ancestry. There is, to be blunt, something rather unpleasant and

---

[12] Max Eastman, *The Young Trotsky* (London: New Park, 1980), p. 3.

suspect about Service's preoccupation with this matter. The fact that Trotsky was a Jew occupies a central place in Service's biography. It is never far from Service's mind. He is constantly reminding his readers of this fact, as if he were worried that it might slip from their attention. Indeed, given the emphasis placed on Trotsky's ethnicity, this book might have very well been titled, *Trotsky: The Biography of a Jew.*

Before we explore this disturbing element of Service's biography in greater detail, let us first respond to the allegation that Trotsky sought to conceal or deflect attention from his ancestry. This claim is as false as the biographer's contention that Trotsky sought to downplay the wealth of his parents. As always, Service assumes that his audience will never bother to read Trotsky's autobiography, in which Trotsky exhibits not the slightest reticence in discussing his ethnic and religious background. And how could he have possibly avoided the subject? The circumstances of his childhood were inextricably intertwined with his Jewish ancestry.

Trotsky's depiction of his Jewish background and its place in his intellectual and political development is entirely consistent with what is known of the broader Odessa-influenced social and cultural milieu within which he lived. Trotsky writes candidly about the place of religion in the life of his family:

> ...In my father's family there was no strict observation of religion. At first, appearances were kept up through sheer inertia: on holy days my parents journeyed to the synagogue in the colony; Mother abstained from sewing on Saturdays, at least within the sight of others. But all this ceremonial observance of religion lessened as years went on—as the children grew up and the prosperity of the family increased. Father did not believe in God from his youth, and in later years spoke openly about it in front of Mother and the children. Mother preferred to avoid the subject, but when the occasion required would raise her eyes in prayer.[13]

As for his own relation to his Jewish origins, Trotsky explained:

> In my mental equipment, nationality never occupied an independent place, as it was felt but little in every-day life. It is true that after the laws of 1881, which restricted the rights of Jews in Russia, my father was unable to buy more land, as he

---

[13] *My Life,* p. 84.

was so anxious to do, but could only lease it under cover. This, however, scarcely affected my own position. As son of a prosperous landowner, I belonged to the privileged class rather than to the oppressed. The language in my family and household was Russian-Ukrainian. True enough, the number of Jewish boys allowed to join the schools was limited to a fixed percentage, on account of which I lost one year.[14]

Trotsky reflected on the relation of his Jewish background to his intellectual development:

This national inequality probably was one of the underlying causes of my dissatisfaction with the existing order, but it was lost among all the other phases of social injustice. It never played a leading part—not even a recognized one—in the list of my grievances.[15]

The Torah and the Rabbi

Service is quite clearly dissatisfied with this explanation, which he does not even bother to quote. He sets out to "correct" Trotsky's account by attempting to make the subject's life conform to the prejudices of the biographer. This effort proves unfortunate for the credibility of Mr. Service. In a key passage, which supposedly refutes *My Life*, Service writes that Trotsky

liked to give the impression that he was integrated into every common aspect of school activities. This was not so. St. Paul's, like all Imperial schools, had to teach religion. Leiba Bronstein entered it as a Jew and did not convert to Christianity. He had to continue his spiritual devotions under the guidance of a rabbi who taught the Jewish pupils, and David Bronstein paid for his services. The rabbi in question failed to make it clear whether the Torah was superb literature or holy writ—and Leiba was later to conclude that he was really an agnostic of some kind. [37]

This account is attributed by Service to Max Eastman's *The Young Trotsky*, which was published in 1926. But has Service been faithful to Eastman's narration? Let us take a look at the original text. This is how Eastman tells this story:

---

[14] Ibid., pp. 86-87.

[15] Ibid., p. 87.

It had been an ambition of his father's—as combining cultural elevation with a certain conventional piety—to have a private tutor read the Bible with his son in the original Hebrew. Trotsky, being only eleven years old, was somewhat abashed before the bearded old scholar who undertook this task. And the scholar, being old and full of his duty, was hesitant about unveiling his own critical views to so young a boy. So it was not quite clear at first whether they were reading the Bible as history and literature, or as the revealed word of God.[16]

There is a quite noticeable difference between the two accounts. Eastman's "Bible" becomes, in Service's account, the "Torah." Eastman's "bearded old scholar," who reveals himself to be an agnostic, is transformed by Service into a "rabbi." It is not beyond the realm of possibility that the text was, indeed, the Torah—though this word generally conveys a wider range of texts than that encompassed in the Pentateuch. But as Service has no additional information to offer, beyond what Eastman wrote, what is the purpose of this change in wording? There is even less justification for Service's transformation of the old agnostic scholar into a rabbi. It should be stressed that this is not a translation issue. Service is referencing an English-language text.

It might be possible to dismiss this as nothing more than a careless exercise of authorial imagination but for the fact that Service's continuous harping on Trotsky's religious background is obsessive, obnoxious and, in its cumulative impact, ugly. He employs the suspect device of noting anti-Semitic attitudes and then proceeding to reinforce them. The reader is offered such passages as the following:

Russian anti-Semites had picked out Jews as a race without patriotic commitment to Russia. By becoming the foreign minister for a government *more interested in spreading world revolution than in defending the country's interests* Trotsky was conforming to a widespread stereotype of the "Jewish problem." ... As things stood he had already become the most famous Jew on earth. America's Red Cross leader in Russia, Colonel Raymond Robins, put this with characteristic pungency. Talking to Robert Bruce Lockhart, head of the British diplomatic mission in Moscow, he described Trotsky as "a four kind son of a bitch, but the greatest Jew since Christ." Trotsky, furthermore, was merely the most famous Jew in

---

[16] Max Eastman, *The Young Trotsky*, pp. 12-13.

a Sovnarkom where Jews were present to a disproportionate degree. The same was true in the Bolshevik central party leadership. If Lenin were to have dispensed with the services of talented Jews, he could never have formed a cabinet (emphasis added). [192]

Robert Service and the Jews

This passage is shortly followed by a chapter entitled "Trotsky and the Jews," which begins: "Trotsky hated it when people emphasized his Jewish background." [199] This emotion may have had something to do with the type of people who were inclined to do the emphasizing. There follow several pages of pointless and ridiculous observations. The reader is helpfully informed that "Trotsky's rejection of Judaism by no means meant that he shunned individual Jews." [201] After naming a few of the Jews with whom Trotsky was on good terms (all major figures in the Russian and European socialist movement), Service notes that "Trotsky also had companions who were cosmopolitans without being Jews." [201] Trotsky, you see, "spoke a lot with August Bebel," the founder-leader of the German Social Democratic Party. The biographer allows that "there was no trace of Judaism in Trotsky's adult lifestyle," although there were many "secularized Jews [who] continued to observe religious food prohibitions and celebrate traditional feast days." [201]

Service then proceeds to call his readers' attention to the fact, in case they had not made the appropriate mental note, that Trotsky's four children—Nina, Zina, Lev and Sergei—"were given names without association with Jewishness." [201]

More important information follows on the next page: Trotsky "was *brash in his cleverness, outspoken in his opinions. No one could intimidate him.* Trotsky *had these characteristics to a higher degree than most other Jews* emancipated from the traditions of their religious community and the restrictions of the Imperial order. He was manifestly an individual of exceptional talent. But he *was far from being the only Jew who visibly enjoyed the opportunities for public self-advancement.* In later years they were to constitute *a model for Jewish youth to follow in the world communist movement* when, like communists of all nationalities, they spoke loudly and wrote sharply regardless of other people's sensitivities. Trotsky can hardly be diagnosed as having suffered from the supposed syndrome of the self-hating Jew. Hatred did not come into the matter. He was too delighted with himself and his life to be troubled by embarrassments about his ancestry." [202, emphasis added]

Having suggested that Trotsky's revolutionary career was an example of Jews taking advantage of opportunities for "public self-advancement," Service develops this idea in the next paragraph:

"Trotsky was one of those tens of thousands of educated Jews in the Russian Empire who at last could assert themselves in situations where their parents had needed to bow and scrape before Gentile officialdom." [202] Many Jews, Service notes thoughtfully, sought advancement in respectable professions. But the "second route was to join the revolutionary parties where Jews constituted a disproportionate element." [202] This is a theory of well-known anti-Semitic parentage: revolution as a form of aggressively ambitious Jewish revenge against a society dominated by Christians. But Service has still more to say on this subject. He declares:

"Young Jewish men and women, trained in the rigors of the Torah, found a congenial secular orthodoxy in Marxist intricacies. Hair-splitting disputes were common to Marxism and Judaism (as they were to Protestantism)." [202] It is now possible to explain Service's previous twisting of the Eastman citation. Trotsky, according to Service's distorted account, had also been trained in the "rigors of the Torah." From there, the reader is led to believe, it was only a hop, skip and jump for the career-minded Bronstein to *Das Kapital*, the theory of Permanent Revolution, and a corner suite in the Kremlin.

Service writes that: "The party's leadership was widely identified as a Jewish gang." [205] No source is given for this statement. He adds, a few sentences down, "Jews indeed were widely alleged to dominate the Bolshevik party." Again, there is no source provided for this allegation. These allegations are not challenged, let alone refuted. Then Service reproduces a paragraph from an "anonymous letter to the Soviet authorities" which is a wild anti-Semitic denunciation of "full-blooded Jews who have given themselves Russian surnames to trick the Russian people." [206]

In another bizarre passage, dealing with the famous negotiations conducted by Trotsky with representatives of Germany and Austria-Hungary at Brest-Litovsk in 1918, Service writes: "As the Germans and Austrians strode to the table for talks they expected to be treated with deference. They acted as if victory was already theirs. They shared the prejudices of their social class. For them, socialists of any kind were hardly human. Russia's communists, who included so many Jews in their leadership, were little better than vermin." [197]

Service fails to provide a source for this assessment of the attitudes of the German delegates. In his autobiography, Trotsky wrote: "At Brest-Litovsk, the first Soviet delegation, headed by Joffe, was treated in a most ingratiating way by the Germans. Prince Leopold of Bavaria received them as his 'guests.' All the delegations had dinner and supper together." Trotsky noted with bemusement that "General Hoffmann's staff was publishing a paper called *Russky Vyestnik (The Russian Messenger)* for the benefit of the Russian prisoners; in its early phases it always spoke of the Bolsheviks with the most touching sympathy."[17]

Naturally, this initial friendliness was politically motivated and did not last long. The deadly seriousness of the issues that confronted the opposing parties at Brest-Litovsk inevitably found expression in the increasingly tense and confrontational atmosphere. This process is depicted brilliantly by Trotsky in *My Life*. His characterizations of his chief adversaries, Kühlmann, Hoffmann and Czernin, are true to life. They are political reactionaries, representatives of the aristocratic elite, but not monsters. Their attitude toward the Bolsheviks is a complex mixture of curiosity, bewilderment, fear, hatred and respect. In Trotsky's account, there is no suggestion that he was dealing with men who viewed the Bolsheviks, with or without Jews, as "vermin." That thought belongs to Service, not to the leaders of the German and Austrian delegates at Brest-Litovsk.

For all Service's preoccupation with Trotsky's religion, his book is remarkably uninformed by any of the very serious and outstanding scholarship on the question of Jewish life and culture in Odessa and Imperial Russia. The important works of Steven J. Zipperstein of Stanford University are not included in Service's bibliography. There is nothing more than a fleeting reference to the bloody anti-Semitic pogroms that killed thousands. Service does not even mention the infamous case of Mendel Beilis, the Jewish worker who was arrested in 1911 for the ritual murder of a Christian youth—a case that provoked international outrage against the tsarist regime. Had he bothered to do so, Service might have taken note of Trotsky's important and influential essay on this case.

This reviewer wishes to register his disgust with Service's inclusion among the biography's illustrations, for no obvious reason, of a Nazi caricature of "Leiba Trotzky-Braunstein." The caption provided by Service states: "In reality, his real nose was neither long nor bent and he never allowed his goatee to become straggly or his hair ill-kempt." Did Service intend this as a joke? If so, it is in very bad taste.

---

[17] *My Life*, p. 363.

What, then, should be made of Service's obsessive fixation with Trotsky's Jewish background? The use of anti-Semitism as a political weapon against Trotsky is so well known that it is impossible to believe that Service's incessant invocation of his subject's Jewish roots is innocent. Whatever Mr. Service's personal attitude to what he refers to as "the Jewish problem," he is all too obviously making an appeal precisely to anti-Semites for whom Trotsky's Jewish background is a major concern. It is fairly certain that the Russian-language edition of this biography will find favor within this reactionary constituency. One cannot help but suspect that Professor Service has taken this into consideration.

Service's Sources

A substantial portion of Service's book is devoted to the blackguarding of Trotsky's personality. He extends his efforts to discredit Trotsky as a revolutionary politician to every aspect of his personal life. Service seems to believe that the theory of Permanent Revolution will be less persuasive if Trotsky can be shown to have been an unpleasant individual. And so, Service's portrait of Trotsky never rises above the level of a vulgar caricature. His subject is always impossibly vain, insensitive, domineering and egotistical. Service is intent to show that these traits were already painfully apparent when Trotsky was still a teenager. He relies entirely on the testimony of a single individual, Gregory A. Ziv, who first met Trotsky in the late 1890s during the first stages of his revolutionary activities. Much later, in 1921, after he had emigrated to the United States, Ziv wrote a bitter memoir which was extremely hostile to the former friend and comrade who had, in the meantime, become the world famous leader of the Russian Revolution.

No one would deny that Ziv's memoir is a document that any serious historian would consult in the preparation of a biography of Trotsky. After all, Ziv knew Trotsky at a critical juncture in the life of the emerging revolutionary. But a historian is obligated to approach documents and sources critically, to carefully consider the degree of trust that can be invested in the information they provide. A highly critical approach is certainly warranted in the case of Ziv. There are many reasons to doubt the objectivity and reliability of his evaluation of Trotsky's personality. First and foremost, Ziv, after he arrived in the United States, became extremely hostile to Trotsky's stand on the imperialist war. Ziv was a supporter of Russia's participation in the "war for democracy." This information is not given to the reader by Service.

But Max Eastman, who was familiar with Ziv's memoir, offered the following background information:

> When Trotsky came to New York [in January 1917] during [the] war—anti-patriot, anti-war, revolutionist—he met Doctor Ziv, who he knew had been publishing a little pro-war paper there in the Russian language. He met him most cordially; and wishing to remember the friendly emotions of these earlier days, he invited him to his house. They talked long and drifted back into the mood of their recollections. But Trotsky, knowing that Ziv could teach him nothing and that he could convince Ziv of nothing, refrained from opening the political question. It was a characteristically courteous, and a very friendly, exercise of judgment. But to the doctor's editorial vanity it seems to have been an unendurable offense, the manifestation of a self-seeking intellectual arrogance which he suddenly discovered had characterized his friend's activities from the cradle. Hence this little volume of weak and ludicrous personal spite.[18]

Prosecutors are legally obligated to make exculpatory evidence available to the defense. Following this general principle, a biographer should not conceal from his readers information that calls into question the credibility of the witness whose testimony he is citing. But Service is indifferent to such principled considerations. While insisting that Trotsky's memoirs must be subjected to the most skeptical scrutiny, Service shows absolutely no inclination to question anything written by Ziv in his memoir. And so he quotes Ziv's statement that Trotsky "loved his friends and he loved them sincerely; but his love was of the kind that a peasant has for his horse, which assists the confirmation of his peasant individuality." [46] This observation makes so deep an impression on Service that he repeats it: "Lëva looked on his revolutionary comrades as the peasant regarded his horse..." [46] What intelligent reader would believe such nonsense?

Enter Schopenhauer

Another claim by Ziv that Service seizes upon concerns the influence of a pamphlet by Arthur Schopenhauer, the nineteenth century German idealist

---

[18] *The Young Trotsky*, p. 21.

philosopher, upon the young Trotsky. Service does not actually provide an extract from this passage, but presents only a summary. For the purpose of clarifying this issue, which sheds light on Service's method, this reviewer has consulted Ziv's original text.

In his memoir Ziv devotes slightly more than one paragraph to this question. He notes that Schopenhauer's pamphlet "somehow fell into his [Trotsky's] hands," and then offers a brief summary of the philosopher's argument. The purpose of the pamphlet is to teach "how to vanquish one's opponent in debate, regardless of whether one was actually correct or not." The pamphlet, according to Ziv, "does not teach rules which must be followed in conducting a debate, but rather exposes devices—more or less crude, or more or less subtle—to which debaters resort in order to be victorious in a debate." Then, in a somewhat surprising admission, Ziv indicates that he does not have any precise information on the impact of the pamphlet on his friend. He writes: "*One can imagine how Bronstein was overjoyed by this small pamphlet that by no means was less valuable for its small size.*" Yes, many things can be imagined, but that does not make them true. Ziv's wording suggests that he did not have any direct evidence that the work made a great impression on Trotsky. He did not write, for example, "Bronstein told me that he was overjoyed by this pamphlet..." If Mr. Ziv was giving sworn testimony, as a witness for the prosecution, the defense attorney would question him carefully on this point. Indeed, after noting that Ziv acknowledges that he does not even know how Trotsky obtained the pamphlet, he would probably ask: "Mr. Ziv, isn't it true that you don't really know for sure if Trotsky read the *Art of Controversy?* Isn't it true that you never actually witnessed him reading the book?" As a matter of fact, based on what Ziv wrote, we cannot know for sure whether Trotsky did read *The Art of Controversy*. But the answer to this question is, for the purpose of evaluating this biography, less important than Service's failure to question Ziv's claims.

Quite the opposite. Service goes far beyond the claims of Ziv. He writes, "Lëva prepared himself as if for a military campaign. He *scrutinized* Schopenhauer's *The Art of Controversy* with the purpose of improving his debating skills (emphasis added)." [45] In fact, as we have shown, Service does not have the evidence to support this claim.

Why is this matter important? Service implies that Schopenhauer's arguments provide a key to understanding the development of not only Trotsky's polemical style, but also his allegedly aggressive and domineering personality. Roaming far from Ziv's actual text and offering his own bowdlerized interpretation of Schopenhauer, Service misrepresents the philosopher as an advocate of an array of unscrupulous debating ploys and tricks. "Victory, crushing victory," declaims Service, "was the only worthwhile objective." The philosopher, according to Service, "went on to declare that the ideas of 'ordinary people' counted for nothing." [45]

Service finally declares: "Schopenhauer *did not belong* to the regular armature of Russian revolutionary thought, and Lëva Bronstein did not *openly acknowledge* his influence on his techniques of argument. *Yet he probably found* much that he needed for his politics and personality in *The Art of Controversy* (emphasis added)." [45]

So, in the end, what are we really left with? Service's claim that Trotsky discovered in Schopenhauer a philosophical justification for his alleged contempt for humanity and poisonous polemics is based on assumptions, suppositions and guesses unsupported by facts.

If we assume, for the sake of argument, that Trotsky read—nay, studied with great care—Schopenhauer's *Art of Controversy*, that does not tell us whether he agreed or disagreed with it; what he accepted and what he rejected. Trotsky read many things as a youth, including, as he tells us in *My Life*, the writings of John Stuart Mill. Yet no one would accuse Trotsky of being an admirer of British empiricism and liberalism. Finally, Service seems to assume that Trotsky's alleged study of *The Art of Controversy* could only have had malign consequences. In the opinion of this reviewer, it is more likely that Trotsky, if he had read *The Art of Controversy*, might have found in this pamphlet material that proved later to be of assistance in exposing the calumnies, distortions, half-truths and lies of his many unscrupulous enemies. Indeed, one suspects that Stalinism taught Trotsky far more than Schopenhauer on the subject of dishonest polemics.

Trotsky and Sokolovskaya

The relentless efforts to malign Trotsky backfire and cast Service himself in a very unflattering light. He appears to be organically incapable of feeling any sympathy whatever for the many emotional injuries and traumas endured by his subject in the course of a life dedicated—or to use the words of his first love and wife Alexandra Sokolovskaya, consecrated—to the revolutionary cause. Even when dealing with the plight of the 19-year-old Lev Davidovich, imprisoned and in solitary confinement, Service's attitude is contemptuous and sneering. For example, he quotes from a deeply moving letter that Trotsky wrote to Sokolovskaya in November 1898. The young man is consumed by loneliness and suffers from insomnia. He confesses that he has contemplated suicide, but then reassures Alexandra that he is "extraordinarily tied to life." And what is the response of Robert Service? He writes: "There was showiness and immaturity in these sentiments. He was a self-centered young man." [52]

Eventually Trotsky and Sokolovskaya marry and are sent into Siberian exile. They have two children. Trotsky's reputation as a brilliant young writer brings him to the attention of the major leaders of Russian socialism. Anxious to expand the scope of his activity in the revolutionary movement, the young man resolves to escape from Siberian exile. In his autobiography, Trotsky writes that Sokolovskaya encouraged him in this decision.

But Service, without presenting any evidence that contradicts Trotsky's narrative, declares: "This is hard to take at face value. Bronstein was planning to abandon her in the wilds of Siberia. She had no one to look after her, and she had to care for two tiny babies all on her own with winter coming on." Service brings his diatribe to a climax with an utterly vulgar comment: "No sooner had he fathered a couple of children than he decided to run off. Few revolutionaries left such a mess behind them." [67] Service, contradicting himself, concedes that Trotsky "was acting within the revolutionary code of behavior." [67] But he then asserts, "Even if Alexandra really did give her consent, Lev showed little appreciation of the sacrifice he had asked of her. 'Life,' he said as if it were a simple matter of fact, 'separated us.' In reality he had chosen to separate himself from his marital and parental responsibilities." [67]

Aside from the libelous character of this allegation, contradicted by everything that is known about the realities of revolutionary struggle, it is hard to imagine a more anachronistic approach to the writing of history. Service presumes to judge the behavior of revolutionaries in late nineteenth century Russia, who were engaged in a struggle to the death against the tsarist autocracy, with the hypocritical standards of a wealthy, conservative and self-satisfied upper-middle class philistine in modern-day Britain.

Let us, by the way, note that Service cuts off Trotsky's sentence before its conclusion. "Life separated us," Trotsky wrote, "but nothing could destroy our friendship and our intellectual kinship."[19]

The enduring character of the profound friendship and mutual solidarity of Trotsky and Sokolovskaya was confirmed by the latter in discussions with

---

[19] *My Life*, p. 133.

Eastman in the 1920s. Alexandra never betrayed that friendship, for which she ultimately paid with her life. Stalin murdered her in 1938. Service makes this cold and contemptuous comment on her tragic fate: "Her troubles had started with a short-lived marriage contracted to keep her and Trotsky together in Siberia—and it was in Siberia that she finally expired." [431]

Service's treatment of the tragic fate of Trotsky's daughter Zina, who committed suicide in Berlin in January 1933, is callous and malicious. He writes, "Trotsky coped with the tragedy by blaming everything on Stalin and his treatment of her." He continues:

> This accusation, frequently repeated in accounts of Trotsky, was ill aimed. Zina had spent all the time she had wanted in Sukhum; it had been Trotsky who summoned her abroad and not Stalin who had deported her—and it had been Trotsky with whom she wanted to live. Trotsky's attempt to politicize the death was not his finest moment. [386]

Service chooses not to quote from the letter Trotsky wrote to the Central Committee of the Communist Party of the Soviet Union on January 11, 1933, less than a week after his daughter's suicide. He does not inform his readers that Zina was unable to return to Russia, where her husband, daughter and mother still lived, because the Stalinist regime had revoked her Soviet citizenship. As Trotsky wrote, "Depriving her of her citizenship was only a wretched and stupid act of vengeance against me."[20]

Determined to discredit Trotsky in any way possible, Service absolves the Stalinist regime of any responsibility for the death of his daughter. And this is despite the fact, as Service knows full well, that Stalin would, within just a few years, murder Trotsky's first wife, his sons, his brothers and his sister, and even his in-laws.

A Shameful Episode

Despite the considerable length of this review, it has left much unsaid. A comprehensive refutation of all of Service's distortions and misrepresentations would easily assume the size of a substantial book. This reviewer will leave for another time the exposure of Service's political falsifications as well as his persistent defense of Stalin against Trotsky. In this regard, another

---

[20] *Writings of Leon Trotsky [1932-33]* (New York: Pathfinder Press, 1972), p. 70.

important issue that remains to be explored is the significance of the Trotsky biographies of Thatcher, Swain and Service as manifestations of the confluence of neo-Stalinist falsification and traditional Anglo-American anti-Communism. Indeed, a striking feature of the ongoing campaign against Trotsky is the degree to which it draws upon the lies and frame-ups of the Stalinists.

There is one final issue that needs to be raised, and that is the role of Harvard University Press in publishing this biography. One can only wonder why it has allowed itself to be associated with such a deplorable and degraded work. It is difficult to believe that Service's manuscript was subjected to any sort of serious editorial review. There are still, or so one would like to believe, professors in Harvard's Department of History who can distinguish serious scholarship from trash.

There was a time when Harvard was justly proud of its role as archivist of the closed section of Trotsky's papers, which it guarded under lock and key—in accordance with the instructions of Trotsky and Natalia Sedova— for nearly 40 years. The Houghton Library considered these papers to be among its historically significant collections. In 1958, Harvard, on its own initiative, published the diary that Trotsky kept in 1935. The publisher's foreword noted respectfully that Trotsky "is to many today one of the heroes of our time."[21] A half-century later, it provides its imprimatur for a slanderous and slovenly work. Is Harvard today, in a period of political reaction and intellectual decay, atoning for its earlier displays of principles and scholarly integrity? Whatever the reason, Harvard University Press has brought shame upon itself. One suspects that at some point in the future, with the recovery of morale and courage, it will look back upon this episode with great regret.

---

[21] Foreword to *Trotsky's Diary in Exile, 1935* (New York: Atheneum, 1963), p. v.

Leon Trotsky as a young revolutionary in 1897 in Nikolaev, prior to his first arrest

Political Biography & the Historical Lie

An Examination of
Professor Robert Service's Biography of Trotsky[1]

It has been reported in the *Evening Standard* that at the public launching of his new biography of Leon Trotsky at Daunt Books in London's Holland Park on October 22, 2009, Professor Robert Service declared: "There's life in the old boy Trotsky yet—but if the ice pick didn't quite do its job killing him off, I hope I've managed it."

One might reasonably wonder what type of historian—indeed, what type of man—would describe his own work, and with evident satisfaction, in such a manner. Is it really the aim of a serious biographer to carry out the literary equivalent of an assassination? Every possible interpretation of this statement speaks against Mr. Service. Leon Trotsky was murdered, and in a particularly gruesome and horrible manner. The blunt side of an alpenstock was driven by the assassin into Trotsky's cranium. His wife, Natalia, was nearby when it happened. She heard the scream of her companion of 38 years and, when she ran into his study, saw blood streaming down over his forehead and eyes. "Look what they have done to me," Trotsky cried out to Natalia.

The death of Trotsky was felt by many as an almost unendurable loss. In Mexico City, 300,000 people paid tribute to him as his funeral cortège made its way through the streets of the capital. A private letter written by the American novelist, James T. Farrell, provides a sense of the traumatic impact

---

[1] Lecture delivered on December 13, 2009 at the Friends Meeting House in London, England.

129

of Trotsky's assassination. "The crime is unspeakable. There are no words to describe it. I feel stunned, hurt, bitter, impotently in a rage. He was the greatest living man, and they murdered him, and the government of the United States is even afraid of his ashes. God!"[2]

A serious biographer of Trotsky would not joke about the "ice pick." It is a despicable icon of political reaction. Mr. Service would, perhaps, protest that his biography has "assassinated" Trotsky only in the sense of bringing an end to all interest in and discussion of this particular individual. But is this a legitimate ambition? A genuine scholar hopes that his work contributes to, rather than stifles, the development of the historical discussion. But this was clearly not the intention of Mr. Service. As he told the *Evening Standard*,[3] he hopes that he will achieve with his biography what Stalin failed to accomplish through murder—that is, to "kill off" Trotsky as a significant historical figure. With this aim in mind, one can only imagine how Service approached the writing of this biography.

Service's remark at his book launch seems to reflect a state of mind that is fairly widespread in the reactionary milieu within which he circulates. A review of the biography written by the right-wing British historian Norman Stone, an admirer of Margaret Thatcher and Augusto Pinochet, is entitled "The Ice Pick Cometh." Another glowing review, written by the writer Robert Harris and published in the London *Sunday Times*, congratulates Service for having "effectively, assassinated Trotsky all over again."[4]

This is the language of people who are very troubled—both personally and politically. Seventy years after Trotsky's death, they are still terrified by the spectre of the great revolutionary. The very thought of the man evokes homicidal images. But do they really believe that Mr. Service's book can accomplish what was beyond the power of Stalin's totalitarian police state? That Mr. Service and his admirers can even entertain such a thought exposes how little they understand of Trotsky and the ideas to which he devoted his life.

Leon Trotsky—co-leader of the October Revolution, opponent of Stalinism, and founder of the Fourth International—was assassinated by an

---

[2] Quoted in *James T. Farrell: The Revolutionary Socialist Years*, by Alan M. Wald (New York: New York University Press, 1978), p. 87.

[3] "Londoner's Diary," *London Evening Standard*, October 23, 2009.

[4] Robert Harris, "Trotsky: A Biography by Robert Service," *The Sunday Times*, October 18, 2009.

agent of the Soviet secret police, the GPU, in August 1940. The last 11 years of his life had been spent in exile. Living on what he called "a planet without a visa," Trotsky moved from Turkey, to France, to Norway and finally, in 1937, to Mexico. The years between his expulsion from the USSR and his arrival in Mexico had witnessed a ferocious growth of international political reaction: the coming to power of Hitler in Germany, the strangulation of the revolutionary movements of the working class in France and Spain by the Stalinist and social democratic bureaucracies under the banner of the "Popular Front," and the orchestration of the Moscow Trials and ensuing Great Terror that physically exterminated virtually all the representatives of Marxist politics and socialist culture in the USSR.

The first of the Moscow Trials, whose 16 defendants included historic leaders of the Bolshevik Party such as Grigory Zinoviev and Lev Kamenev, was held in August 1936. The defendants were accused of plotting assassinations and various acts of terrorism. Not a single piece of evidence was produced at the trial, other than the confessions of the accused. All were sentenced to death by the tribunal. The defendants' appeals were denied within a few hours of the trial's conclusion, and they were executed on August 25, 1936. Though not present, the chief accused were Leon Trotsky and his son, Lev [Leon] Sedov. From his exile in Norway, Trotsky vehemently denounced the trial as "one of the biggest, clumsiest, and most criminal plots of the secret police against world opinion."[5]

Under pressure from the Soviet regime, the social democratic government of Norway interned Trotsky in order to prevent him from continuing his public exposure of Stalin's murderous frame-up of the Bolshevik leaders. For nearly four months he was held incommunicado, virtually cut off from any contact with the outside world, while the Stalinist regime broadcast its lying denunciations of him. The Norwegian confinement did not end until December 19, 1936 when Trotsky was placed aboard a freighter bound for Mexico, whose government had granted him asylum.

The last message that Trotsky wrote before his departure was to his eldest son, Lev Sedov. Not knowing what awaited him on the voyage to Mexico, Trotsky informed Lev that he and his younger brother Sergei were his heirs, entitled to whatever royalties accrued from his writings. Trotsky noted that he had no other possessions. His letter ended with a poignant request to Lev Sedov: "If you ever meet Sergei," wrote Trotsky, "tell him that we have never

---

[5] *Writings of Leon Trotsky [1935-1936]* (New York: Pathfinder Press, 1977), p. 413.

forgotten him and never will forget him for a single moment."[6] But Lev Sedov was never to see or speak with his younger brother again. Sergei was executed, on Stalin's orders, on October 29, 1937. Nor was Lev ever to be reunited with his father and mother. He died on February 16, 1938, the victim of an assassination carried out by agents of the Soviet secret police.

Trotsky and Natalia Sedova arrived in Mexico on January 9, 1937. They lived as guests of Diego Rivera in his famous "Blue House" in Coyoacán, a suburb of Mexico City. Trotsky immediately threw himself into the struggle to expose Stalin's frame-ups. The second trial of Old Bolsheviks was about to begin. This time there were to be 21 defendants, including Yuri Pyatakov and Karl Radek. In a speech filmed on January 30, 1937, which is easily viewed today on the Internet, Trotsky declared:

> Stalin's trial against me is built on false confessions, extorted by modern Inquisitorial methods, in the interests of the ruling clique. *There are no crimes in history more terrible in intention or execution than the Moscow trials of Zinoviev-Kamenev and of Pyatakov-Radek.* These trials develop not from communism, not from socialism, but from Stalinism, that is, from the unaccountable despotism of the bureaucracy over the people!
>
> What is my principal task now? To reveal the *truth*. To show and to demonstrate that the true criminals hide under the cloak of the accusers.[7]

Trotsky issued a call for the establishment of an international commission of inquiry to investigate and pass judgment on the charges made by the Soviet regime. He pledged to present to this commission "all my files, thousands of personal and open letters in which the development of my *thought* and my action is reflected day by day, without any gaps. I have nothing to hide!"[8] Trotsky declared that there was not a stain on his honor, either personal or political.

Within less than three months, on April 10, 1937, the commission was convened in Coyoacán under the chairmanship of the renowned American philosopher, John Dewey. Immense pressure had been brought to bear by the Stalinists and their legions of liberal friends—including luminaries such as Lillian Hellman, Malcolm Cowley and Corliss Lamont—to prevent the

---

[6] Ibid., p. 502.

[7] *Writings of Leon Trotsky [1936-37]* (New York: Pathfinder, 1978), p. 179.

[8] Ibid.

formation of the commission, and, when those efforts failed, to sabotage the proceedings. For one week, Trotsky testified before the commission, answering scores of questions relating to the allegations made by the Stalinist regime. No one who witnessed him testify, hour after hour, ever forgot the experience. James T. Farrell, who observed the proceedings, recalled in later writings the overwhelming moral force of Trotsky's presence.

His final oration, delivered in English and lasting more than four hours, left the commissioners deeply moved. "Anything I can say will be an anti-climax," Dewey remarked upon the conclusion of Trotsky's speech.[9] In December 1937, the Dewey Commission issued its findings. Trotsky was declared "Not Guilty" and the proceedings in Moscow were found to be a "frame-up."

The findings of the Dewey Commission represented a great moral victory for Trotsky. But the powerful momentum of political reaction had not been exhausted. Within the Soviet Union, Stalin's police were murdering more than 1,000 people every day. In Spain, the victory of Franco was being assured by the counter-revolutionary politics of the Communist Party and the homicidal frenzy of Stalin's secret police. Paralyzed by the betrayals of the Stalinists, the European working class was unable to stop the spread of fascism and the movement toward war. Trotsky concentrated his energies on the founding of the Fourth International. "The world political situation as a whole," he wrote in early 1938, "is chiefly characterized by a historical crisis of the leadership of the proletariat."[10]

The Stalinists countered Trotsky's efforts by escalating their violence against his closest co-thinkers and supporters. In July 1937, Erwin Wolf, one of Trotsky's political secretaries, was murdered in Spain. Two months later, Ignace Reiss—who had defected from the GPU, publicly denounced Stalin and declared his allegiance to the Fourth International—was assassinated in Switzerland. In February 1938, the GPU killed Sedov. And in July 1938, Rudolf Klement, the secretary of the Fourth International, was kidnapped in Paris and murdered.

Despite this reign of Stalinist terror, the Fourth International held its founding conference in September 1938. In a speech recorded one month

---

[9] *The Case of Leon Trotsky*, Report of Hearings on the Charges Made Against Him in the Moscow Trials, by the Preliminary Commission of Inquiry (New York: Merit Publishers, 1968) p. 585.

[10] *The Death Agony of Capitalism and the Tasks of the Fourth International. The Transitional Program* (New York: Labor Publications, 1972) p. 7.

later, Trotsky declared that the aim of the Fourth International "is the full material and spiritual liberation of the toilers and exploited through the socialist revolution." He scoffed at the terror of the Soviet bureaucracy. "The hangmen think in their obtuseness and cynicism that it is possible to frighten us. They err! Under blows we become stronger. The bestial politics of Stalin are only politics of despair."[11]

Less than two years of life remained for Trotsky after the founding of the Fourth International. His intellectual creativity and political far-sightedness were undiminished. Not only did he recognize the inevitability of a second world war, Trotsky predicted that Stalin would attempt to extricate himself from the disastrous consequences of his international policies by seeking an alliance with Hitler. Trotsky's analysis was confirmed with the signing of the Stalin-Hitler Non-Aggression Pact in August 1939. But Trotsky also warned that Stalin's treachery would not spare the Soviet Union from the horrors of war. It would be only a matter of time before Hitler hurled his military forces against the USSR.

During the final months of his life, with war already raging in Western Europe, Trotsky defended the historical perspective of socialism in the face of widespread skepticism and despair. He did not seek to reassure wavering followers with predictions of imminent revolution.

Rather than offering a prediction, Trotsky posed a question: "Will objective historical necessity in the long run cut a path for itself in the consciousness of the vanguard of the working class; that is, in the process of this war and those profound shocks which it must engender, will a genuine revolutionary leadership be formed capable of leading the proletariat to the conquest of power?"[12]

He recognized that the many defeats suffered by the working class had created widespread skepticism as to its revolutionary capacities. There were many who shifted blame for these defeats away from the political leaders and onto the shoulders of the working class itself. For those who believed that past defeats "proved" that the working class was incapable of taking and holding state power, the historical condition of mankind could only appear hopeless. But against that perspective of despair and demoralization, Trotsky advanced another: "Altogether differently does the case present itself to him who has clarified in his mind the profound antagonism between the organic, deep-going, insurmountable urge of the toiling masses to tear themselves free from

---

[11] *Writings of Leon Trotsky [1938-39]* (New York, Pathfinder, 1974), pp. 86-87.

[12] *In Defense of Marxism*, (London, New Park, 1971) p. 15.

the bloody capitalist chaos, and the conservative, patriotic, utterly bourgeois character of the outlived labor leadership."[13]

Trotsky did not expect to survive the war. He assumed that Stalin would spare no effort to kill him before the Soviet Union was drawn into open conflict with Nazi Germany. In the early morning hours of May 24, 1940, a Stalinist assassination squad, led by the painter David Alfaro Siqueiros, penetrated the villa in which Trotsky and Natalia were living. Robert Sheldon Harte, a Stalinist agent working inside the compound, had unlocked the gates of the villa. The Stalinist hit men made their way into the bedroom of Trotsky and Natalia and unleashed a barrage of machine gun fire. Almost miraculously, the two survived the assault. But Trotsky knew that the May attack would not be the last. He understood better than anyone else the danger that he confronted. "In a reactionary epoch such as ours," he stated, "a revolutionist is compelled to swim against the stream. I am doing this to the best of my ability. The pressure of world reaction has expressed itself perhaps most implacably in my personal fate and the fate of those close to me. I do not at all see in this any merit of mine: this is the result of the interlacing of historical circumstances."[14]

On August 20, 1940, Trotsky was assaulted by a GPU agent, and died the next day of the injuries that he had suffered. He was 60 years old.

Several months after the assassination, Max Eastman wrote a final tribute to Trotsky. It was published in, of all places, the prestigious bourgeois journal, *Foreign Affairs*. Eastman had known Trotsky very well for almost 20 years. He had written Trotsky's biography and translated into English many of his most important works, including *The History of the Russian Revolution*. Eastman was not an uncritical admirer of Trotsky. Their relationship had been marked by periods of sharp conflict. During the last years of Trotsky's life, Eastman repudiated his radical inclinations, definitively rejected Marxism and moved ever more sharply to the right. When Trotsky and Eastman met in Mexico for the last time, in February 1940, it was not as comrades but as old friends who had become somewhat estranged. At this point, neither man was interested in attempting to persuade the other of the correctness of his own position.

The fact that Eastman was no longer politically connected to Trotsky endows his final tribute with exceptional probative value. His memorial essay, entitled "The Character and Fate of Leon Trotsky," began as follows:

---

[13] Ibid.

[14] *Writings of Leon Trotsky [1939-40]* (New York, Pathfinder, 2001), p. 299.

Trotsky stood up gloriously against the blows of fate these last fifteen years—demotion, rejection, exile, systematized slanderous misrepresentation, betrayal by those who had understood him, repeated attempts upon his life by those who had not, the certainty of ultimate assassination. His associates, his secretaries, his relatives, his own children were hounded to death by a sneering and sadistic enemy. He suffered privately beyond description but he never relaxed his monumental discipline. He never lost his grip for one visible second, never permitted any blow to blunt the edge of his wit, his logic or his literary style. Under afflictions that would have sent almost any creative artist to a hospital for neurotics and thence to the grave, Trotsky steadily developed and improved his art. His unfinished life of Lenin, which I had partially translated, would have been his masterpiece. He gave us, in a time when our race is woefully in need of such restoratives, the vision of a man.

Of that there is no more doubt than of his great place in history. His name will live, with that of Spartacus and the Gracchi, Robespierre and Marat, as a supreme revolutionist, an audacious captain of the masses in revolt.[15]

These words provided a sense of the enduring significance of Trotsky's life. Eastman was telling his readers that Trotsky would still be remembered in 2,000 years as one of the great fighters for human freedom.

But here we are, 70 years after Trotsky's assassination, in the midst of a politically reactionary and intellectually dishonest campaign to deprive him of "his great place in history." The publication of Robert Service's biography of Trotsky is a milestone in this campaign of historical distortion and falsification, whose stated aim is the discrediting of the actions and ideas of this key figure in modern history.

Before proceeding to a review of Service's *Trotsky*, it is necessary to make a few preliminary remarks about the treatment of Trotsky by historians both within and outside the USSR. Of course, within the USSR during Stalin's dictatorship, Trotsky was totally anathematized. From the early 1920s, the political struggle waged by the rising Soviet bureaucracy against Trotsky proceeded first and foremost on the basis of the falsification of history: of the development of the Russian Social Democratic Labor Party, the protracted conflict between its Bolshevik and Menshevik factions, the role of different

---

[15] *Foreign Affairs*, Volume 19, No. 2 (January 1941, p. 332).

tendencies and individuals in that generally heated struggle, and finally, of the October Revolution. Trotsky's role in the latter event, and in the civil war that followed, was so immense that the campaign to discredit him, which began in earnest in 1923, required the systematic falsification of history.

The campaign of lies began in 1923-1924 with the charge that Trotsky "underestimated the peasantry." This absurd allegation, which reflected pre-1917 programmatic differences as well as emerging disputes within the Soviet state over economic and foreign policy, set the stage for a generalized attack on Trotsky's theory of Permanent Revolution, which had provided the strategic foundation for the Bolshevik conquest of state power and its goal of world socialist revolution. The fight against Trotsky reflected the repudiation of the internationalist program of the October Revolution by a bureaucracy increasingly focused on the defense of its social privileges within a national framework. Thus there existed a symbiotic relationship between the ever more vindictive denunciation of Trotsky's supposed heresies—supported by the misrepresentation of pre-1917 factional conflicts between Trotsky and Lenin—and the promulgation of the program of "socialism in one country." The lies that began in 1923 led to tragic consequences. As Trotsky wrote in 1937, the judicial frame-ups of the Moscow Trials had their source in supposedly "minor" historical distortions.

Even after the exposure of Stalin's crimes in 1956, the Soviet bureaucracy desperately resisted Trotsky's historical and political rehabilitation. Even if it no longer claimed officially that he had been in league with the Gestapo, the Soviet regime and its allies defended and supported the struggle against "Trotskyism" that had been waged by Stalin in the 1920s. The systematic falsification of Trotsky's role in the history of Russian socialism, in the leadership of the October Revolution, in the creation of the Red Army and its victory in the Civil War, and, above all, in the fight against the Soviet bureaucracy, continued—even up until the dissolution of the USSR. Mr. Service claims that Gorbachev ordered Trotsky's posthumous rehabilitation in 1988. [2] This is just one of Professor Service's innumerable errors. Trotsky was never officially rehabilitated by the Soviet government.

Outside the USSR, the treatment of Trotsky was very different. The role played by Isaac Deutscher's trilogy—*The Prophet Armed, Unarmed* and *Outcast*—in reawakening interest in Trotsky is well known. But it must be noted that Deutscher's recounting of Trotsky's extraordinary life found a receptive audience within a broad spectrum of scholars who, though usually hostile to Marxism, accepted as an indisputable fact his gigantic role in the history of the twentieth century. Thus, even an historian as unfriendly to Trotsky's ideas as Richard Pipes could bring himself to admit, in a review of Deutscher's "magnificent" second volume: "Personal courage and intellectual honesty Trotsky undoubtedly possessed, in sharp contrast to the other contenders for Lenin's mantle who were cowardly and deceitful to a remarkable degree."[16]

The growing appreciation of Trotsky's role in Soviet history was not, by any means, attributable solely to Deutscher's biography. The work of other important historians writing in the 1950s, 1960s and 1970s contributed to a significant deepening of the understanding of Russian revolutionary history and Trotsky's role within it. Of particular significance was the work of scholars such as E. H. Carr, Leopold Haimson, Moshe Lewin, Alexander Rabinowitch, Richard B. Day, Pierre Broué, Robert V. Daniels, Marcel Liebman and Baruch Knei-Paz.

Significantly, a fundamental change in the treatment of Trotsky became apparent in the last years of the USSR and in the aftermath of its dissolution. First, as the crisis of the Stalinist regime mounted within the USSR, it was inevitable that the old historical falsifications would lose credibility. This process, one might have expected, would work to the advantage of Trotsky's historical reputation. Certainly, in the aftermath of 1956, dissident elements hungered for whatever information they could find about him. However, from the 1970s on, the movement of the Soviet intelligentsia was to the right. Solzhenitsyn's *Gulag Archipelago*, which paid little attention to the left-wing opposition to Stalinism, became the leading text of the dissident movement. This opposition did not reject Stalinism as a perversion of Marxism; rather, it rejected Marxism and the entire revolutionary project. Thus, within the "dissident" literature of the 1970s and early 1980s, the treatment of Trotsky was markedly hostile.

Emphasis was generally placed not on his opposition to Stalinism, but rather on the alleged continuity between Trotsky's policies and those implemented by Stalin after Trotsky had been expelled from the Communist Party and exiled from the USSR. This tendency became particularly pronounced during the era of Gorbachev, when, for the first time, genuine historical documents relating to Trotsky's role, including some of his books, became available. As if to counter the favorable impression these documents and books would make on a public that was asking whether an alternative had existed to Stalin and Stalinism, the new opposition to Trotsky assumed the form of

---

[16] *The American Historical Review*, Vol. 65, No. 4 (July 1960), p. 904.

unfavorable commentaries on his personality. Another increasingly common form taken by anti-Trotskyism in the last years of the USSR, and in the immediate aftermath of its dissolution, was a heavy-handed and overtly anti-Semitic emphasis on Trotsky's Jewish origins.

The reactionary environment of political triumphalism that followed the collapse of the Stalinist regime in 1991 was reflected no less sharply in the treatment of Trotsky outside the former USSR. A campaign was initiated to undermine and even destroy the historical image of Trotsky as the representative of an historical alternative to Stalinism. In the early 1990s, the University of Glasgow sponsored the publication of the *Journal of Trotsky Studies*. As soon became clear, the purpose of this journal was to discredit Trotsky by claiming that his historical reputation was undeserved, that it was based on an all-too-uncritical acceptance of a narrative based on Trotsky's writings. These writings, it was claimed, were self-serving and even false. The chief target of this attack was Trotsky's autobiography, *My Life*, which had achieved, over many decades, recognition as a masterpiece of twentieth century literature.

Every facet of Trotsky's career—as it had been presented in his autobiography and in the works of other historians—was challenged. Trotsky led the October insurrection? No, he spent the crucial night of the Bolshevik seizure of power attending to insignificant secretarial functions. Trotsky led the Red Army to victory? No, he was a vainglorious poseur, who liked to strut around in military dress. Trotsky opposed the bureaucracy? No, he was an inveterate factionalist and trouble-maker who simply loved to argue.

The principal specialist in this sort of rewriting of history was Ian Thatcher, who served as co-editor of the *Journal of Trotsky Studies* at the University of Glasgow, before moving on to Leicester University and then to Brunel University in West London. Thatcher's career has been almost entirely based on creating a new school of anti-Trotskyist falsification. The climax of his efforts in this sphere was his writing of a biography of Trotsky that was published by Routledge in 2003. There is no need for me to spend time on Thatcher's work today, as I have already written an extensive analysis of this miserable compendium of distortions and lies.[17] He is relevant to today's discussion only as the precursor and principal inspirer of Robert Service's biography. Mr. Service pays special tribute to Thatcher in his preface. "Ian," he writes, "has spent his career writing about Trotsky; I appreciate his generosity of spirit in scrutinizing my draft and making suggestions." [xx] Indeed, Ian

---

[17] See Part II of this book.

Thatcher's "spirit" pervades Service's biography. Claiming that his work exposes Trotsky's "evasive and self-aggrandizing" autobiography, Service's basic approach is borrowed entirely from Thatcher.

"The Full-Length Biography"

In introducing his book, Service describes it as "the first full-length biography of Trotsky written by someone outside of Russia who is not a Trotskyist." [xxi]

What is meant by the term "full-length"? Merely that it is long? Generally, the term "full-length biography" implies not merely the length of a book, but, rather, its breadth and depth. Every important biography examines its subject in the context of the epoch in which he or she lived. It not only recounts the actions of the individual, but also examines the origins and development of his or her thought. It strives to uncover and explain the influences, objective and subjective, that shaped the subject's emotional and intellectual characteristics. The Service biography does none of these things—and not merely because its author is pathologically hostile to his subject (though that is, indeed, a serious handicap). The fact is that Mr. Service simply does not know enough about the life and thoughts of Trotsky. Far too little time and intellectual effort went into the preparation of this book for it to be anything else than a piece of hack-work.

The genuine scholar who possesses the necessary knowledge, audacity and even perhaps foolhardiness to attempt a "full-length" biography of a major historical figure imposes immense demands upon himself. The biographer must be prepared, to the extent that it is possible, to recreate in his or her own mind the life of the subject. To undertake such a project is, more often than not, extremely taxing on the biographer, often requiring years of study, research and writing. It is both intellectually and emotionally demanding—both for the author and for those with whom he lives and works. That is why so many historians include in their prefaces or forewords expressions of gratitude to their wives or husbands, children, friends and colleagues who provided intellectual, moral and emotional support.

One might cite as an example of this process the writing of the biography of G. V. Plekhanov by Professor Samuel Baron. Many years after the publication of this book in 1963, Baron wrote an essay in which he described the ordeal through which he had passed. The project had begun in 1948, when Baron chose to make an aspect of Plekhanov's work the subject of his doctoral dissertation. Its completion required four years. But Baron decided that this dissertation was too narrowly focused to be worthy of publication:

> [And so] with scant appreciation of the implications I resolved to write a full-scale biography. Because the sources were so voluminous, the subject so complex, and my free time so limited, it required eleven years to see the plan through. During these years, although I was burdened with a heavy teaching load and had a home and family to care for, Plekhanov was rarely out of mind. I spent many an evening during the teaching year, as well as weekends, holidays and vacations, in research and writing... My sleeping as well as my waking hours were often filled with reflections and refractions of my subject. The task I had set myself seemed so interminable that sometimes I wondered out loud whether it would finish me before I finished it. Yet there could be no thought of quitting, for I had too much invested, and so I continued doggedly at my Sisyphean labor.[18]

How long did it take Professor Service to research and write his biography of Trotsky? His previous large volume, a rambling and inchoate work entitled *Comrades: A History of World Communism*, was published in 2007. Before that Service brought out, in 2004, a biography of Stalin. I will not discuss the quality of either work, other than to state, quite briefly, that both were abysmally bad. But let us leave that problem for some other time. What interests us here is that Service has brought out his "full-length" biography of Trotsky only two years after the publication of his *History of World Communism*. At that point, judging from the content of the earlier volume, Service's knowledge of Trotsky's life was very limited. The references to Trotsky are of a desultory character and include a number of glaring factual errors. He gets the date of the first attempt on Trotsky's life by David Alfaro Siqueiros wrong. It occurred in May 1940, but Service writes that it took place in June. Even more astonishingly, he gets the date of Trotsky's death wrong.

But only two years after the publication of *Comrades*, Service's *Trotsky* has hit the bookstores. Consider what is involved in writing a biography of Trotsky. His political career spanned 43 years. He played a major role, as chairman of the Petrograd Soviet, in the 1905 Revolution. In 1917, after returning

---

[18] Samuel H. Baron, "My Life With G. V. Plekhanov," in: *Plekhanov in Russian History and Soviet Historiography* (Pittsburgh: University of Pittsburgh Press, 1995), p. 188.

to Russia and joining the Bolshevik Party, Trotsky again became the chairman of the Petrograd Soviet. He also became the chairman of the Military Revolutionary Committee, which, under Trotsky's direction, organized and led the October 1917 insurrection that brought the working class to power. He became, in 1918, the Commissar for Military Affairs, and, in that position, played the leading role in the organization and command of the Red Army. Between 1919 and 1922, Trotsky was, alongside Lenin, the most influential political figure in the Communist International. Beginning in late 1923, with the formation of the Left Opposition, he emerged as the central figure in the struggle against the Stalinist bureaucracy. After his expulsion from the Soviet Union in 1929, Trotsky inspired the formation of the International Left Opposition and, between 1933 and 1938, elaborated the theoretical and programmatic foundations of the Fourth International.

In addition to the immense scope of his political and practical activities, Trotsky was among the most prolific writers of the twentieth century. It has been estimated that a complete collection of his published writings would run well over 100 volumes. Even today, a substantial portion of his writings, including letters and diaries, has not been published or translated into English. The point is that the writing of a serious full-length biography of Trotsky is a task that would require years of rigorous work by a conscientious scholar.

Moreover, the biographer would have to be deeply knowledgeable of the historical and social environment within which his subject lived, and with the political and theoretical premises that formed the foundations of his outlook. Professor Service makes a major point of the fact that his biography has not been written by a Trotskyist, and refers disparagingly to the late Pierre Broué, who was politically affiliated to the Trotskyist movement, as an "idolater." [xxi] Aside from the fact that Broué was, quite apart from his political commitments, an outstanding historian, there is a very good reason why his personal involvement with socialist politics, like that of Deutscher (who was not a Trotskyist) was a significant advantage in the writing of a biography of Trotsky. Both Broué and Deutscher possessed, even before they set to work, a genuine familiarity with Marxist and socialist culture, acquired over many decades of political involvement.

Service possesses none of the qualifications required to write a biography of Trotsky. One must allow that the lack of personal involvement in the Marxist movement need not be an absolute barrier to the writing of such a biography. Indeed, it may allow a degree of scholarly "detachment," which a politically committed historian might find more difficult to attain. But Professor Service is neither detached nor politically uncommitted. Having chosen to describe the late Broué as an "idolater," Service can be described, with far greater justification, as a "hater." And hate, particularly of the subjective and vindictive character that so obviously motivates Service, is incompatible with genuine scholarship. Moreover, there is still one more failing that disqualifies Mr. Service as a biographer and historian—and that is an utter lack of intellectual integrity and curiosity.

I have already written a lengthy critique of Professor Service's biography that was circulated widely in November at the annual conference of the American Association for the Advancement of Slavic Studies (AAASS).[19] Several thousand specialists in the field of Russian history were in attendance. A significant number of historians received and read my critique. In subsequent discussions, a few of these historians have expressed some degree of disapproval of its harsh tone. But no one has challenged or contradicted me on a single issue of fact.

This published critique, "In the Service of Historical Falsification," ran well over 10,000 words. One might ask oneself: what more is there to say about Service's book? The truth is, my initial critique barely scratched the surface of Professor Service's falsifications, distortions, half-truths and outright lies.

I do not intend today to simply repeat the points that I have already raised. But I will resume my enumeration of Professor Service's distortions by returning to the issue that plays so central a role in his biography of Trotsky—that is, Trotsky's Jewish origins. As I stated in my earlier review: "There is, to be blunt, something unpleasant and suspect about Service's preoccupation with this matter. The fact that Trotsky was a Jew occupies a central place in Service's biography. It is never far from Service's mind. He is constantly reminding his readers of this fact, as if he were worried that it might slip from their attention."[20] As I noted, his descriptions of Trotsky are rife with ethnic stereotyping (e.g., Trotsky "was brash in his cleverness, outspoken in his opinions. No one could intimidate him. Trotsky had these characteristics to a higher degree than most other Jews...", "...he was far from being the only Jew who visibly enjoyed the opportunities for public self-advancement..." [202], "his real nose was neither long nor bent" and so on).

[19] See Part I, Lecture 2 of this book.

[20] "In the Service of Historical Falsification: A Review of Robert Service's *Trotsky: A Biography*" (Oak Park, MI: Mehring Books, 2009), p. 15.

Among Service's favorite techniques is to present openly anti-Semitic attitudes without citation, such as, "Jews indeed were widely alleged to dominate the Bolshevik Party." [205] Alleged by whom? The deliberate use of the passive voice to present a position without a citation that properly identifies the source allows Service to introduce an anti-Semitic slur without assuming any responsibility for it. This is not an innocent mistake. There are definite rules that govern scholarly work. Service, who has worked for decades as a professional historian, violates these rules deliberately and repeatedly.

I would like to call attention to another example of Service's efforts to emphasize Trotsky's Jewish origins to which I have not previously referred. And that is his persistent reference to the young person as "Leiba Bronstein." Service writes that "Trotsky was Leiba Bronstein until the age of twenty-three when he adopted his renowned pseudonym." [11] And, so, for the first 40 pages of Service's biography, he refers to the young man only as "Leiba." Finally, on page 41, Service announces a major turning point. "Leiba," already eighteen and increasingly involved in revolutionary activity, has made new acquaintances in the provincial town of Nikolaev: Ilya Sokolovsky, Alexandra Sokolovskaya and Grigory Ziv. They were Jews, Service writes, "but they did not talk, read or write in Yiddish. Moreover, they had Russian first names and liked to be called by very Russian diminutives: Ilya as Ilyusha, Alexandra as Sasha, Shura or Shurochka and Grigori as Grisha. Leiba, wanting to be like them, decided that he wanted to be known as Lëva. Pronounced 'Lyova', this was the Russian diminutive of Lev. Semantically it had nothing to do with the Yiddish name Leiba; but it was a common first-name and helpfully it sounded a little the same." [41-42]

This story of the transformation of Leiba into Lëva reinforces a central theme of Service's argument: that Trotsky was ashamed of his Jewish origins and even sought to downplay them in his autobiography (one of the examples of its "serious inaccuracies"). So Service would have his readers believe that he has uncovered the real story whereby little "Leiba Bronstein" —the son of the "plucky Jew" David Bronstein—became Lyova Bronstein, and, somewhat later, Lev Trotsky.

An interesting story, but is there any truth in it? In his autobiography, Trotsky remembers that he was called, from his earliest childhood, Lyova. In *My Life*, a footnote written by the translator Max Eastman states: "Trotsky's full and original name was Lev Davydovich Bronstein, his father's name being Davyd Leontiyevich Bronstein. 'Lyova' is one of the many similar diminutives of Lev, which literally means 'Lion.' In English and French usage, Trotsky has become known as Leon, in German as Leo."[21]

Service offers no documentary evidence that the young boy was ever called anything other than Lyova, or related diminutives, such as "Lyovoch-ka." The Bronstein family did not speak Yiddish—the language used at home was a mixture of Russian and Ukrainian—so there is no apparent reason why he would have been called Leiba.

So what about Service's story of the young "Leiba's" adoption of the name Lëva so that he could have a Russian-sounding first name like his friends? For this story Service does provide a footnoted reference to two items: 1) a bitterly hostile memoir written by Grigory Ziv, who had been one of the young Trotsky's earliest associates in the revolutionary movement; and 2) a letter written by the young Trotsky in November 1898 to his love, Alexandra Sokolovskaya.

A reader would reasonably assume that these documents provide the factual substantiation of Service's story. Most readers, however, would have neither the time nor the means to access the original documents. Neither document exists in English. Ziv's book, published in 1921, is available in a few libraries in the original Russian. The letter to Sokolovskaya, which is also in Russian, exists on microfiche in the archives of the Hoover Institution at Stanford University.

An examination of these documents has yielded the not entirely surpris-ing discovery that they include absolutely no information that corroborates Service's story. The first chapter of the Ziv memoir, in which his initial con-tacts with the young Trotsky are recounted, is entitled "Lëva." It says noth-ing at all about Trotsky changing his first name from "Leiba" to "Lëva" or Lev. The young man he met was known as Lëva. The name "Leiba" does not appear, even once, in the memoir. Inasmuch as Ziv discusses at length the change in his former comrade's last name—from Bronstein to Trotsky (which occurred when the young revolutionary escaped from exile and apparently took the name of a former jailer)—there is no reason to believe that Ziv sim-ply forgot the name Leiba. Ziv did not write about it, because he had never heard Lëva referred to by that name.

What about the second document cited by Service, the letter of No-vember 1898 from Trotsky to Alexandra Sokolovskaya? This is an intensely personal and intimate letter, from a young man to a woman with whom he

---

[21] *My Life* (Mineola, NY: Dover Publications, 2007), p. 3.

is deeply in love. This letter is an important document, to which Service refers on several occasions. Does the young Trotsky, in this very personal letter, explain to his love how he came to adopt the name Lëva? The answer is: No! There is nothing at all about such a transformation. The letter, by the way, is signed "Lëva," the name by which he had been known his entire youth.

So until Professor Service is able to produce proper documentation for his story about the transformation of "Leiba" into "Lëva," we are entitled to assume that he simply, and quite dishonestly, made the whole thing up.

The issue of Trotsky's original name is of both historical and political significance. It is well known that references to Trotsky as Bronstein, a name that he had not used since 1902, became increasingly common in the mid-1920s as the Stalinist bureaucracy intensified its campaign against the Left Opposition. References to Trotsky as Bronstein (and to Zinoviev as Radomyslsky and Kamenev as Rosenfeld) became part of the stock-in-trade of the Stalinists. During the Moscow Trials, Trotsky drew attention to the anti-Semitic subtext of the proceedings, in which so many Jews were among the defendants. Curiously, many bourgeois liberals of Jewish origin in the United States, including the politically prominent Rabbi Stephen Wise, denounced Trotsky for calling attention to this aspect of the trials. This willingness to maintain a polite silence on the anti-Semitic stench emanating from the Kremlin reflected the indulgent attitude of liberals toward Stalinism during the era of Popular Frontism.

Decades later, during glasnost in the 1980s, and continuing after the dissolution of the USSR, Trotsky's Jewish origins assumed obsessive dimensions among a wide variety of Russian anti-Semites. As the eminent historian Walter Lacqueur has pointed out:

> ...it would be wrong to underrate the real hatred for Trotsky among sections of the Russian Right and the neo-Stalinists. He was the personification of all evil, and he was doubly vulnerable as a Communist and a Jew; his "original name," Leiba Bronstein, was always stressed with loving care by his enemies, a practice that had once been the monopoly of the Nazis. No one would have dreamed of referring to Lenin as Ulyanov, to Gorky as Peshkov, or to Kirov as Kostrikov.[22]

---

[22] Walter Lacqueur, *Stalin: The Glasnost Revelations* (New York: Charles Scribner's Sons, 1990), pp. 59-60.

In a footnote, Lacqueur writes that Trotsky's childhood name was Lyova.

In a number of meetings related to the book launch of the biography, Professor Service has been questioned about his treatment of Trotsky's Jewish background. Rather than explain his approach in a professional manner, Service has replied aggressively, as if threatening a lawsuit: "Are you calling me an anti-Semite?" Only Service and, perhaps, his closest associates know what his innermost feelings about Jews are. But that is not the issue. An individual who, for whatever reasons, appeals to, arouses, and exploits anti-Jewish prejudice is *practicing* anti-Semitism. That Service may include Jews among his personal friends is beside the point. It is a well-known historical fact that Karl Lüger—the founder of the anti-Semitic Christian Socialist Party and mayor of Vienna in fin-de-siècle Austria—had a number of Jewish friends. For Lüger, anti-Semitism was merely a political device to rally the embittered Viennese petty bourgeoisie to his politically reactionary banner. When asked to explain how he reconciled his anti-Semitic demagogy with his genial dining engagements with Jews, Lüger replied cynically: "In Vienna, I decide who is a Jew." Professor Service practices similar moral double bookkeeping.

One final point on this matter. In his 2004 biography of Stalin, Professor Service made a point of absolving Stalin of the charge of anti-Semitism. He cites a comment that Stalin made at the conclusion of an early congress of the Russian Social Democratic Labor Party. Stalin, noting that a higher percentage of Jews was to be found among the Mensheviks than among the Bolsheviks, remarked that "It would do no harm if we, the Bolsheviks, carried out a small pogrom in the party." Service, with remarkable indulgence, observes that Stalin's remarks "were later used against him as proof of anti-Semitism. They were certainly crude and insensitive. But they scarcely betokened hatred of *all* Jews... For many years into the future he would be the friend, associate or leader of countless individual Jews [emphasis added]." [77] What an extraordinarily generous explanation of Stalin's attitude toward Jews! Inasmuch as he did not hate *all* Jews, and even included Jews among his friends, Stalin was not an anti-Semite! By the way, it should be noted that Service's citation of Stalin's remarks at the RSDLP conference left out the following passage: "Lenin is outraged that God sent him such comrades as the Mensheviks. What kind of people are they, really? Martov, Dan, Axelrod—circumcised Jews... Do Georgian workers really not know that the Jewish people are cowardly and no good for fighting?"[23] The central purpose of Service's biogra-

---

[23] Cited in Hiroaki Kuromiya, *Stalin* (London: Longman, 2005), p. 12.

phy—and in this he is continuing where his mentor Ian Thatcher left off—is to discredit Trotsky not only as a political figure, but also as a man. To some extent, Service's concentration on Trotsky's personality is dictated by the fact that the biographer has sufficient sense to realize that he lacks the intellectual equipment to deal with Trotsky's ideas. It is easier to attack Trotsky personally, to misrepresent his actions and his motives.

Service's portrayal of Trotsky has been welcomed by innumerable right-wing critics. For example, Robert Harris has written in the London *Sunday Times*:

> If one can imagine the most obnoxious middle-class student radical one has ever met—bitter, sneering, arrogant, selfish, cocky, callous, callow, blinkered and condescending—and if one freezes that image, applies a pair of pince-nez and transports it back to the beginning of the last century, then one has Trotsky.[24]

I would imagine that most of the adjectives employed by the overheated Mr. Harris would serve very well as a description of his own person.

The real purpose of Service's grotesque portrayal of Trotsky—which reverberates throughout the bourgeois press and will eventually be echoed in subsequent pseudo-historical works that dutifully cite Professor Service's "authoritative" and "magisterial" volume—is the concoction of an entirely new historical persona. All traces of the real Trotsky—as he was described and remembered by comrades and friends, and, above all, as found expression in his words and his deeds—are to be effaced, obliterated and replaced with something monstrous and grotesque that bears no resemblance to the real human being. The historical persona of the great revolutionary, political genius, military leader and master of the written word is to be replaced with something abominable and contemptible. Trotsky, à la Service, one of the political monsters of the twentieth century! This is what Service and his friends have in mind when they talk of his book as a second assassination of Trotsky!

But because the concoction grossly falsifies reality, the author loses himself in countless contradictions. The book begins, oddly enough, with a fairly honest and objective summary of Trotsky's role in the Russian Revolution. Service writes, in the opening paragraph:

---

[24] Robert Harris, "Trotsky: A Biography by Robert Service," *The Sunday Times*, October 18, 2009.

Trotsky moved like a bright comet across the political sky. ... [H]e was the finest orator of the Russian Revolution. He led the Military-Revolutionary Committee which carried out the overthrow of the Provisional Government in October. He did more than anyone to found the Red Army. He belonged to the Party Politburo and had a deep impact on its political, economic and military strategy. He was a principal figure in the early years of the Communist International. The whole world attributed the impact of the October Revolution to his partnership with Lenin. [1]

Within little more than a page, however, Service sets to work repudiating his opening paragraph. Trotsky, he tells us, "exaggerated his personal importance. His ideas before 1917 were nowhere near to being as original and wide-ranging as he liked to believe. His contribution to the Bolshevik advance on power was important but not to the degree that he asserted." [4]

The two assessments are not compatible with each other. If Trotsky did all that Service states that he did in the first paragraph of the biography, then how could Trotsky have "exaggerated his personal importance"?

After the first paragraph, Service piles insult upon insult, indifferent to the accumulation of obvious absurdities and contradictions. There are times when he even manages to make a declaration in one sentence that he proceeds to contradict in the same paragraph! "Leiba," he writes, "had no compunction about living at his father's expense while despising his hopes and values." The two sentences that follow immediately after read: "The son, furthermore, was as stubborn as his father. He would no longer be told what to do, and rather than submit to the paternal will he fled his comfortable apartment and took up residence in Shvigovski's house." [41] Thus, contrary to what Service declared in the first sentence—that "Leiba had no compunction about living at his father's expense"—the reader learns in the third sentence that the young man gave up the comforts of home in order to pursue his ideals!

Service claims repeatedly that Trotsky edited drafts of his autobiography in order to remove material that might prove embarrassing to him. In fact, he does not provide a single example of such an excision. Quite the opposite. Service notes that in an early draft of the autobiography, Trotsky recounts a story in which he displayed exceptional personal and physical courage in defying a cruel and sadistic prison warden. Trotsky told the warden to his face that he would not tolerate his abusive comments. It was the warden who retreated. In the published version of *My Life*, this story—for which there were witnesses—was not included.

Service comments: "As with several such episodes of daring in his life, Trotsky did not include this information in his published memoirs. It had to be dragged out of him by admiring writers. Although he liked to cut a dash in public, he disliked boasting: *he preferred others to do the job for him. He was noisy and full of himself. People did not have to wait long before discovering how vain and self-centred he really was.*" [56, emphasis added]

Through a rather clumsy sleight of hand, Service finds a way of insulting Trotsky for his modesty and dislike of boasting!

Service devotes an enormous amount of space to blackguarding Trotsky as a faithless husband who cruelly abandoned his first wife and their two children. "As a husband," writes Service, "he [Trotsky] treated his first wife shabbily. He ignored the needs of his children especially when his political interests intervened. This had catastrophic consequences even for those of them who were inactive in Soviet public life—and his son Lev, who followed him into exile, possibly paid with his life for collaborating with his father." [4]

One would hardly guess, based on Service's telling of the story, that either the oppressive conditions of tsarist Russia or, later, the persecutions of Stalin had anything to do with the tragic fate of Trotsky's family and loved ones. In fact, Service actually criticizes Trotsky for assigning responsibility to the Soviet regime for the death of his daughter Zina in 1933.

But the circumstances of the deaths of his children and his first wife are of little interest to Service. What interests him is portraying Trotsky as some sort of irresponsible and callous philanderer, who thoughtlessly and egotistically abandoned his first wife, Alexandra Sokolovskaya.

Service treats the relationship between Trotsky and Alexandra Sokolovskaya with a truly offensive crudeness. Repeatedly, he attempts to drag both the young Lyova and Alexandra down to his own level.

In this regard, Service's use of the letter of November 1898—to which I have already referred—is especially significant. This letter was written by the 19-year-old Lyova to Alexandra while they were both imprisoned in Odessa. They could not communicate with each other in person. When Lyova wrote this letter, he was ill and depressed. Nearly a year had passed since they had been arrested. Trotsky had spent several months of imprisonment in solitary confinement.

Citing a brief passage from this letter, in which Trotsky admits that he had thought of, and rejected, suicide, Service comments:

> There was showiness and immaturity in these sentiments. He was
> a self-centred young man. Unconsciously he was trying to induce

Alexandra to do more than love him: he wanted her to understand and look after him and perhaps this could be achieved by admissions of weakness. He was never genuinely suicidal; his comment was designed to make her want to protect him. He saw that he had been haughty and unfeeling towards her. What better, then, than to own up to possessing a stony exterior and to say he was "shedding tears" about this? [52]

This sort of facile psychologizing, even when offered with the best of intentions, is of rather dubious value. But it assumes a maliciously absurd character when the passage upon which the analysis hinges has been falsified. Trotsky, Service tells us, is slyly attempting to appeal to Alexandra's vulnerability by insincerely confessing that he was "shedding tears" about his "stony exterior."

The problem with this "interpretation" is that Service has misrepresented the text of Lyova's letter. The exposure of this falsification requires that the relevant passage be fully and correctly quoted. The young revolutionary wrote:

Sasha [Alexandra] is so good, and when I feel like kissing and caressing her so much.... And all that is beyond reach: instead, there is loneliness, insomnia, repulsive thoughts about death ... brrr ... The hour of redemption will arrive, "The people will sing their hymn, They will remember us with tears. They will visit our graves." Our graves, Sasha: our g-r-a-v-e-s. – O, with what horror will they speak at some time about today's social order ... beyond my doors right now at this very moment I can hear the familiar clang of so many chains: after all they are on people. Sasha, how much we have become used to this, and yet how terrible it is. Chains on people ... And this is all according to the law. Are you surprised by my burst of "Weltschmerz"?... An unusual sensitivity is developing in me: I have become capable of "shedding tears" while reading the civil poems of P. Ya /in "Mir B."/... or while reading works of fiction ... It's simply that my nerves are extremely strained, that's all. The Siberian taiga will temper this tender civic sensitivity. On the other hand, how happy we will be there. Like Olympian gods. We will always, always be inseparably together.—How many times I have always repeated this, and yet I feel like repeating it over and over again ... You and I have gone through so much together, we have suffered so much that, to be sure, we deserve our hour of happiness.

This letter is, in its own right, an extraordinary and deeply moving document. That its author was the future leader of the October Revolution imparts to it immense significance. To interpret this letter as an expression of "showiness" and "immaturity" speaks to Service's cynicism and insensitivity. However, from a professional standpoint, Service's treatment of this letter is dishonest and misleading.

First of all, Trotsky's admission to "shedding tears," which he places in quotation marks, does not refer to his weeping about his efforts to conceal his "stony exterior." Rather, it refers directly to his response to the poetry of Pyotr Yakubovich. Were Service a serious historian, he would—after having carefully reflected on this matter—explain to his readers the significance of this reference. Yakubovich (1860-1911) was an important poet and revolutionary, active in the populist People's Will. His poems, which evoked the heroism and tragedy of the doomed struggle of the revolutionary terrorists against tsarism, made a deep moral impact upon the youth of the 1890s. The images employed by Yakubovich in his poetry, particularly those of death and sacrifice, are evoked by Trotsky in his letter to Alexandra. She, of course, would have understood these references very well. A conscientious historian would find in this complex letter—from which I have cited only a small section—valuable material for developing an understanding of his subject and his times. But Service is simply not interested.

An odor of indifference and laziness pervades the entire volume. The author shows no curiosity at all about the sources of Trotsky's intellectual and artistic creativity. Service's comments on Trotsky's early literary efforts, written during his first Siberian exile, are generally so banal and perfunctory that it seems their only purpose is to provide the author with the page count he requires in order to advertise his biography as "full-length." A typical example of Service's talent for producing penetrating intellectual commentary is his remark that Trotsky "adored French novels, was an admirer of Ibsen and was impressed by Nietzsche. *He treated all of them as examples of contemporary world culture.*" [207, emphasis added] Did he really? Who would have imagined? But there is something here that does not seem quite right. The reference to Nietzsche raises doubts. The reader may be tempted to wonder: what was it about Nietzsche that impressed Trotsky?

If the critical reader is in a position to investigate the issue, he might discover an essay, written by Trotsky shortly after the death of Nietzsche in 1900, entitled "Something about the Philosophy of the 'Overman.'" Upon reviewing this essay, the reader will quickly learn that "impressed" is hardly the word that describes the young Trotsky's response to Nietzsche. Trotsky saw in the latter's philosophy of the "overman" a justification for a new and ever more powerful social type:

> The financial adventurists, "overmen" of the stock exchange, political and newspaper blackmailers *sans scruple*, in short, that entire mass of parasitical proletariat which has tightly attached itself to the bourgeois organism and in one way or another lives—and usually lives quite well—at society's expense without giving back anything in return. ... But the entire group (rather numerous and ever growing) still needed a theory which would give the intellectually superior the right to "dare." It awaited its apostle and found him in Nietzsche.

Trotsky concludes his essay with the observation that the social soil from which Nietzscheanism emerged "has turned out to be decayed, malignant and infected..."[25]

Does it still appear that Trotsky was "impressed" with Nietzsche? Or is it not more likely that Service did not bother to read Trotsky's essay, and simply does not know what he is talking about? With Service, as with others of his type, intellectual dishonesty goes hand in hand with ignorance and charlatanry.

As I have previously noted, an exhaustive review of all the errors and false statements that appear in this volume would require a "full-length" book at least as long as Service's biography. It is not an exaggeration to state that there is hardly a page in which an informed reader will not find passages that are objectionable from the standpoint of the basic standards of historical scholarship. It is not even possible to accept, without direct investigation, the author's references and citations. Again and again it emerges that the source material cited by Service does not support his claims.

In bringing this review to a conclusion, it is appropriate to return to Service's treatment of the relationship between Trotsky and Alexandra Sokolovskaya. The distortion of the circumstances of their separation plays a major role in Service's effort to discredit Trotsky—as a husband, a father, and as a man. All the reviewers in the right-wing British press have picked up the theme with enthusiasm.

---

[25] L. Trotskii, *Works*, Series 6, Volume 20, Culture of the Old World, M.-L., State Publishing House, 1926, pp. 147-162 (new translation from the original Russian text).

In discussing the circumstances of his first escape from Siberian exile in 1902, Trotsky wrote in *My Life:*

> At that time we already had two daughters. The younger was four months old. Life under conditions in Siberia was not easy, and my escape would place a double burden on the shoulders of Alexandra Lvovna. But she met this objection with the two words: "You must." Duty to the revolution overshadowed everything else for her, personal considerations especially. She was the first to broach the idea of my escape when we realized the great new tasks. She brushed away all my doubts.
>
> For several days after I had escaped, she concealed my absence from the police. From abroad, I could hardly keep up a correspondence with her. Then she was exiled for a second time; after this we met only occasionally. Life separated us, but nothing could destroy our friendship and our intellectual kinship.[26]

Service, who does not actually quote Trotsky's statement, writes: "He [Trotsky] later made the claim that Alexandra had wholeheartedly blessed his departure. This is hard to take at face value" [67].

On what basis is this statement made? Service does not produce a single piece of evidence—documents, letters, personal testimony—that contradicts Trotsky's account, which, it should be stressed, was written in 1929 when Alexandra was still alive. She did not contradict it, even though—given the fact that Trotsky had been exiled from the Soviet Union and was publicly reviled as the greatest enemy of the Soviet people—the Stalinist regime would have welcomed her personal denunciation of her former husband.

Service employs a series of loaded phrases to cast Trotsky's actions in the worst possible light: "Bronstein was planning to abandon her in the wilds of Siberia... No sooner had he fathered a couple of children than he decided to run off." [67] Service, however, proceeds to discredit his own unsubstantiated claims by acknowledging that Trotsky "was acting within the revolutionary code of behavior. The 'cause' was everything for the revolutionaries. Marital and parental responsibilities had an importance but never to the point of preventing young militants from doing what their political conscience bade them to do." [67] If that were the case, as Service acknowledges explicitly, then on what grounds can he claim that Trotsky's statement that Alexandra

---

[26] *My Life*, pp. 132-133.

supported, and even proposed, his escape from exile "is hard to take at face value"?

The fact is that Service's condemnation of Trotsky's action is not based on an honest appraisal of the historical context within which the two young revolutionaries lived. One must add that Service's reference to Alexandra being "abandoned" is maliciously motivated conjecture. As a matter of historical fact, there is good reason to believe that efforts were made to provide assistance for Alexandra and the children. Indeed, in a later chapter, Service includes material that indicates that the Bronstein family played a significant role in providing support for Trotsky's children. During a trip to Western Europe to visit Trotsky in 1907, Trotsky's parents brought his daughter Zina with them. Service notes that Trotsky's family "lived a complicated existence. Zina at that time lived with his [Trotsky's] sister Elizaveta and her husband in their family home on Gryaznaya Street in Kherson. Alexandra wrote regularly to them." [108]

So it seems that Trotsky did not "abandon" his family. As revolutionaries, both Lev Davidovich and Alexandra Lvovna coped as best they could in exceedingly difficult circumstances. At some point in the future, as more documents are discovered, it may be possible to reconstruct accurately the details of their complicated personal arrangements. But Robert Service will not be the man who undertakes that assignment.

Finally, with regard to the personal relation between Trotsky and Alexandra, there is a document that testifies to their deep and enduring bond of comradeship and friendship. It is a letter written by Alexandra to Trotsky on August 8, 1935. The final act of the terrible human tragedy is about to begin. Alexandra addresses the letter to "Dear Lyova." She tells Trotsky of the difficult conditions that confront different members of their family. Alexandra includes, in a reference to efforts by Trotsky to provide material support for her, "I am very much touched, as always, by your thoughtful attitude toward me." And she closes the letter, "Love and Embraces, Yours, Alexandra."[27]

Lev Davidovich Trotsky and Alexandra Lvovna Sokolovskaya were extraordinary human beings, the representatives of a revolutionary generation whose capacity for self-sacrifice, in the interest of the betterment of mankind, seemed to know no limits. How pathetic it is for Professor Service and his ilk to believe that he will succeed, with insults, falsifications and slanders, in dragging these titans down to his miserable level.

---

[27] *Trotsky's Diary in Exile, 1935* (New York: Atheneum, 1963), pp. 159-160.

Trotsky in his study at Coyoacán, Mexico in 1937

Trotsky's Enduring Significance[1]

Last week Professor Robert Service spoke at an event sponsored by Foyle's Books in London. He noted that his biography of Trotsky had become the subject of a counter-campaign by the Socialist Equality Party, and that his book was being criticized at public meetings all over the world—including this one being held in Sydney, Australia. He stated: "I've had a lot of problems with Trotskyist sectarians in the last two or three months because I don't idolize Trotsky. I don't worship at the shrine of Trotsky."

We are not the only ones whom Professor Service has accused of being "idolaters." In the opening pages of his biography, he made the exact same accusation against the well-known authors of two significant biographies of Trotsky: Isaac Deutscher and Pierre Broué. Deutscher, according to Service, was the principal "idolater" of Trotsky. As for Broué, he "worshipped at Trotsky's shrine."

The use of the word "idolater" and the phrase "worshipping at Trotsky's shrine" implies that Trotsky is the object of a quasi-religious or cult-like veneration. He is an "idol"—i.e., a "false god"—worshipped by mindless pagans immune to facts and reason. This is a case of the pot calling the kettle black. It is Service who shows himself incapable of treating Trotsky as a genuine historical personage to be examined in the context of the times in which he lived. For Service, Trotsky is not a god to be worshipped, but a devil to be exorcised.

This exorcism requires that Trotsky be exposed as a monster—a man without humanity, without any redeeming features. He is cold-blooded,

---

[1] Lecture given at a meeting of readers at Gleebooks bookstore in Sydney, Australia on February 3, 2010.

mean-spirited, arrogant, and egotistical; a soulless calculating machine, who is prepared to consign humanity to the flames in demonic pursuit of an unrealizable utopia. And that is not all: Service's Trotsky is an ungrateful son, contemptuous of his father's faith and material achievements. He is also a faithless husband, who casually impregnates and then deserts his first wife; an uncaring and absentee father, ultimately responsible (as a consequence of his political obsessions) for the suffering and death of his children; and a sexual libertine who (according to rumors) made advances to a well-known British sculptress and even wrote his wife a sexually explicit letter when they were both in their late fifties (which, of course, Service quotes in detail).

Trotsky, Service goes on, postured as an intellectual, writing on subjects about which he knew nothing. He was also a liar and falsifier, who wrote an autobiography from which Trotsky—in the course of several drafts—removed systematically anything that might compromise the public image that he had dishonestly constructed. Among the most important details that Trotsky sought to downplay, according to Service, was the fact that he was Jewish.

This attempt to suppress his Jewish background, argues Service, was the key to Trotsky's life. Service presents the transformation of young "Leiba" Bronstein into the Russified "Lev" Bronstein as a critical turning point in the young man's life. Having dispensed with a hated Jewish-sounding first name, the stage was finally set for the next act of self-reinvention: the creation of Lev Davidovich Trotsky! The problem with this story, as with so much of what Service writes, is that it is without any factual foundation. The first name by which Bronstein was known from his birth was "Lev," or the diminutive, Lyova.

Service's book is a catalog of insults: Trotsky "was noisy and full of himself. People did not have to wait long before discovering how vain and self-centred he really was." [56] "Any woman who lived with him had to accept that he would do as he pleased." [67] "Always he wrote whatever was in his head." [79] "Intellectually he flitted from topic to topic and felt no stimulus to systematize his thinking." [110] "He himself made no claim to intellectual originality: he would have been ridiculed if he had tried." [109]

And though Trotsky allegedly tried to conceal his heritage, Service sees everywhere the mark of his Semitic ethnicity: Trotsky "was brash in his cleverness, outspoken in his opinions. No one could intimidate him. Trotsky had these characteristics to a higher degree than most other Jews..." [202] "He was far from being the only Jew who visibly enjoyed the opportunities for self-advancement..." [202] As for the roots of Trotsky's attraction to Marxism,

Service asserts that, "Young Jewish men and women, trained in the rigours of the Torah, found a congenial orthodoxy in Marxist intricacies. Hair-splitting disputes were common to Marxism and Judaism." [202]

The Bolshevik Party provided a congenial home for Trotsky. "The party's leadership was widely identified as a Jewish gang," Service informs his readers, adding for good measure: "Jews indeed were widely alleged to dominate the Bolshevik Party." [205] But Trotsky did not conform to all Jewish stereotypes. Including in his collection of photos a grotesque Nazi caricature of "Leiba Trotzky-Braunstein," Service adds a caption that notes helpfully: "In reality, his real nose was neither long nor bent and he never allowed his goatee to become straggly or his hair ill-kempt." [Image 11, 136-137]

Amidst all this muck, what does Service have to say about Trotsky's political ideas and his writings? The answer, in brief, is virtually nothing. Indeed, Service states emphatically that he was determined not to make Trotsky's written and spoken words, or even his public deeds, the focus of his biography. In contrast to the "idolater" Deutscher and the "shrine-worshipper" Broué, Service proclaims that "it is as important to pinpoint what Trotsky was silent about as what he chose to speak or write about. His unuttered basic assumptions were integral to the amalgam of his life." [5]

What an extraordinary approach for a biographer to take—particularly of a man who was widely considered (as by Bertolt Brecht, for example) to be the greatest European writer of his time! How can a biographer declare—and expect to be taken seriously—that what his subject did *not* write, say or do is as important as what he wrote, said and did?

This absurd conception, however, is central to Service's purpose, and explains the animus he bears against biographers—especially Deutscher and Broué—for whom Trotsky's vast literary output forms the essential intellectual and political foundation for an appraisal of the man. This is an approach that Service rejects—for reasons that have far more to do with concerns relating to contemporary politics than with historical method.

As Service himself acknowledges, both in his book and in a number of public statements, he has written his biography to overcome the lingering influence of Deutscher's trilogy—*The Prophet Armed, Unarmed* and *Outcast*—published between 1954 and 1963. Service does not tell us anything about his own political affiliations during the 1960s and 1970s (if I had the opportunity, I would ask Professor Service whether there was any truth to the many rumors that he was a member, or on the periphery, of the virulently anti-Trotskyist British Communist Party), but he was clearly angered, if not traumatized, by the enormous growth of Trotskyist movements during that period. It is widely and justly believed that Deutscher's biography contributed significantly to this important political phenomenon. There is no disputing the fact that Deutscher's trilogy provided thousands of radicalized youth in Europe, the United States and, may I add, Australia, with their initial introduction to the life and ideas of Leon Trotsky.

When the first volume of Deutscher's biography *The Prophet Armed* appeared—covering the years between 1879 (the year of Trotsky's birth) and 1921 (the end of the Civil War)—Trotsky's reputation had been buried beneath the vast and monstrous edifice of Stalinist lies. There was not another figure in the twentieth century, perhaps not in world history, who had been subjected to such an unrelenting campaign of falsification and slander. The virtually unlimited resources of the Soviet regime, and of Stalinist-run parties throughout the world, were devoted to blackguarding Trotsky as an anti-Soviet saboteur, terrorist and fascist agent. Within the Soviet Union, his political co-thinkers, past and present, were ruthlessly exterminated. The Stalinist regime killed almost every member of the Bronstein family, including Trotsky's siblings, nieces and nephews, his in-laws and his two sons. Even before the years of mass killings, the death of Trotsky's two daughters was related to conditions created by the Stalinist regime's persecution of their father.

Trotsky was assassinated by a Soviet agent in August 1940. By then, World War II had begun. After the Soviet Union was invaded in June 1941—bringing the infamous Stalin-Hitler Pact of 1939 to a bloody conclusion—Western European and American intellectuals were hardly in a mood to remind themselves of Stalin's innumerable crimes against the international socialist movement. With the encouragement of the Roosevelt administration, Hollywood produced a cinematic portrayal of US Ambassador Joseph Davies' disgusting pro-Stalin account of the Moscow Trials, entitled *Mission to Moscow*. The film portrayed Trotsky as an enemy of the Soviet people.

The onset of the Cold War following the end of World War II lessened the ardor of intellectuals for Stalin, particularly in the United States. But Trotsky—as a major historical and political presence—had by then faded into the background.

Stalin's death in March 1953 marked the beginning of the protracted crisis and death agony of the bureaucratic regime. In 1956 Khrushchev's secret speech exposed Stalin as a mass murderer. By this time, Deutscher's first volume had been published, and it contributed enormously to a renewed interest in the life of Stalin's implacable adversary. The second volume came out in

1959 and the third in 1963. By this point, the political radicalization of youth had begun. The reading of Deutscher's trilogy became a major generational experience.

At this point, I must speak of my own experience: I was in Washington in November 1969. A mass demonstration had been called against the Vietnam War. By this time, virtually nothing remained of my earlier hopes that the Democratic Party represented a progressive, let alone socialist, opposition to imperialism. On the eve of the mass rally, I witnessed a demonstration outside the White House. The protestors marched around the presidential residence holding candles in their hands. The scene struck me as utterly futile. Did the protestors really believe that the candles would awaken Nixon's conscience?

Across the street from the White House on Pennsylvania Avenue, I found a bookstore. A book attracted my attention. Its cover carried the photo of a young man, whose eyes gazed out confidently through a set of pince-nez. The book's title was *The Prophet Armed*. I bought the book, began reading it that night, and could hardly allow myself to put it down until I had completed it. That was the beginning of what was to become a life-long engagement with the life and ideas of Leon Trotsky.

Wherein lay the power of Deutscher's biography? Without question, Deutscher was a masterful writer, whose command of the English language recalls that of his great compatriot Joseph Conrad. But Deutscher's great achievement was his re-creation—on the basis of the historical record—of Trotsky's towering revolutionary persona, as a writer, artist, orator, military leader, political strategist, socialist visionary and, yes, human being. The drama and tragedy of the October Revolution and its reflection in the life of its greatest figure found powerful expression in the pages of Deutscher's biography. However, to describe the work as an uncritical exercise in hagiography is utterly false. As a matter of fact, a substantial portion of Deutscher's biography—particularly its final volume—is devoted to an increasingly emphatic exposition of the author's deep and irreconcilable political differences with many critical aspects of Trotsky's political perspective.

Notwithstanding Deutscher's criticisms, he left his readers in no doubt of Trotsky's immense and enduring historical significance. Those who wished to understand the Russian Revolution, the twentieth century, and, beyond that, the historical destiny of mankind, had to engage themselves with the ideas of Leon Trotsky. At the end of his great work, Deutscher left his readers with the conviction that Trotsky's life represented a harbinger of a better and more humane world, a world in which the great ideals that had inspired the Russian Revolution would finally be realized. He understood Trotsky as a Promethean figure who, though overcome in his own lifetime by the overwhelming force of reaction, would find vindication in the ultimate triumph of his ideals. And Deutscher closed his biography with a quote from the final stanza from Shelley's *Prometheus Unbound*:

> *To defy Power, which seems omnipotent;*
> *To love, and bear; to hope till Hope creates*
> *From its own wreck the thing it contemplates;*
> *Neither to change, nor falter, nor repent;*
> *This, like thy glory, Titan, is to be*
> *Good, great and joyous, beautiful and free;*
> *This is alone Life, Joy, Empire, and Victory.*

In the presence of these noble sentiments, so appropriate to Trotsky's life and historical role, what is left of Professor Service's petty and spiteful work?

Trotsky and his first wife Alexandra Sokolovskaya in exile in Siberia

The Biographer as Character Assassin[1]

Since the publication last autumn of Robert Service's biography of Leon Trotsky, I have written one lengthy review and delivered two lectures, the first in London and the second in Sydney. This is my third lecture on this book. What, one might reasonably wonder, is there to add to what I have already written and said? This thought crossed my mind as I began to prepare for this evening's meeting. Would I find myself in the position of having to repeat what I have already said, albeit before a new audience? This will not, at least for the most part, be the case. Some repetition is unavoidable, but there is much that remains to be said.

Returning to Mr. Service's biography after a hiatus of several months, two things became clear to me. First, the book is even worse than I had remembered it to be. Second, I had not identified all the factual errors, half-truths, distortions, falsifications and outright slanders that are to be found in Mr. Service's biography. Indeed, the work of identifying all the errors in his book is a job that could keep a number of Oxford history department graduates busy for months. What I wrote in my initial review was not an exaggeration: the refutation of every statement that is factually incorrect, lacks the necessary substantiation and violates accepted standards of scholarship would require a volume almost as long as Service's book. There are statements and assertions that are completely unacceptable, from a purely professional standpoint, in every chapter.

Previously, I called attention to some of the most malicious passages in Mr. Service's biography—that is, his scurrilous portrayal of Trotsky's character

---

[1] Lecture given on Robert Service's biography of Leon Trotsky at St. Catherine's College, University of Oxford, England on May 5, 2010.

and personal life. As he acknowledged in his introduction, Service set out to discredit the heroic image of Trotsky that had emerged from the pages of Isaac Deutscher's magisterial biographical trilogy, *The Prophet Armed, Unarmed* and *Outcast*, which had exerted significant influence on a generation of radicalized youth in the 1960s. Service's intention was to discredit Trotsky not only as a political figure, but also as a man: to present him as an ungrateful son, a faithless and philandering husband, a cold and uncaring father, a rude, disruptive and untrustworthy comrade; and, finally, as a mass murderer, a man who "revelled in terror." [497] In short, Trotsky is portrayed as one of the monsters of twentieth-century political history. I also questioned Mr. Service's obsessive fixation with Trotsky's Jewish ancestry, which he dealt with in a manner that would not fail to delight anti-Semites.

The detailed exposure of Service's blackguarding of Trotsky's personality left insufficient time to examine his treatment of Trotsky's politics and ideas. I should point out, however, that Service had declared that he was not particularly interested in examining what Trotsky said, wrote or for that matter did. Service wrote that he intended "to dig up the buried life." [4] Service proclaimed that he was as interested in "what Trotsky was silent about as what he chose to speak or write about." According to Service, Trotsky's "unuttered basic assumptions were integral to the amalgam of his life." [5]

This approach suited Mr. Service's purposes, both commercial and political. First, it spared him the trouble of actually reading Trotsky's major works, let alone working systematically through his vast legacy of published and unpublished papers. At any rate, Service would not have been able to engage in serious research, even if he had been inclined to. His biography of Trotsky was produced in accordance with a commercial formula that he had worked out with his publishers (Macmillan in Britain, Harvard University Press in the United States). The Trotsky biography is the third large book by Service brought on to the market in the space of just five years. The first book, a biography of Stalin, was published in 2005. It consisted of 604 pages of text, neatly packaged in five parts. Each part had 11 chapters, between 10 and 13 pages in length. Service's second book *Comrades* was published two years later, in 2007. Marketed as an authoritative history of world communism, this volume consisted of 482 pages of text, organized in six parts. Each part had six chapters. Each chapter consisted of 10 to 12 pages.

Comrades is a travesty of political and intellectual history. Service's introduction to the volume, a wild romp through the origins of Marxism, reads like the first draft of a Monty Python skit. Service informed his readers, among other things, that "Marx claimed to have turned Hegel upside down" and that he never "condoned Ricardo's advocacy of private enterprise." Having so expeditiously dealt with philosophy and political economy, Service proclaimed: "Crucial to Marxism was the dream of apocalypse followed by paradise. This kind of thinking existed in Judaism, Christianity and Islam."[2] The volume sparkles with scores of such brilliantly thoughtful observations.

Service set to work on his next venture. With *Trotsky*, published in 2009, Service and his publishers achieved a perfect equilibrium between the commercial timetable and the content manufacturing process. *Trotsky* has 501 pages of text, packaged in four parts, 13 chapters each. A total of 52 chapters, each consisting of nine to 10 pages. Thus, one can reasonably assume, Service was expected to churn out a chapter a week, and complete the writing in just one year. Considering the additional months required for editing, proofreading, typesetting and printing, the biennial publishing schedule did not leave Service all that much time for reading, sifting through and evaluating documents, and thinking. This would partly explain the astonishing number of factual mistakes in his biography.

However even if Mr. Service had negotiated a more relaxed schedule, the result still would have been largely the same. Service set out to produce an anti-Trotsky and anti-Trotskyist hatchet job that, by its very nature, precluded a principled and thoughtful engagement with Trotsky's writings and ideas. Ignoring Trotsky's writings facilitated the distortion of his ideas. For Service, the truth or untruth of any particular statement, or whether one or another judgment was based on credible evidence, were not matters about which he needed to concern himself. In writing about Trotsky, no absurdity was too grotesque.

That Trotsky was one of the great revolutionary intellectuals of the twentieth century is not a statement that serious historians—including those who have no sympathy for his politics—would challenge. He was indisputably a writer of exceptional force. He was the rarest of political figures—one who commanded the attention of the world through the power of his writings. Separated from all the conventional trappings of power, living in isolated exile—on an island off the coast of Istanbul in Turkey, later in provincial villages in France and Norway, and finally in a suburb of Mexico City—Trotsky's words influenced world opinion.

His enemies continued to fear him. The very mention of his name would send Hitler into a rage. Even the mighty Stalin, ensconced in the Kremlin,

---

[2] Robert Service, *Comrades! A History of World Communism* (London: MacMillan, 2007), p. 14.

with a vast apparatus of terror at his command, feared Trotsky. The Soviet historian, the late General Dmitri Volkogonov, wrote, "Nearly everything about or by Trotsky was translated for him [Stalin], in one copy. ... He had a special cupboard in his study in which he kept ... virtually all of Trotsky's works, heavily scored with underlinings and comments. Any interview or statement that Trotsky gave to the Western press was immediately translated and given to Stalin."[3] In a remarkable passage, Volkogonov, who had access to Stalin's private papers, wrote that

> Trotsky's spectre frequently returned to haunt the usurper. ... [Stalin] feared the thought of him. ... He thought of Trotsky when he had to sit and listen to Molotov, Kaganovich, Khrushchev and Zhdanov. Trotsky was of a different calibre intellectually, with his grasp of organization and his talents as a speaker and writer. In every way he was far superior to this bunch of bureaucrats, but he was also superior to Stalin and Stalin knew it. ... When he read Trotsky's works, such as *The Stalinist School of Falsification, An Open Letter to the Members of the Bolshevik Party*, or *The Stalinist Thermidor*, the Leader almost lost his self-control.[4]

Seventy years after his death, Trotsky's works remain in print in many languages throughout the world. Indeed, of all the principal representatives of classical Marxism—with the possible exceptions of Marx and Engels—Trotsky remains the most widely read. The words "Revolution Betrayed," "uneven and combined development," "Permanent Revolution," and "Fourth International"—linked with the name of Trotsky—evoke key motifs of the political experience of modern history. As long as the Russian Revolution remains a subject of interest, controversy and inspiration—that is, for generations to come—Trotsky's monumental *History of the Russian Revolution* will retain its hold on readers' intellect, imagination and emotions. Trotsky was clearly a major political thinker. As a well-known contemporary historian, Baruch Knei-Paz (who is not a Trotskyist) aptly wrote in a 1978 study of Trotsky's thought:

> A great deal has been written about Trotsky's life and revolutionary career—both in and out of power—but relatively little about his social and political thought. This is perhaps only natural since

---

[3] Dmitri Volkogonov, *Stalin: Triumph and Tragedy* (New York: Grove Weidenfeld, 1988), p. 228.

[4] Ibid., pp. 254-256.

his life contained many sensational moments and he is, even now, and perhaps not unjustly, considered to be the quintessential revolutionary in an age which has not lacked in revolutionary figures. Yet his achievement in the realm of theory and ideas is in many ways no less prodigious: he was among the first to analyse the emergence, in the twentieth century, of social change in backward societies, and among the first, as well, to attempt to explain the political consequences which would almost invariably grow out of such change. He wrote voluminously throughout his life, and the political thinker in him was no less an intrinsic part of his personality than the better-known man of action. [5]

Now, let us listen to Service: "Always he [Trotsky] wrote whatever was in his head." [79] Trotsky "made no claim to intellectual originality: he would have been ridiculed if he had tried." [109] "He refused to bother himself with research on most questions currently bothering the party's intellectual elite..." [109] "Intellectually he flitted from topic to topic..." [110] "He simply loved to be seated at a desk, fountain pen in hand, scribbling out the latest opus..." [319] "His thought was a confused and confusing ragbag..." [353] "He spent a lot of time in disputing, less of it in thinking. ... This involved an ultimate lack of seriousness as an intellectual." [356] "His articles were full of schematic projections, shaky reasoning and ill-considered slogans." [397]

As one reads such passages, one is simply amazed by their sheer stupidity and crudity. Does their author expect such nonsense to be taken seriously? Does he himself believe it? Service provides no examples of Trotsky's "confused and confusing ragbag of ideas." Service does not attempt to analyze, or even present an adequate summary of, a single work by Trotsky. Characterizations such as those cited above are dished up without any examination of or citation from the actual texts. Even the most significant concepts and ideas associated with Trotsky—such as the theory of Permanent Revolution and his analysis of the socio-economic foundations of the Soviet Union as a *degenerated workers' state*—are not explained. To the extent that even brief references are made to specific works of Trotsky, it is done in a manner calculated to make their author and his ideas appear ridiculous.

Service is not the first to employ this technique against Trotsky. In fact, his method bears a striking resemblance to that used in the international

---

[5] Baruch Knei-Paz, *The Social and Political Thought of Leon Trotsky* (Oxford: Clarendon Press, 1978), p. viii.

anti-Trotsky campaign mounted by the Soviet bureaucracy and allied Stalinist parties, such as the Communist Party of Great Britain, in the late 1960s and early 1970s. As a young graduate student during that period studying Soviet history, Mr. Service would have been aware of this campaign. The writings of the Stalinist Betty Reid, the CPGB's anti-Trotsky specialist, were widely circulated on university campuses in Britain. During those years, the Soviet bureaucracy became increasingly concerned about the spread of Trotskyist influence among radicalized youth. But as Stalin's crimes had already been discredited by the revelations of Khrushchev, it was no longer possible for the Kremlin's ideological operatives to simply denounce Trotsky as a "fascist wrecker," as had been the style in the 1930s and 1940s. Other forms of insidious falsification had to be developed. The gross misrepresentation of Trotsky's writings—specifically, making them appear absurd or the ravings of a lunatic—played a central role in the renewed assault on Trotskyism. Of course the attempt to discredit Trotsky's ideas required that citations from his writings be kept to a minimum. In an important article entitled "The Revival of Soviet Anti-Trotskyism," written in 1977, the late Robert H. McNeal, a noted American scholar, described the Stalinist method:

> There is quite a lot that cannot be stated in the revived version of Soviet anti-Trotskyism. His writings cannot be cited in full bibliographical form, nor very frequently. One finds relatively frequent reference to the titles (never additional publication information) *Permanent Revolution* and *My Life*, but very little else. This is a sensible precaution. No need to service the enemy by providing subversive reading lists, particularly considering the readers in countries whose libraries contain Trotskyist works. This vagueness on primary sources facilitates their interpretation. ... It is vaguely asserted that Trotsky slandered the Soviet Union, denied that it was socialist, an assertion that is regarded as too absurd to require rebuttal, but the content of Trotsky's critique of Stalinism is never described.[6]

Service writes that Trotsky's "written legacy should not be allowed to become the entire story" and that "It is sometimes in the supposedly trivial residues rather than in the grand public statements that the perspective of his career is most effectively reconstructed." [5] He goes on to claim that

---

[6] *Studies in Comparative Communism*, Vol. X, Nos. 1 & 2, Spring/Summer 1977, p. 10.

Trotsky's published autobiography is a dishonest attempt to conceal the truth of his life, and that "The excisions and amendments tell us about what he did not want others to know." [5] These statements exemplify a method of falsification that is a variant of the Stalinist method identified quite precisely by McNeal.

The method employed by Service is connected to the political outlook that suffuses his writing. Service's detestation of Trotsky is the mirror reflection of his admiration of Stalin. Having reviewed Service's mocking and derisory characterizations of Trotsky, let us examine the professor's evaluation of Stalin. In the 2005 biography, Service describes Stalin as "an excellent editor of Russian-language manuscripts."[7] Service does not cite a single manuscript in which this excellence is demonstrated. Nor does he mention that Stalin, as dictator, did most of his editing with an executioner's bullet. Rather, the tributes continue. "In fact," writes Service, "Stalin was a fluent and thoughtful writer even though he was no stylist." [*Stalin,* 221] Not an opinion. A fact! This is in contrast to Trotsky, who as Service told us, "wrote whatever was in his head." Yes, Stalin was by no means perfect. "He was a mass killer with psychological obsessions," Service notes dolefully. But "he thought and wrote as a Marxist." [*Stalin,* 379] His *Foundations of Leninism* was "a work of able compression." [*Stalin,* 221] "Stalin," writes Service, "was a thoughtful man and throughout his life tried to make sense of the universe as he found it. He had studied a lot and forgotten little. ... He was not an original thinker nor even an outstanding writer. Yet he was an intellectual to the end of his days." [*Stalin,* 569-570] Summing Stalin up at the biography's conclusion, Service declares, "But exceptional he surely was. He was a real leader. He was also motivated by the lust for power as well as by ideas. He was in his own way an intellectual, and his level of literary and editorial craft was impressive. About his psychological traits there will always be controversy." [*Stalin,* 603]

Service's aim in his Trotsky biography was to discredit the favorable image that emerged from the earlier biographies written by Isaac Deutscher and the French historian Pierre Broué. The purpose of Service's biography of Stalin was the exact opposite. While, for Service, the writing of the Trotsky biography was a labor of hate, his work on *Stalin* was a labor of love. The existing image of Stalin was "overdue for challenge," he wrote. "This book is aimed at showing that Stalin was a more dynamic and diverse figure than has

---

[7] Robert Service, *Stalin: A Biography* (Cambridge, MA: Belknap Press of Harvard University Press, 2005), p. 115..

conventionally been supposed." [*Stalin,* x] Service conceded that Stalin "was a bureaucrat and a killer." But "he was also a leader, a writer and editor, a theorist (of sorts), a bit of a poet (when young), a follower of the arts, a family man and even a charmer." [*Stalin,* x] Much of the same, by the way, could be said of Goebbels and Goering, not to mention Hitler.

Perhaps Service imagined that he was providing his readers a nuanced portrait, a blending of contradictory characteristics. But what he really presented was a variation of the worst of movie clichés—the mass murderer who tucks his children into bed and gently kisses them goodnight. But what did Service leave us with? Actually, with a political portrait quite similar to that drawn by Mikhail Gorbachev, the last Soviet leader, in his notorious speech on history in November 1987:

> There is now much discussion about the role of Stalin in our history. His was an extremely contradictory personality. To remain faithful to historical truth we have to see both Stalin's incontestable contribution to the struggle for socialism, to the defense of its gains; the gross political errors, and the abuses committed by him and by those around him, for which our people paid a heavy price and which had grave consequences for the life of our society.[8]

Both Service and Gorbachev are prepared to accept that Stalin committed crimes. But the emphasis is on his positive achievements. In the first paragraph of the Stalin biography, Service declared: "Although Lenin had founded the USSR, it was Stalin who decisively strengthened and stabilised the structure. Without Stalin, the Soviet Union might have collapsed decades before it was dismantled in 1991." [*Stalin,* 3] These words could have been written by a member of the Soviet Politburo! A more emphatic apology and justification for Stalin's policies is hard to imagine. Stalin *decisively* strengthened and stabilized the structure of the USSR! It would have collapsed without him, decades before its dissolution in 1991!

With these words, all of Stalin's actions and crimes are rationalized and justified: the crushing of the Left Opposition in the 1920s; the horrors of collectivization, the Moscow Trials and the Terror of the late 1930s; the disorientation and betrayals that facilitated the victories of fascism in Europe; the decapitation of the Red Army leadership in 1937-1938 and the Stalin-Hitler

---

[8] "Gorbachev on History; Revolution's Road from 1917 to Now: The Leader Takes Stock," *The New York Times,* November 3, 1987.

Pact, which led to the unnecessary loss of millions of Soviet lives after the German invasion in June 1941; the mismanagement of the Soviet economy and the stultification of its intellectual life; the murder of its finest writers, philosophers, and scientists; the revival of anti-Semitism; and the besmirching of Marxism and socialist ideals, within the Soviet Union and internationally. All this is legitimized by Service as necessary for the stabilization and preservation of the USSR! Service overlooks the fact that the structure left behind by Stalin staggered from crisis to crisis, and that the generation of bureaucrats that rose to power under his tutelage presided over the stagnation and breakdown of the Soviet Union.

Service goes so far to imply that the terror was a legitimate response by Stalin to threats confronting the USSR:

> Chief among his considerations was security, and he made no distinction between his personal security and the security of his policies, the leadership and the state. Molotov and Kaganovich in their dotage were to claim that Stalin had justifiable fears about the possibility of a "fifth column" coming to the support of invading forces in the event of war. Stalin gave some hints of this. He was shocked by the ease with which it had been possible for General Franco to pick up followers in the Spanish Civil War which broke out in July 1936. He intended to prevent this from ever happening in the USSR. Such thinking goes some way to explaining why he, a believer in the efficacy of state terror, turned to intensive violence in 1937-8. [*Stalin*, 347-348]

Service accepts as credible the lying justifications for the terror given by Stalin's co-butchers, Molotov and Kaganovich, who affixed their names to thousands of execution orders in the 1930s. There exists no evidence whatever that Stalin's decision to exterminate the Bolshevik Old Guard and vast sections of the revolutionary socialist intelligentsia had anything to do with "justifiable fears" that a right-wing coup against the Soviet state was being prepared. By implying that events in Spain—where well-known army officers, long identified with the extreme right, launched a coup against the Republican government in Spain—spurred Stalin to launch the terror, Service bestows legitimacy on the monstrous allegations hurled by State prosecutor Vyshinsky against the Old Bolshevik defendants at the Moscow Trials. It must be pointed out that plans for the physical destruction of the Old Bolsheviks were far advanced by the time the Spanish Civil War broke out in July 1936. The murder of Kirov had taken place in December 1934. Zinoviev and Kamenev and countless others had been in prison since 1935. Preparations for the first Moscow trial—which included placing Zinoviev, Kamenev and other imprisoned potential defendants under extreme pressure, including torture, to provide confessions—had been underway for months. If there was any foreign event that "inspired" Stalin to wipe out his old comrades, it was not the right-wing coup in Spain. Rather, it was the "Night of the Long-Knives" in Germany in June 1934—that is, Hitler's assassination of his old party associates in the leadership of the SA storm troopers.

It is true that Stalin launched the terror to deal with threats to his regime. But those threats came not from the fascist right, but from the socialist left. Stalin's fear that social discontent within the Soviet Union would lead to a resurgence of Bolshevik tendencies, above all that led by Trotsky, has been well-documented—especially by the brilliant Russian Marxist historian, Vadim Z. Rogovin. Not surprisingly, Rogovin's seven-volume history of the struggle of the socialist left and Trotskyist opposition to Stalinism is not included by Service in the bibliographies of his Stalin and Trotsky biographies.

Service's defense of Stalin is continued in his biography of Trotsky. He notes with disapproval that, "Trotsky had provided arguments that discredited the reputation of Stalin and his henchmen, and it was all too easy for writers unthinkingly to adopt them as their own." [*Trotsky*, 3] Service continues:

> Trotsky was wrong in many cardinal aspects of his case. Stalin was no mediocrity but rather had an impressive range of skills as well as a talent for decisive leadership. Trotsky's strategy for communist advance anyway had little to offer for the avoidance of an oppressive regime. [3]

As for the unpleasant aspects of Stalin's regime, the source of these problems lay with Trotsky, whose "ideas and practices laid several foundation stones for the erection of the Stalinist political, economic, social and even cultural edifice." [3] Later in the biography, blatantly falsifying Trotsky's famous work of literary criticism *Literature and Revolution* and attributing to the author views that are the exact opposite of what is written in the book, Service states: "When all is said and done ... it was Trotsky who laid down the philosophical foundations for cultural Stalinism." [318]

Service's defense of Stalin against Trotsky's writings is extraordinarily vituperative: "As for the charge that Stalin was an arch-bureaucrat, this was rich coming from an accuser who had delighted in unchecked administrative authority in the years of his pomp." [3] The tirade continues:

> Even Trotsky's claim that Stalin was uninterested in aiding foreign communist seizures of power fails to withstand scrutiny. Moreover, if communism had been victorious in Germany, France or Spain in the inter-war years, its banner-holders would have been unlikely to have retained their power. And if ever Trotsky had been the para-mount leader instead of Stalin, the risks of a bloodbath in Europe would have been drastically increased. [3]

Whose scrutiny? Service himself does not examine in detail any of the major revolutionary conflicts—in Britain, China, Germany, France and Spain, to name a few—that were the subject of Trotsky's polemics during the 1920s and 1930s. But the statement itself is not one that could be made by any reputable and honest historian. The destructive role of Stalinism dur-ing the "low dishonest decade"[9] that preceded the outbreak of World War II, the devastating impact of its duplicitous, cynical and murderous activities on the European and international workers' movement, was burnt into the consciousness of an entire generation who lived through the terrible events of the 1930s. George Orwell's *Homage to Catalonia* is only the most famous account of the Stalinist nightmare.

There are countless books in which the Stalinist subversion of the Spanish revolution, including the repression of the left and the murder of POUM leader Andrés Nin, has been recorded for history. The transformation of the Communist International into a corrupt instrument of Soviet foreign policy, led by functionaries selected and controlled by the Kremlin, is a massively documented historical fact. The Seventh Congress of the Comintern, held in 1935, committed the national Communist parties to the class collaboration-ist perspective of "Popular Front" alliances with "liberal" and "democratic" bourgeois parties. Service fails to mention this Congress, which Trotsky pre-dicted would set the stage for the formal dissolution of the Comintern. As later noted by the historian E. H. Carr, who wrote a famous book in which he subjected Stalin's foreign policy to "scrutiny":

> ...It was significant that no further congress, and no major session of IKKI [Executive Committee of the Communist International], was ever again summoned. Comintern continued to discharge

---

[9] W. H. Auden, "September 1, 1939" (http://www.poemdujour.com/Sept1.1939.html).

subordinate functions, while the spotlight of publicity was directed elsewhere. Trotsky's verdict that the seventh congress would
"pass into history as the liquidation congress" of Comintern was
not altogether unfair. The seventh congress pointed the way to the
dénouement of 1943.[10]

Alongside his outright falsifications, Service issues *ex cathedra* pro-
nouncements whose nonsensical character must become apparent to any
reader who actually thinks about what he is reading. How does Service know
that "if communism had been victorious in Germany, France or Spain in the
interwar years, its banner-holders would have been unlikely to have retained
their power"? What is the basis of this judgment? If the working class would
actually have come to power in two of the most economically and cultur-
ally advanced countries in Western Europe, and, in addition, held power in
the strategic Iberian peninsula, how would these revolutionary regimes have
been overthrown? Through the efforts of a capitalist Britain, perhaps led by
Winston Churchill? Does Service assume that the British working class—
whose opposition to the anti-Bolshevik efforts of the imperialist Lloyd
George government in 1918-1920 contributed significantly to the survival of
Soviet Russia—would have supported a military campaign to restore capitalism in France, Germany and Spain?

Service never poses another essential question: What would have
been the impact of such revolutionary advances by the working class in the
major European centers of capitalism on the development of the Soviet
Union? Trotsky always stressed that the defeat suffered by the revolutionary movement in Western Europe was the decisive factor in the development of the Stalinist dictatorship. The repudiation of the revolutionary
internationalism of the early Bolshevik regime and its replacement by the
Stalin-Bukharin theory of socialism in one country was a political adapta-
tion to setbacks in Western Europe, particularly in Germany. Conversely,
Trotsky held that a renewal of revolutionary struggles in the capitalist centers would transform the political situation in the Soviet Union. As he
wrote in 1936:

> The first victory of a revolution in Europe would pass like an elec-
> tric shock through the Soviet masses, straighten them up, raise
> their spirit of independence, awaken the traditions of 1905 and

---

[10] E. H. Carr, *Twilight of the Comintern, 1930–1935* (New York: Pantheon Books, 1982), p.
427.

1917 ... and acquire for the Fourth International no less significance than the October Revolution possessed for the Third.[11]

Service never directly explains Trotsky's conception of the relationship between the fate of the Soviet Union and the development of international revolution. But his biography is not the work of a politically neutral scholar. That would not necessarily condemn the work. What does condemn the biography is that the political views and objectives that motivate the work require historical falsification. Service's political hatred of Trotsky's perspective of world revolution, and his support for Stalin's nationalist program, is apparent to those who recognize the pro-Stalin subtext that pervades the Trotsky biography. Service writes:

> Trotsky prided himself on his ability to see Soviet and international affairs with realism. He deceived himself. He had sealed himself inside preconceptions that stopped him from understanding the dynamics of contemporary geopolitics. [3]

For Service, the "preconceptions" are those of revolution and Marxian internationalism. The "dynamics of contemporary geopolitics," as Service (much like Stalin) conceives them, proceed from the primacy of the national state and its interests and the indestructibility of capitalism.

Let us return to the most bizarre assertion of all, that is to Service's claim that "if ever Trotsky had been the paramount leader instead of Stalin, the risks of a bloodbath in Europe would have been drastically increased." One is compelled to ask: What could Trotsky possibly have done that would have made the loss of human life in the Europe of the 1930s and 1940s worse than it actually was? Apart from the atrocities committed by Stalin within the USSR, his policies—beginning with the defeat of the German working class in 1933—set into motion a chain of events that culminated in the very real bloodbath of World War II. The war cost the lives of approximately 50 million people in Europe—including 27 million Russians, six million Germans, six million Jews and three million Poles. Service seems to be arguing, however circuitously, that millions more would have died if Trotsky's perspective of socialist revolution had prevailed. The actual loss of life that occurred as a consequence of the failure of revolution—the victory of fascism in Germany and the outbreak of World War II—was less than it would have been had the socialist revolution succeeded. The conclusion that Service invites his readers

---

[11] Leon Trotsky, *The Revolution Betrayed* (Detroit: Labor Publications, 1991), p. 247.

to draw is that given the choice between victory of socialist revolution and the victory of fascism, the latter is the lesser evil.

The claim that underlies this position is that Trotsky was a violent man, indifferent to human life and suffering, willing to sacrifice countless lives for the sake of revolution. As Service states at the conclusion of his biography, Trotsky "fought for a cause that was more destructive than he had ever imagined." [501]

Portraying Trotsky as a cold-blooded fanatic, brutally indifferent to human life, Service provides an example of his subject's ruthlessness. Trotsky, he writes, "displayed his complete moral insouciance when telling his American admirer Max Eastman in the early 1920s that he and the Bolsheviks were willing 'to burn several thousand Russians to a cinder in order to create a true revolutionary American movement.' Russia's workers and peasants would have been interested to know of the mass sacrifice he was contemplating." [313] This passage is calculated to send a shudder down the spines of its readers. What type of monster of political fanaticism, they must wonder, could contemplate such an act?

But did Trotsky actually say this? And, if he did, in what context? Why did Max Eastman, despite learning of the terrible plan, become one of Trotsky's most devoted international supporters during the 1920s? And, still later, the principal translator of Trotsky's writings into English? The passage that I have just quoted appears on page 313 of Service's *Trotsky*, in Chapter 33, entitled "On the Cultural Front." Service cites as his source the memoirs of Max Eastman, *Love and Revolution: My Journey Through an Epoch*. And indeed on page 333 of that book, we find Eastman's account of his discussion with Trotsky.

Eastman's story is wonderfully told. It is of his first meeting with Trotsky, which took place in Moscow in 1922, during the Fourth Congress of the Communist International. Eastman was anxious to speak to Trotsky about a problem that had been troubling him. The American socialist movement was dominated by Russian immigrants. They were monopolizing the leadership of the young Communist Party. An opportunity arose for Eastman to approach Trotsky during a session of the congress. Eastman was surprised to find that Trotsky's appearance was very different from the well-known Mephistophelian caricatures of the newspapers. Trotsky, Eastman recalled, looked "more like a carefully washed good boy in a Sunday School class than like Mephistopheles."[12] Eastman requested an appointment, which Trotsky

---

[12] Max Eastman, *Love and Revolution: My Journey Through an Epoch* (New York: Random

immediately granted. They met again the next day at Trotsky's office at the Military Revolutionary Soviet.

Trotsky, as Eastman humorously described him, was "certainly the neatest man who ever led an insurrection." But what particularly surprised Eastman was Trotsky's "quietude." Newspaper descriptions of Trotsky that portrayed him as nervous and excitable, wrote Eastman, "seemed almost a libel against this gracious person who listened with such courtesy to the bad French in which I wrestled forth my ideas." Eastman explained to Trotsky that the dominant role played by Russian socialists "made it impossible to get an American revolutionary movement started." To make matters worse, though most of them were Mensheviks before October 1917, "they think they created the October Revolution." Adopting a jocular tone, Eastman compared the posturing ex-Mensheviks to a young rooster who crows "in a loud falsetto voice because some hen who is old enough to be his grandmother has laid an egg." Trotsky, Eastman remembered, was amused by this comment. He then made the remark in French which Eastman recalled verbatim: "*Mais nous sommes prêts à brûler quelques milliers de Russes afin de créer un vrai movement révolutionnaire Américain.*" Eastman places within parentheses the English translation: "But we are ready to burn up a few thousand Russians in order to create a real American revolutionary movement."[13]

Service, it is clear, has deliberately and maliciously misrepresented the remark made by Trotsky. He was jesting with Eastman, who understood that Trotsky was not talking about incinerating Russian workers and peasants, but rather of reducing the influence of pompous ex-Menshevik Russian immigrants in the American socialist movement. Moreover, Service, with the intention of enhancing the impact of his lie, adds words that are not found in Eastman's text. The words "to a cinder" do not appear in the original. So Service has transformed a humorous anecdote, recalled by Eastman many decades later—one which presents Trotsky in a favorable light, as a patient, humorous and cultured man—into an example of a revolutionary fanatic's horrifying inhumanity.

Is this a trivial, let alone innocent, mistake? Hardly. This sort of falsification has consequences. The falsification, once it has escaped detection, becomes part of the accepted historical narrative, repeated over and over in essays and books. As time passes, it becomes ever more difficult to expose the lie, let alone identify the liar who put it into circulation.

House, 1964) p. 332.

[13] Ibid., pp. 332-333.

Service's biography is a shameful and shameless compendium of distortions and falsifications. It is not sufficient for Service to misrepresent the ideas for which Trotsky lived and died. He seeks to belittle the man, to make him appear deserving of the reader's contempt. He repeats the same insults. On page 336 Service describes Trotsky as "intensely self-righteous." On page 381, he writes of Trotsky's "matchless self-righteousness." Even Trotsky's writings are subjected to ridicule. "The mixture of tub-thumping and slipperiness," Service writes, "was preserved in *The History of the Russian Revolution*." [403] He expresses amazement that people have "automatically believed" Trotsky's account of his struggle against Stalin. "In fact the gap between the Politburo and the Opposition was never as wide as he pretended." [356] Service does not offer this statement, wholly unsubstantiated, as his own interpretation. He declares it to be a *fact*, and, therefore, beyond dispute! Thus, Service finds it "surprising" that a great many people "who had no sympathy for communism" nevertheless "accepted the idea that the USSR would not have been a totalitarian despotism under Trotskyist rule." [356]

In what are among the most degraded passages in his book, Service refers contemptuously to liberal and socialist intellectuals who rallied to Trotsky's defense during the Moscow Trials, supporting his call for a Commission of Inquiry. Their position, Service states, "reflects their naivety. They were blind to Trotsky's contempt for their values. They overlooked the damage he aimed to do to their kind of society if he ever got the chance. Like spectators at a zoo, they felt sorry for a wounded beast." [466]

I have already shown that Mr. Service practices his profession incompetently and dishonestly. These lines expose Service as a man bereft of any respect for democratic principles. Trotsky's right to answer his accusers and defend himself was not contingent upon his endorsement of the political institutions of the United States. Mr. Service would be well-advised to read the words with which John Dewey, the great American liberal philosopher, explained the *raison d'être* of the Commission of Inquiry over which he presided as chairman. Leon Trotsky, he explained, had been declared guilty of terrible crimes by the highest tribunal of the Soviet Union. Trotsky had demanded that the Soviet government seek his extradition, which would have enabled him to answer the charges against him in either a Norwegian or Mexican court. This demand had been ignored by the Soviet Union. What followed from this situation? Dewey stated:

> The simple fact that we are here is evidence that the conscience of
> the world is not as yet satisfied on this historic issue. This world

conscience demands that Mr. Trotsky be not finally condemned before he has had full opportunity to present whatever evidence is in his possession in reply to the verdict pronounced upon him in hearings at which he was neither present nor represented. The right to a hearing before condemnation is such an elementary right in every civilized country that it would be absurd for us to reassert it were it not for the efforts which have been made to prevent Mr. Trotsky from being heard, and the efforts that now are being made to discredit the work of this Commission of Inquiry.[14]

In another public statement, Dewey answered, with evident anger, the claims that Trotsky did not deserve, on account of his political views, to be defended.

In the cases of Tom Mooney in San Francisco and Sacco-Vanzetti in Boston, we got used to hearing reactionaries say that these men were dangerous nuisances anyway, so that it was better to put them out of the way whether or not they were guilty of the things for which they were tried. I never thought I would live to see the day when professed liberals would resort to a similar argument.[15]

Service's animus for the proceedings of the Commission is evident. He writes nothing of the international Stalinist campaign to sabotage and discredit the Commission, which included threats of violence against public supporters of the inquiry. Dewey's family feared for the life of the 78-year-old philosopher. Service writes, as if something was amiss, that Dewey was Trotsky's "favored choice as chairman" [466], and that "they agreed to avoid examining the broadest questions of Trotsky's political and moral record." [467] He applauds the resignation of the journalist Ferdinand Lundberg from the Commission before its first session. "Lundberg had come to think, justifiably, that Trotsky was a prime architect of the suppression of civil rights in the USSR which he now, as a victim, complained about." [467]

Service does not cite even one line from the transcript of the Commission's hearing in Mexico in April 1937. He ignores Trotsky's famous speech with which the hearing concluded, which made an overwhelming impression on

---

[14] *John Dewey: The Later Works, 1925-1953*, Volume 11: 1935-1937, Essays and *Liberalism and Social Action*, edited by Jo Ann Boydston (Carbondale and Edwardsville: Southern Illinois University Press, 1991), p. 307.

[15] Ibid., p. 317.

the commissioners. Service states that the Commission "went on for a whole week until Dewey felt he could summarize an agreed verdict. Nobody had been in serious doubt about what it would be. Trotsky was exculpated." [467] This is a trivialization and slur on the Commission's work. No "agreed verdict" was arrived at and delivered in Mexico. In fact, Dewey and other Commission members had traveled to Mexico as members of the "Preliminary Commission" to conduct a *preliminary investigation*, which included the questioning of Trotsky and the collection of relevant documents in his possession. After leaving Mexico, it prepared a preliminary report, which found that Trotsky "has established a case amply warranting further investigation."[16] The Preliminary Commission recommended that the Commission of Inquiry continue its work. It was not until December 1937, eight months after it had questioned Trotsky in Mexico, that the Dewey Commission issued its verdict, found Trotsky to be not guilty and the Moscow Trials to be a frame-up.

Upon submitting the report of the Preliminary Commission, Dewey stated:

> The work of investigation is only begun. Various lines of inquiry have been opened which must be pursued until all the available facts are disclosed. Final judgment must be reserved until the different lines of investigation have been carried through to the end.[17]

Explaining the principles that motivated the work of the Commission, Dewey stated that "friendship for truth comes before friendship for individuals and factions." He insisted that the Commission of Inquiry was "committed to one end and one end only: discovery of the truth as far as that is humanly possible. Lines are being drawn between devotion to justice and adherence to a faction, between fair play and a love of darkness that is reactionary in effect no matter what banner it flaunts."[18]

Dewey summed up all that was at stake in the struggle to defend historical truth against lies. If there is a question in your mind as to why our party has devoted so much time and effort to the exposure and refutation of attempts to falsify Trotsky's life and the history of the epoch in which he lived, I urge you to read and ponder Dewey's words, so relevant to our times, and, hopefully, adopt them as your own credo.

---

16 Ibid., p. 314.

17 Ibid.

18 Ibid., p. 320.

This year marks the seventieth anniversary of Trotsky's assassination, on August 20, 1940, at the hands of a Stalinist agent, Ramon Mercader, in Coyoacán, Mexico. That Trotsky still remains a subject of intense controversy is not unusual. That is the fate of all truly important historical figures. But what is extraordinary is the degree to which he remains, so many years after his assassination, the subject of such unrelenting misrepresentation, falsification and outright slander. History will record that the Soviet bureaucracy never formally rehabilitated Leon Trotsky (contrary to the claim of Service, who gets even this fact wrong). Even as he was pursuing pro-capitalist policies that were to result, within little more than four years, to the dissolution of the Soviet Union, Mikhail Gorbachev publicly declared:

> Trotskyism was a political current whose ideologists took cover behind leftist pseudo-revolutionary rhetoric, and who in effect assumed a defeatist posture. This was essentially an attack on Leninism all down the line. The matter practically concerned the future of socialism in our country, the fate of the revolution.
>
> In the circumstances, it was essential to disprove Trotskyism before the whole people, and denude its antisocialist essence.[19]

Service is at the back of a long line of anti-Trotsky slanderers who have been at work, in the service of political reaction, for more than 85 years. The conservative reaction against the revolutionary internationalist program of the October Revolution began in 1923 under the banner of the fight against Trotskyism. By the mid-1930s, this fight had assumed the form of the systematic physical extermination of all the surviving representatives of the Marxist political and intellectual tradition within the Soviet Union. And beyond the borders of the USSR, the Trotskyists were persecuted within the imperialist countries—both fascist and democratic. Hitler, as I have already mentioned, would fly into a rage when Trotsky's name was mentioned. In the United States, the Roosevelt administration organized the indictment and imprisonment of leaders of the Trotskyist movement.

And if there was anyone in the world who hated Trotsky even more than Stalin did, it was none other than Winston Churchill. In 1937, Churchill published a book entitled *Great Contemporaries*. One chapter was devoted to Hitler, of whom Churchill wrote with unabashed admiration. He still

---

[19] "Gorbachev on History; Revolution's Road from 1917 to Now: The Leader Takes Stock," *The New York Times*, November 3, 1987.

had high hopes for the German *Fuehrer*. But another chapter was devoted to Trotsky. The language was out of control. "Like the cancer bacillus," Churchill wrote, "he grew, he fed, he tortured, he slew in fulfillment of his nature."[20] It should be noted that Churchill's most vile slanders, directed against Trotsky as a man, are picked up and expanded upon by Service.

The rage of Hitler, the vituperation of Churchill, and the sadistic vindictiveness of Stalin are not difficult to explain. They were Trotsky's contemporaries, his *lesser* contemporaries. They were engaged in what they knew to be life and death struggles against the revolutionary cause that he, more than any other person of his time, represented and embodied. Read the newspapers of the day. How often one finds on the front page, beneath the banner headlines reporting one or another spectacular event of the 1930s, a smaller headline that reads: "Trotsky says..." or "Trotsky predicts..." The press in this way informed its readers of Trotsky's response to the great events of the day. But why the interest in the reaction of one man? Because that one man was the authoritative voice of world socialist revolution. Trotsky was the revolution in exile. On August 31, 1939—on the very eve of the outbreak of World War II—the French newspaper *Paris-Soir* reported a discussion between Hitler and the French ambassador Coulondre. Hitler expresses his regrets that war is inevitable. Coulondre asks Hitler if it had occurred to him that the only victor in the event of war will be Trotsky. "Have you thought this over," he asked. And Hitler replied, "I know." Reading this account, Trotsky wrote: "These gentlemen like to give a personal name to the spectre of revolution."[21]

Service's portrayal of Trotsky is drawn entirely from the slanders of those who stood in the camp of reaction, both Stalinist and imperialist. He cannot permit the introduction of any testimony that contradicts the caricature that he presents to his readers. Moreover, Service relies on the fact that, so many years after his death, there is no one left who actually knew, respected and loved the "Old Man," as he was known to so many of his followers. I was fortunate to have met and spoken with witnesses to Trotsky's life: Arne Swabeck and Al Glotzer—both of whom spent weeks with Trotsky in Prinkipo in the early 1930s; the Belgian revolutionary Georges Vereeken; the German revolutionist, Oskar Hippe, and the captain of Trotsky's guard in Coyoacán,

---

[20] Cited in *Trotsky, Great Lives Observed*, edited by Irving H. Smith (Englewood Cliffs, NJ: Prentice-Hall, 1973), p. 86.

[21] Leon Trotsky, "On the Nature of the USSR," in *In Defence of Marxism* (London: New Park, 1971), p. 39.

Harold Robins. Not all of these men remained Trotskyists. But of Trotsky's greatness and humanity they were never in doubt. Even after the passage of decades, they viewed the time they had spent with Trotsky as the most important period of their lives.

I have also met survivors of Stalin's terror, who experienced firsthand the bestiality of the bureaucracy's counter-revolutionary nationalist pogrom against the genuine representatives of Bolshevism, such as Revekka Mikhailovna Boguslavskaya, Tatiana Ivarovna Smilga and Zorya Leonidovna Serebriakova, whose fathers, members of the Left Opposition, were shot in 1937 or 1938. They met Trotsky when they were still children, and he seemed like a giant in their eyes. They recalled how their fathers—Mikhail Boguslavsky, Ivar Smilga and Leonid Serebriakov—would speak of "Lev Davidovich" with respect and genuine love. Though Tatiana Smilga and Zorya Serebriakova are still alive, they were not interviewed by Service. Nadezhda Joffe was the daughter of Adolf Joffe, Trotsky's close friend, who committed suicide in November 1927 to protest Trotsky's expulsion from the Communist Party. She had first met Trotsky as a child, in Vienna, before the 1917 Revolution. She played together with Trotsky's young son, Lev Sedov. In contrast to Service's portrayal of Trotsky as an uncaring father, Nadezhda remembered a man who loved children and was infinitely patient as he mediated their squabbles. Though Service cites Joffe's memoirs, he makes no reference to her personal recollections of Trotsky.

There exist a number of important literary portraits of Trotsky, in which his extraordinary personality is memorably portrayed. The American writer, James T. Farrell, travelled with John Dewey to Mexico in April 1937. Years later, in the 1950s, he wrote an account of that trip. Farrell had observed Trotsky closely, during the week in which the latter spent hours answering questions put to him by the members of the preliminary commission. Trotsky was under crushing political and personal pressure. He was all too aware of the horror that was unfolding in Moscow, where his old comrades had already been murdered or were awaiting execution. His youngest son Sergei had already disappeared. Trotsky was compelled to answer questions in a language that was not his own.

Trotsky, Farrell recalled

> gave the impression of great simplicity, and of extraordinary control over himself. He was a decisive and noncasual person. He spoke with remarkable precision. His manners were as impeccable

as his clothes, and he was a man of charm. His gestures were very graceful. He was extraordinarily alert. At times it seemed as though his entire organism were subordinated to his will. His voice was anything but harsh. ...

He was taut, like a bow drawn tightly. It would never snap, but it would vibrate at the slightest ripple of one's breath. His temperament was vibrant. He was a man of tremendous intellectual pride and of self-confidence. He was intolerant of stupidity, of what he deemed to be stupid, and his simplicity and extraordinary graciousness seemed like an acquisition of experience. He was a man of genius, of will, and of ideas. He might even be called an archetype of the civilized, highly cultivated Western European. He was a man of the West, and in this unlike the majority of current men in power in the Soviet Union. His Marxian faith was a faith in ideas. We can properly say that Trotsky was a great man.[22]

Farrell offered this account of Trotsky's testimony:

In Mexico, Dewey remarked that Trotsky had spoken for eight days and had said nothing foolish. And what Trotsky said exposed a world of horror, of tragedy, of degradations of the human spirit. "When people get accustomed to horrors," wrote the Russian poet Boris Pasternak, "these form the foundations of good style." The horrors of history were a basic ingredient of Trotsky's style. His masterful irony is, like all great irony, a protest because the horrors of history loom so overwhelmingly in the face of the reason of man. And he was a man of history in the sense that most of us are not and cannot be. ... And as he talked, his style, his thought, his irony gave the hearings a tone which reduced the impact of the horrors of history which were revealed—the tale of war, of revolution, of idealism turned to cynicism, of the breaking of brave men, the betrayals of honor, truth, and friendship, the perversions of truth, the sufferings of families and of the innocent, the revelation of how the Revolution and the society which had become the hope of so many in the West was really a barbarism practically unparalleled in modern history. Read the cold print of his testimony

---

[22] James T. Farrell, "Dewey in Mexico," in *Reflections at Fifty* (New York: The Vanguard Press, 1954), pp. 108-109.

and all this is clear. Some of Trotsky's interpretive and causal explanations may vary from our own, but the facts, the revelations, the horrors are all there. And as Trotsky talked, accepting full moral responsibility for all of his own acts when he was in power, his style gave this testimony an almost artistic character.[23]

I have quoted this passage at such length because you must hear it. You have an intellectual and moral right to hear it. The younger generation has been largely cut off intellectually from the revolutionary experiences of the twentieth century. For so many years, we have lived in an environment of political and intellectual reaction. The events of the past century are falsified, or, almost as bad, simply not written and talked about. There is a danger that the young generations, coming to maturity in the first decades of the twenty-first century, will not know what they must know of the great events of the twentieth century, of its revolutions and the counter-revolutions. Of the wars, and the efforts to put an end to them. And they will not know of the great voices of the past, and the words they spoke.

We are entering into a new epoch of revolutionary struggle. Of this there are growing and increasingly apparent signs. The gulf between the few who are rich, rich beyond anything that is rational and comprehensible, and the great mass of the world's human beings grows ever greater. The economic system, designed to perpetuate and add to the wealth of the rich, assumes before our eyes an ever more irrational character. The global problems metastasize, producing social and ecological catastrophes. The operations of privately owned corporations ever more obviously endanger the very survival of the planet. The growing awareness of these dangers, the anger over inequality and injustice, is mounting. A change in mass consciousness is now underway. But the development of consciousness must be nourished with the lessons of history. The great voices of the past, including that of Leon Trotsky, must be heard again, so that we can learn from and be inspired by them.

---

[23] Ibid., pp. 111-112.

Leon Trotsky, ca. 1920

Assessing Leon Trotsky Seventy Years After his Assassination[1]

The subject of this panel is a man who remains, even 70 years after his assassination by a Stalinist agent, a relentlessly contemporary figure. Trotsky was one of the titans of the political and intellectual life of the 20th century. But the efforts to blackguard Trotsky, misrepresent his theoretical work, and manufacture false accounts of his life continue. Trotskyism remains as politically heretical in the 21st century as *Spinosisme* was in the 18th. Indeed, in recent years, the hostility to Trotsky has grown more intense, and this hostility has assumed a particularly vicious character. We are, it must be said, very far from the time when principled liberal adversaries of Trotsky read his work with intense interest and even admiration. To the extent that liberalism retained a certain level of intellectual integrity and still believed sincerely in its democratic ideals, it was possible, in the 1930s, for a man such as John Dewey (though not, of course, for the liberal fellow travelers of the Soviet regime, such as the publishers of the *Nation*) to disagree with Trotsky while readily acknowledging his genius, courage and honesty. Not only that. Dewey felt obligated—on the basis of his principles—to provide Trotsky with the means to defend himself against the accusations of the Stalinists.

Later, in the 1950s, 1960s and 1970s, a new generation of historians sought to deal objectively and honestly with the October Revolution and its greatest figures, including Leon Trotsky. Alexander Rabinowitch, on the basis of meticulous archival research, established the decisive role played

---

[1] Report given at the annual convention of the Association for Slavic, East European and Eurasian Studies, November 21, 2010.

by Trotsky in the development of the strategy of the October insurrection and its tactical implementation. Richard B. Day investigated the economic thought of the Left Opposition. Baruch Knei-Paz produced a detailed examination of Trotsky's political and social thought. As it turned out, the publication of Knei-Paz's study in 1978 proved to be the high water mark in formal academic work on Leon Trotsky—excluding the efforts of Pierre Broué, who was not only an outstanding historian but also a Trotskyist.

The last 20 years have witnessed an anti-intellectual counterrevolution in the field of Soviet studies in general and, in particular, the study of Leon Trotsky. The initial cause of this reaction is not difficult to identify. The dissolution of the Soviet Union had a demoralizing effect on broad sections of the liberal intelligentsia in the United States and Western Europe. Whatever their individual political convictions, all the historians who did serious work on the Russian Revolution were motivated by the belief that October 1917 represented a major turning point in world history. Its origins, the event itself, its aftermath, and those who played an important role in this historical drama demanded conscientious study. The collapse of 1991 seemed to invalidate that fundamental belief. The era of bourgeois triumphalism and its house intellectual, Francis Fukuyama, had arrived, courtesy of the RAND Corporation. The October Revolution, it was now proclaimed, was not only a political crime. It was a mistake, and a pointless one at that!

The very idea that the October Revolution posed even the possibility of a historically viable alternative to capitalism had been massively refuted.

This argument had a substantial impact on the academic community, whose confidence in human progress had already been undermined, even before the dissolution of the Soviet Union, not only by the blather of the Reagan years but also by the subjectivism and irrationalism of the Frankfurt School and Postmodernism. However, the effort to deny the substance and legitimacy of October 1917 rested from the start on very shaky historical and intellectual foundations. After all, the Soviet state, which arose out of the revolution, had survived not merely for 71 days, as in the case of the Paris Commune, but for 73 years. In the course of its existence, the Soviet Union had undergone an extraordinary industrial transformation, defeated Nazi Germany in war, vastly raised the living standards and cultural level of its people, recorded remarkable achievements in science, and exercised immense global influence. Moreover, the claim that the outcome of December 1991 was the inexorable product of October 1917 required that historians either belittle or ignore alternatives to the course of Soviet development under Stalin and his successors—alternatives that were not only imagined, but which were actually programmatically formulated and fought for. One particularly cynical example of this approach is to be found in the writings of British historian Eric Hobsbawm, a long-time member of the Stalinist British Communist Party, who justified Stalin's regime as "the only game in town."

Ironically, the claim by anti-Marxists that the final outcome of Soviet history followed inevitably from the 1917 Revolution—that the political and economic policies that were pursued from the early days of War Communism and the NEP through to collectivization, the Liberman reforms and Gorbachev's Perestroika represented the sole conceivable path of development—mirrored the arguments of the Stalinist regime, which sought to cloak its errors by depicting bureaucratic arbitrariness as an expression of "historical necessity." This perversion of a genuinely materialist and dialectical conception of Marxist determinism by Stalin was capably exposed by Professor Day in 1990 in his perceptive refutation of the "Blackmail of the Single Alternative."[2] Day's essay was written on the very eve of the definitive failure of Gorbachev's Perestroika, the Stalinist bureaucracy's dissolution of the USSR, and the restoration of capitalism.

As Day correctly noted: "When Stalin canonized 'Leninism' in the mid-1920s, he excluded from Lenin's thought every element of sophistication and fastened on every plausible justification for the authoritarian organization of political and economic life."[3] Significantly, Day linked his opposition to the "blackmail of the single alternative" (or Hobsbawm's "only game in town") to an examination of the alternative posed by Trotsky. Stressing the connection between Trotsky's philosophical conceptions and his programmatic opposition to the nationalist line of socialism in one country, Day explained:

> Trotsky looked upon historical contradictions as the material of social policy. Following the Hegelian and Marxist commitment to universality, he also believed that contradictions had to be comprehended within the "whole" of world economy, of which capitalism and socialism were now "parts." With the emergence of the world market, the nation-state—whether capitalist or socialist—could no longer exist as "an independent economic arena."

---

[2] "The Blackmail of the Single Alternative: Bukharin, Trotsky and Perestrojka," in *Studies in Soviet Thought*, Volume 40, No. 1/3, August-November 1990, pp. 159-188.

[3] Ibid, p. 163.

The world division of labor was "not disrupted by the fact that a socialist system prevails in one country while a capitalist one prevails in the others."[4]

In an environment shaped by post-Soviet capitalist triumphalism, few historians were prepared to develop historical work along the path suggested by Day and explore systematically historical alternatives to Stalinism. The one great exception to the prevailing pattern of intellectual prostration before the force of political and ideological reaction was the work of historian and sociologist Vadim Rogovin in Russia, who entitled the first volume of his seven-volume history of the Trotskyist opposition to Stalinism between 1923 and 1940 *Was There an Alternative?*

The renewed assault on the historical reputation of Trotsky in the 1990s grew out of the need of bourgeois ideologists to deny the possibility that the path of Stalinist dictatorship was not the only one that might have been followed in the USSR. Trotsky's very existence as a revolutionary opponent of the regime—and, moreover, one who posed a major political threat to the Stalinist bureaucracy—had to be denied. Thus, by its very nature and purpose, this assault demanded the revival of the methods of falsification and even the same lies that had been used by the Stalinist regime in its relentless war against Trotsky. All the facts that had been established by historians over the previous 40 years (since the publication of the first volume of Deutscher's biography in the 1950s) about the life and work of Trotsky had to be, to use what was to become a favorite catch-phrase of the distortionists, "called into question." This was the self-proclaimed agenda of the so-called *Journal of Trotsky Studies* that was established at the University of Glasgow in the early 1990s. Professor Ian Thatcher was among its co-founders. The journal did not last long. Only four issues were produced. But the *Journal* developed the mode of falsification that was to guide all the anti-Trotsky works that were to be written over the next decade and a half. The main components of this modus operandi were: 1) claims that well-established facts about the life of Trotsky—such as his leadership of the October 1917 insurrection, his critical role as creator and commander of the Red Army, his commitment to internationalism, and his uncompromising opposition to Stalinism—were "myths" ripe for exposure; 2) assertions that Trotsky's writings, including such acknowledged literary masterworks as his autobiography and his monumental *History of the Russian Revolution*, were unreliable; and 3) slurs against Trotsky's intellectual, political and moral integrity.

---

[4] Ibid, p. 170.

The succession of economic crises and mounting geo-political insta-
bility in the first decade of the new century provided a further impulse for
the assault on Trotsky. As the triumphalism of the 1990s gave way to anxiety about the future of capitalism, reactionary academics recalled with fear
the impact of Isaac Deutscher's biographical trilogy—*The Prophet Armed,
Unarmed* and *Outcast*—on a generation of politically radicalized youth in
the 1960s. Deutscher's biography led students to even more dangerous material, the writings of Trotsky himself! Throughout Europe and the Americas,
tens of thousands of young people experienced the overwhelming intellectual
impact of the writings of this political and literary genius. In a period of new
and—quite possibly, even greater crisis, was there not a danger that this process might be repeated? How was this to be prevented? Thus, within the space
of six years, the three anti-Trotsky biographies of Professors Swain, Thatcher
and Service appeared. Each of these biographies began with an explicit denunciation of Deutscher's work. "Deutscher went along with, and indeed
helped to foster the Trotsky myth," declared Swain.[5] Thatcher mockingly described Deutscher's biography as reading like "a boy's own adventure story"
and complained that he relied too much on Trotsky's own writings.[6] Service
dismissed Deutscher as one who "worshipped at Trotsky's shrine."[7] These
books were written with the obvious purpose of inoculating readers against
the influence of Trotsky. As Swain bluntly wrote in the second sentence of
his book: "Readers of this biography will not find their way to Trotskyism."[8]

None of these authors emerged from their anti-Trotsky project with either their integrity or reputation intact. I have spent a significant part of the
last three years exposing the innumerable falsifications and distortions contained in these books. At times, I have felt something like a lawyer who has
only one client. But any hope that I might find some respite from the task
of refuting anti-Trotsky slanders and falsification is premature. In October I
went to Germany to speak at a meeting in Berlin that had been called to com-
memorate the seventieth anniversary of Trotsky's assassination. I was compelled to devote a substantial portion of my remarks to rebutting a diatribe
against Trotsky that had been recently written by a member of the history

---

[5] Geoffrey Swain, *Trotsky* (New York: Pearson Longman, 2006), p. 1.

[6] Ian D. Thatcher, *Trotsky* (London: Routledge, 2003), pp. 14-16.

[7] Robert Service, *Trotsky: a biography* (London: Macmillan, 2009), p. xxi.

[8] Swain, p. 1.

faculty at the Humboldt University. The campaign against Trotsky is clearly not an exclusively Anglo-American enterprise.

In fact, yet another addition to anti-Trotskyist literature has been recently provided by the Russian historian Roy Medvedev. This is a name with which students of Soviet historiography are familiar. He established an international reputation with the publication of *Let History Judge*. The first English-language edition of this work was published in 1972. The second, revised, edition appeared in 1989. *Let History Judge* was widely seen as the first significant attempt by a Soviet historian to expose the crimes of Stalin and Stalinism. Medvedev's political outlook was that of a moderate reformer. His writings were directed toward and reflected the outlook of the Khrushchevite and later the Gorbachevite wings of the Soviet bureaucracy. He was never politically sympathetic to Trotsky. Nevertheless, he wrote in *Let History Judge*: "Specifically in regard to Leon Trotsky, his activities and tragic fate require a precise and carefully weighed political and legal evaluation."[9]

That was written 21 years ago. In his recent essay, which appears as the introduction to a new biography of Leon Trotsky by the Ukrainian-American scholar Georgii Cherniavskii, Medvedev resorts to the same falsifications that he refuted in *Let History Judge*. Ironically, Medvedev's introductory essay contradicts the generally favorable portrait of Trotsky provided by Cherniavskii. It is as if the publishers felt an obligation to counter-balance Cherniavskii's positive presentation with Medvedev's harshly negative and dishonest declarations.

There is a staggering contrast between what Medvedev wrote in 1989 and what he writes in 2010. In *Let History Judge*, Medvedev stated:

> It is well known that the Petrograd Soviet played the key role in the organization and preparation of the insurrection and that it was headed by Trotsky. ... The result of the victorious armed insurrection in Petrograd was the transfer of power to the Soviets. The Provisional Government was overthrown.[10]
>
> ... Trotsky's role in the practical preparation and implementation of the October Revolution was exceptionally important, as a

---

[9]   Roy Medvedev, *Let History Judge*, (New York: Columbia University Press, 1989), p. 18.

[10]   Ibid, pp. 47-48.

great many accounts by direct participants and eyewitnesses of the October insurrection attest.[11]

But what does Medvedev say now?

> Yes, in October 1917 Trotsky headed both the Petrograd Soviet and the Military-Revolutionary Committee of this Soviet. An armed uprising was prepared, but it was not needed: power passed from the Provisional Government into the hands of the Soviets swiftly and peacefully; the Red Guards had to take by force only the Moscow Kremlin.[12]

Thus, in order to belittle Trotsky's role in the October Revolution, Medvedev does away with the insurrection in Petrograd. There really was, you see, nothing for Trotsky to do on the evening of October 24–25, 1917. This version is a variant on the approach taken by Ian Thatcher's former colleague at Glasgow University, Professor James White, who wrote in the *Journal of Trotsky Studies* that on the evening of the insurrection, the inept and hapless Trotsky was left behind in the Smolny Institute by his more capable comrades, such as Stalin, to simply answer the phone.

Medvedev wrote in 1989:

> There is no question that Trotsky's activity played a fundamental role in transforming the Red Army from a conglomerate of guerilla and semi-guerilla formations into a fairly disciplined military machine. Trotsky was able to organize tens of thousands of former tsarist officers to work in the army, from noncommissioned officers up to and including generals. If it is true that the Red Army would not have been able to win the civil war without military commissars, it is also true that it could not have done so without military specialists.[13]

But now Medvedev asserts: "To over-emphasize Trotsky by name as the 'commander-in-chief' of the Red Army was primarily to the advantage of the White-Guard generals."[14]

---

[11]   Ibid, pp. 102.

[12]   Roy Medvedev, "Predislovie" [Foreword], in: Georgii Cherniavskii, *Lev Trotskii* (Moskva: Molodaia Gvardiia, 2010), p. 9 (unpublished English translation from the Russian).

[13]   *Let History Judge*, p. 104.

[14]   "Predislovie", p. 10.

In *Let History Judge*, Medvedev acknowledged that Trotsky's role in the leadership of the Bolshevik Party was second only to that of Lenin. He wrote:

> In 1921–1922 Trotsky was considered the second most important figure in the Bolshevik leadership. Greetings in honor of comrades Lenin and Trotsky were announced at many rallies and meetings, and portraits of Lenin and Trotsky hung on the walls of many Soviet and party institutions. Trotsky's name occurred in songs and military marches. This period was undoubtedly the high point of Trotsky's career as a revolutionary and political leader of the Soviet state. Lenin's attitude toward Trotsky at this time was one of emphatic respect, as was Trotsky's toward Lenin.[15]

But Medvedev's 2010 essay offers a very different appraisal:

> However, in actual fact the Bolshevik Party of 1917 had no "second leaders." ... Trotsky often called himself "second" [after Lenin], and was inwardly convinced that he was. This belief formed the basis of his pretensions to power and to Lenin's heritage after the leader had died.
>
> However, as the great Niccolo Paganini once noted, there are many "seconds." It is therefore more precise to speak not about a "second leader," but about a "second rank" of leaders, among whom we can see in 1917–1920 not only Lev Trotsky, but also Yakov Sverdlov, Joseph Stalin, Lev Kamenev, Grigory Zinoviev, Feliks Dzerzhinsky, as well as Nikolai Bukharin and Nikolai Krestinsky.[16]

Medvedev's attempt to demote Trotsky is, as he knows all too well, a blatant falsification of the historical record. Yakov Sverdlov played a significant role in the organizational structure of the Bolshevik Party. He was not, however, an independent political leader, let alone a theoretician. As for Stalin, Kamenev and Zinoviev, their checkered political roles in 1917 are well known. All three, at one point or another, opposed the independent struggle for power by the working class. In March 1917, Stalin and Kamenev (as well as Sverdlov) adopted a conciliatory position toward the bourgeois Provisional Government. In October 1917, Kamenev and Zinoviev opposed the insurrection. Dzerzhinsky played an important role in the early years of the revolution

---

[15] *Let History Judge*, p. 109.

[16] "Predislovie", p. 8.

as leader of the Cheka, the state police organization established by the Soviet regime to fight the counterrevolutionary forces. Bukharin, without question, was a significant, though erratic, leader. But neither Dzerzhinsky nor Bukharin remotely approached the stature of Trotsky as revolutionary leaders. As for Krestinsky, a future member of the Left Opposition (and victim of Stalin's purges), he would have been the last person to denigrate Trotsky's role as the co-leader of the October Revolution.

In his current effort to diminish Trotsky's role in 1917, Medvedev minimizes the significance of a well-known comment by Lenin:

> On 1 November 1917, at a session of the Petrograd Party Committee, Lenin called Trotsky "the best Bolshevik." But this was a deliberate exaggeration, since Trotsky had only joined the Bolsheviks in the summer of 1917 and had been elected a member of the RSDLP (b) at the Sixth Congress.[17]

In fact, there was nothing off the cuff in this assessment. It was made by Lenin in the midst of a bitter life-and-death struggle against his opponents within the leadership of the Bolshevik Party who were demanding that he accept the formation of a coalition government with the Mensheviks. The fate of the Bolshevik Party and the revolution was at stake. As recounted by Alex Rabinowitch in his *Bolsheviks in Power*:

> At the Petersburg Committee meeting, evidently struggling to maintain his composure with only mixed success, Lenin charged that the behavior of the Central Committee's representatives in the Vikzhel meetings was treasonous. The only Bolshevik leader he singled out for praise was Trotsky. "Trotsky recognized long ago that unification is impossible and from that time on there has been no better Bolshevik."[18]

In his essay on Trotsky in *Revolutionary Silhouettes*, Anatole Lunacharsky, the Bolshevik commissar of culture, described Trotsky as "the second great leader of the Russian revolution." Attempting to compare Lenin and Trotsky, Lunacharsky credited Lenin as a revolutionary politician of "infallible instinct," less prone to be swayed by his emotions, if only temporarily.

---

[17] Ibid.

[18] Alexander Rabinowitch, *Bolsheviks in Power*, (Bloomington: Indiana University Press, 2007) p. 33.

Lunacharsky's assessment, written in 1919, included the following significant qualifications:

> It would be wrong to imagine, however, that *the second great leader of the Russian revolution* is inferior to his colleague in everything: there are, for instance, aspects in which Trotsky incontestably surpasses him—he is more brilliant, he is clearer, he is more active. Lenin is fitted as no one else to take the chair at the Council of People's Commissars and to guide the world revolution with the touch of genius, but he could never have coped with the titanic mission which Trotsky took upon his own shoulders, with those lightning moves from place to place, those astounding speeches, those fanfares of on-the-spot orders, that role of being the unceasing electrifier of a weakening army, now at one spot, now at another. There is not a man on earth who could have replaced Trotsky in that respect.[19] [Italics added]

Medvedev's essay, contemptuous of the historical record, abounds with numerous derogatory comments: "Trotsky little distinguished himself as People's Commissar of Foreign Affairs,"[20] "In the 1930s Trotsky's role and influence were inflated and exaggerated by European governments ..."[21] "No one, either in the past or present, could coherently outline even in a small pamphlet certain 'foundations of Trotskyism.'"[22]

Such statements indicate the extent of Medvedev's intellectual regression. But even worse, in the light of Medvedev's past work, is his new appraisal of Stalin. The greatest strength of *Let History Judge* was its denunciation of Stalin's role in Soviet history. Medvedev explained that *Let History Judge* was written, in part, to answer "stubborn attempts to rehabilitate Stalin that have persisted since 1969."[23] He argued against those in the Soviet bureaucracy who sought, in one way or another, to justify or minimize Stalin's criminal activities. Medvedev opposed the widespread claim that Stalin's activities in the 1920s were correct, and that only his later actions should be condemned.

---

[19] Anatole Lunacharsky, *Revolutionary Silhouettes*, (London: Penguin Press, 1967), p. 68.

[20] "Predislovie", p. 9.

[21] Ibid, p. 10.

[22] Ibid.

[23] *Let History Judge*, p. xiv.

Stalin had inflicted devastating damage to the cause of socialism in the Soviet Union and internationally. Medvedev explained that while Stalin used Marxist phrases to legitimize his actions, he was never a Marxist.

But now Medvedev offers an entirely different appraisal of Stalin, who, he writes:

> ... much better than Trotsky studied all of Lenin's works, many of which Trotsky never even read. It was Stalin, therefore, who was able rather quickly and successfully to rework Lenin's theoretical heritage into a rather integral conception of the 'foundations of Leninism'... Neither Trotsky, nor Bukharin, nor Kamenev, nor Zinoviev was able to do this, although they tried. All of Trotsky's attempts to base himself on Lenin's theoretical and political heritage proved unsuccessful and were easily refuted by Stalin. But without the support of Lenin's heritage, Trotsky had no chance at winning recognition and achieving victory.[24]

And so the reader is led to conclude that it was Stalin who represented the heritage of Lenin, and that accounts for his victory over Trotsky. Medvedev gives other reasons for Stalin's victory: "[W]hen it came to the force of character, to political will, ruthlessness and many other qualities that are needed in the struggle for power, Stalin greatly surpassed Trotsky."[25] But in *Let History Judge*, Medvedev wrote scornfully of those who spoke with admiration of Stalin's "will":

> An assassin who shoots from ambush hardly needs a stronger will than his victim. An honorable man abstains from crimes not because he lacks a strong character; his character is simply directed toward other goals. Too often we call a man strong who violates all the accepted norms of human relations and all the rules of honorable struggle; the more he flouts these rules, the stronger and more resolute he seems to some people. In fact, most crimes evince not strength of will, but weakness of moral principles.[26]

What accounts for Medvedev's terrible intellectual degeneration? He is clearly another victim of the collapse of the USSR, which has destroyed his

---

[24] "Predislovie", p. 9.

[25] Ibid.

[26] *Let History Judge*, p. 593.

political and moral equilibrium. Medvedev has become a fervent admirer of Vladimir Putin, whom he compares to Peter the Great! This disorientation is not simply a matter of Medvedev's personal weakness. Notwithstanding his earlier condemnation of Stalinism, his political opposition to Trotskyism foreclosed the possibility of achieving a comprehensive critique of the Soviet regime. Its collapse took him by surprise, and he drifted, like so many other Soviet intellectuals, into the reactionary milieu of Russian nationalism and chauvinism. This is what has drawn him to Stalin.

In his better years, Medvedev wrote that Stalinism might legitimately be described as a "serious and prolonged disease of Soviet society." This was a fruitful and suggestive idea, which can be of use in an investigation of anti-Trotskyism. There is a distinctly pathological element in the persistence, over many decades, of the falsification of every aspect of Trotsky's thought and activities. But the source of this disease is not biological, but social. It is a manifestation of intense contradictions in society. In periods of mounting crisis, anti-Trotskyism flares up as an ideological defense mechanism against the revolutionary critique of the existing social order and the growing potential for working class resistance to capitalist oppression.

Alexander Rabinowitch—one of the few contemporary historians who, though not a Marxist, still deeply believes in the historical significance of October—made this same point in a more direct and simple way. Why, I asked him recently, did the attacks on Trotsky continue 70 years after his death. "Because," he replied, "Trotsky is still a threat." Indeed, to all those who defend injustice and inequality, he certainly is.

Part IV

Three Lectures
in Germany

Leon Trotsky, Commissar of War 1918-1925

Seventy Years Since the Assassination of Leon Trotsky[1]

Seventy years, more than two-thirds of a century, have passed since the assassination of Leon Trotsky. In political terms, this is a substantial period of time. It is a platitude to state the obvious: that so much has changed since 1940. The world of Churchill, Roosevelt and Hitler *seems*—the verb has been chosen with deliberation—to belong to a long-past era. Whether it is really so far behind us is a question that demands very serious consideration, especially when one examines the reception of Leon Trotsky by historians. Whatever else has changed in the world, Trotsky remains an extraordinarily contemporary figure. Even after the passage of 70 years, the passions evoked by his name have not subsided.

Two days after Trotsky's assassination, the *New York Times*, in an editorial that welcomed his death, wrote spitefully: "The victims of his cold cruelty ... can be numbered in the millions. ... It was not enough for him that Russia should be drenched in blood and suffering; the whole world had to wade through a sea of violence so that the triumph of the proletariat could be assured."

The vitriol of the editorialists who penned those lines can be understood. They feared Trotsky as the greatest revolutionary of their time. He represented a threat to their interests and way of life. They were writing about an enemy whose deeds had shaped the world in which they lived. However, the editorialists could not help but acknowledge the immense scale of their adversary's achievements:

---

[1] Report given to a meeting in Berlin on October 17, 2010.

He was a powerful writer, an orator who could sway vast crowds, an organizer of sheer genius ... It was Trotsky, newly arrived in Russia from New York's East Side, who took a nondescript, ragged mass of Russians and welded them into the Red Army. He drove every "white" general from the soil of Russia, he broke every Allied attempt to restore the old regime, he gave a semblance of order to a transport and supply system that had been sunk in utter chaos.

Seventy years after Trotsky's death, the anger of his enemies has not subsided. In the course of the last seven years, three biographies of Trotsky, by British historians, have been published. The first, by Ian Thatcher, appeared in 2003. The second, by Geoffrey Swain, was brought out in 2005. The most recent, by Robert Service, was published, amidst great fanfare, last year. There is not a trace of historical detachment, objectivity, let alone basic honesty, in these biographies. The authors write about Trotsky as if he were a living political opponent and their personal enemy. Oddly enough, the editorialists of the *Times*, writing in 1940, for all their politically-embittered anger, were more scrupulous in their attitude toward the facts. They, at least, acknowledged the vast historical role played by Trotsky.

I have spent no small amount of time answering and refuting the books of Thatcher, Swain and Service, which are all shameless exercises in historical distortion and falsification. My essays and lectures on these three authors have been collected and brought together in a book that runs to approximately 200 pages. I am indebted to the Mehring Verlag for having produced a German-language edition of this book. I would like to be able to say that my critique was exhaustive in its refutation of Swain, Thatcher and Service. Unfortunately, I was compelled, under the pressure of time and other responsibilities, to concentrate my attention on only the most egregious of these writers' falsifications of the historical record.

I had hoped, with the publication of *In Defense of Leon Trotsky*, that it might be possible to take a welcome respite from the less than pleasant task of answering so-called historians who make a career of falsifying and distorting. Alas, that wish is not likely to be fulfilled. Before my coming to Germany, the comrades of the Partei für Soziale Gleichheit (PSG—Socialist Equality Party) informed me of the decidedly hostile attitude of the faculty of the Department of History at the Humboldt University to the scheduled public lecture of Professor Alexander Rabinowitch on the October Revolution. The department was unwilling to make available a suitable lecture hall, or even formally welcome Rabinowitch's presence at the Humboldt—if only by inviting him for a cup of coffee.

I was interested to discover the source of the history faculty's hostility to Professor Rabinowitch's lecture. Certainly, something more than bad manners was involved. And, as a review of the writings of members of this faculty quickly established, that is most definitely the case.

The online archive of the history faculty at the Humboldt includes a review of Robert Service's *Trotsky*[2] by university lecturer Andreas Oberender. He is a junior member of the faculty working under the direction of Professor Jörg Baberowski. Oberender's work demonstrates, if nothing else, that the contemporary campaign to discredit Trotsky is not a uniquely Anglo-American exercise.

Oberender's enthusiasm for Service's biography knows no bounds. He joyfully welcomes Service's long-overdue demolition of the "myth" of Trotsky's world-historical significance. As if following a script written by Service himself, Oberender repeats the latter's dismissal of the renowned Trotsky biographies of Isaac Deutscher and Pierre Broué. These writers were mere "apologists" and "worshippers" of Trotsky.

In contrast, Oberender praises Service as the "ideal biographer" of Trotsky: "Completely above suspicion of any connection to Trotskyism, he possesses the required critical distance to his protagonist..." Oberender fails to consider that Service's association with the virulently anti-communist Hoover Institute at Stanford University calls into question his claim of "critical distance" and objectivity.

Despite his unqualified praise for Service's biography, Oberender has nothing concrete to say about it. He does not cite even a single sentence from this supposedly brilliant work. Instead, he devotes almost all of his review to his own vicious denunciation of Trotsky.

Oberender writes, "Without his already early apparent writing and speaking talents he would have merely remained a young revolutionary among many. He had no other means of drawing attention to himself apart from his rhetoric."

How is one to answer such a banal and absurd statement? What would one think of a biographer of Count Leo Tolstoy who wrote, "Without his talent as a writer, Tolstoy would have simply remained a wealthy landowner

---

[2] See, http://www2.h-net.msu.edu/reviews/showrev.php?id=30601
for German review (not available in English).

among many others. Had he not written *War and Peace, Anna Karenina, Resurrection,* and *The Death of Ivan Ilyitch,* no one would care about Tolstoy. Except for his skill as a writer, he had no means to call attention to himself." Yes, how profoundly true!

Underlying Oberender's diatribe against Trotsky is a bitter hatred of the socialist movement. He continues:

> Trotsky's development hardly differed from that of the typical left-wing member of the radical intelligentsia alienated by the Tsarist regime. The milieu of his socialization was the unhealthy hotbed of fractional in-fighting predominating in the circle of émigrés and editorial boards with their endless scholastic debates over the purity of the Marxist doctrine and the correct path to revolution.

Trotsky, according to Oberender, "never emerged from the suffocating influence of Russian social democracy; the reader looks in vain for any signs of candor and willingness to reach out to other intellectuals and ideological milieus."

What astonishing ignorance! Trotsky's activities and influence, before 1917, was not confined to the milieu of the Russian social democracy. He was a major figure in the European socialist movement, well known to all the major leaders of the Second International—including Ramsey MacDonald, the British Fabian and future prime minister. Trotsky spoke and wrote fluently in French and German. He was, at least before 1914, on close personal terms with Karl Kautsky and his articles appeared in *Die Neue Zeit.* Trotsky was considered an outstanding authority on the politics of the Balkans. As for the range of his cultural interests, not even Service denies that Trotsky wrote on a wide range of intellectual, literary and artistic trends. Trotsky wrote on subjects such as Nietzsche, Ibsen, and the European artistic avant-garde.

Oberender continues: "The adoption and reception of Marxism by the young Trotsky graphically demonstrates what happens when an undoubtedly agile and responsive intellect submits to an ideology, which walls itself within a hermetically sealed conceptual structure and recognizes reality only through the prism of rigid dogma and irrefutable truths."

Oberender, in a manner typical of vulgar pragmatists, attempts to deride as "dogmatic" those like Trotsky who are conscious of theoretical method and who think systematically. He fails to identify the "rigid dogmas" and "irrefutable truths" that supposedly marred Trotsky's thinking. Presumably, Oberender has in mind the entire opus of Marxist thought, its foundations in philosophical materialism, and the materialist conception of history. It does not occur to Oberender that his own assertions, laid down without supporting arguments, exemplify the sort of dogmatic thinking of which he accuses Trotsky.

Oberender goes on: "Impartial analysis and objective argumentation were not Trotsky's cup of tea; he was a master of grandiose phrases and abrasive polemics, gifted with the dubious talent of masking the most abstruse and outlandish ideas in dazzling rhetorical pomp. His stylistic excesses went hand in hand with a striking lack of substance and profundity."

Oberender assumes that his readers are totally ignorant of Trotsky's literary opus and the immense influence that he exerted through his writings on public opinion. Brecht said in 1931, in conversation with Walter Benjamin and Emil Hesse-Burri, that Trotsky could be justly considered the greatest writer in Europe. And Brecht, it should be noted, was not a political supporter of Trotsky. Any professional academic capable of writing such dishonest and unadulterated rubbish forfeits all right to be taken seriously as a historian.

Trotsky's writings on European and world politics over a period of nearly 40 years are unequaled in their perspicacity. Nevertheless Oberender continues:

> Trotsky wrote vast numbers of texts in quick succession, assuming the competence to address all manner of issues, with the result that his unrestrained urge to communicate descended into empty verbiage. Significantly, in June 1926 the Politburo called upon Trotsky to rein in his mass production of texts and concentrate more on the posts and tasks given to him by the party.

Oberender's sympathies are with Stalin and the rest of Trotsky's factional opponents in the Soviet Politburo. He fails to note that the Stalinist efforts to censure Trotsky were part of an expanding campaign to silence and legally proscribe the greatest and most popular opponent of the growing bureaucracy.

Oberender descends ever lower. In a ludicrous exercise in counter-factual history, he asks: "What would have become of Trotsky if the Tsarist regime had not collapsed as a result of the First World War? He would have then had to make his way through life as a left radical journalist and aging revolutionary in waiting."

And what, we might similarly ask, would have happened to Lincoln without the crisis of the union? He would have remained a small town lawyer. Or what would have happened to Luther without the conflict between Rome

and the German princes that set the stage for the Reformation? On a somewhat more modest scale, what, one might wonder, would have happened to
Frau Merkel without the fall of the Berlin Wall? Oberender asks us to consider, in essence, what would have become of Trotsky if the 20th century hadn't
happened! But, without Herr Oberender's permission, it did happen, and he
is not pleased with the results.

> In times of revolution and civil war he quit his desk in order to agi-
> tate among the masses and the Red Army to take up arms against
> the Whites. His rhetorical and organizational talents, together
> with his undoubtedly unsentimental approach to the use of vio-
> lence, allowed him to quickly become one of the best known and
> most influential party leaders.

In other words, in the maelstrom of war and revolution, in which millions
of people became engaged in massive political struggles, Trotsky emerged as
one of the great figures of world history!

Oberender now wants to undo what occurred in history. "What remains
from Trotsky and his mystique? ... Having read the [Service] biography there
can be no doubt that on the basis of a critical examination not much remains
of Trotsky's once overblown reputation. His writings belong mostly in a cabinet of curiosities, and the extravagance of his thought strikes one today, in our
own non-ideological age, as strange, if not bizarre. The Fourth International
he founded is barely a footnote in the history of the workers' movement."

Mr. Oberender, I understand, was born in what was once East Germany.
How would he assess today the place of the Stalinist ruling SED in the history
of the workers' movement? Or, for that matter, that of the Communist Party
of the Soviet Union? What remains of these reactionary bureaucratic structures? Trotsky foretold the fate of the Stalinist parties: "Of these reactionary
organizations," he wrote, "not one stone will be left on another."

As Mr. Oberender indulged in speculation as to what would have been
Trotsky's fate had not War and Revolution intervened, he cannot object when
I pose the question: What would have happened to Mr. Oberender had the
German Democratic Republic not collapsed? Frankly, I doubt that his life
would have proceeded all that differently. A place would have been found for
his meager talents somewhere within the academic structures of the GDR.
He might have even found a place within the Humboldt University. Indeed,
the review he has written of the Service biography could have been published
in a Stalinist journal without a single word being changed!

Oberender claims that Trotsky's writings belong in a cabinet of curiosities, which have no relevance to our times. A strange verdict, coming from a historian—especially one whose specialty, supposedly, is the history of the Soviet Union. To say that Trotsky is irrelevant is tantamount to dismissing the historical significance of what must be counted among the most important events of the 20th century—the Russian Revolution. Is it possible to understand the political strategy that guided the October Revolution without reference to the writings of Leon Trotsky? No serious historian could exclude from his study of 1917 a careful reading of Trotsky's *History of the Russian Revolution*, which also happens to be one of the indisputable masterpieces of world literature. Similarly, a study of Trotsky's *Revolution Betrayed* remains the essential work not only for historians, but for anyone today who wishes to understand what the Soviet Union was and the origin and nature of the social, economic and political contradictions that led to its dissolution in 1991—a fate foreseen by Trotsky in 1936!

To a degree unequalled by any other writer of his lifetime, Trotsky's literary work remains extraordinarily contemporary. For all the many changes in the world over the last 70 years, Trotsky dealt with issues, processes and problems that remain with us to this day: the nature of world economy and its relationship to the nation-state; the significance and implications of the global hegemony of American imperialism; and the fragility of bourgeois democracy. Of course, Mr. Oberender does not even provide the title of a single work by Trotsky. But of all his omissions, the most troubling is his failure to even note what must be considered, at least by a German historian, among Trotsky's greatest achievements: his analysis of German fascism and his impassioned warning of the colossal menace that Nazism posed to the German and international working class.

Does Mr. Oberender believe that these writings, too, belong in a cabinet of historical curiosities? Have these no relevance to our supposedly "non-ideological" age? Even as we meet, a major exhibit on the Nazi regime has been mounted in Berlin's Museum of History. To this day, German politics and culture is scarred by the Nazi victory in January 1933 and its aftermath. But this victory was achieved by the fascists only as a consequence of the cowardly and irresponsible policies of the Social Democratic and Communist parties, which refused to unite the millions of socialist workers in Germany for a common struggle against Hitler.

Trotsky's warnings on the danger posed by fascism rank among the most prescient political documents written in the 20th century. They are all the more extraordinary for having been written by Trotsky while he lived in enforced exile in Turkey. Trotsky called for a united front of the working class against the Nazis, and denounced both the SPD's pathetic subordination to Hindenburg and the Stalinist party's criminally irresponsible identification of the Social Democracy with fascism. While the Stalinist KPD claimed, with a mixture of demagogy and terrified fatalism, that a Nazi victory would lead quickly to a communist revolution, Trotsky warned that Hitler's assumption of power would represent a political catastrophe of unimaginable dimensions.

All claims that it would have made no difference if Trotsky had emerged victorious from the inner-party struggle are refuted by the events in Germany. If no other issue had divided Trotsky and Stalin, the collision over Germany was of sufficient historical moment to justify the claim that Trotsky's defeat had the most tragic consequences.

Permit me to refer to one document written by Trotsky in April 1932, nine months before Hitler's victory. What would be the appropriate response of the Soviet government to a fascist victory? Trotsky wrote:

> ... My relations with the present Moscow government are not such that I have any right to speak in its name or refer to its intentions, about which I, like every other reader and man of politics, can judge only on the basis of all the information accessible. But I am all the more free to say how in my opinion the Soviet government *ought* to act in case of a fascist state victory in Germany. Upon receiving the telegraphic communication of this event I would sign an order for the mobilization of the reserves. When you have a mortal enemy before you, and when war flows with necessity from the logic of the objective situation, it would be unpardonable lightmindedness to give that enemy time to establish and fortify himself ... and thus grow up to the dimensions of a colossal danger.[3]

Does Mr. Oberender believe that these words, too, belong in a cabinet of historical curiosities?

What assessment is to be made of Leon Trotsky, 70 years after his death? We now have the advantage of historical perspective. We know the outcome of the political conflicts in which Trotsky played so central a role. We know the fate of the Soviet Union, and of the Stalinist regime that came to power on the basis of the political struggle against Trotsky.

---

[3] Leon Trotsky, *Writings of Leon Trotsky, 1932* (New York: Pathfinder Press, 2002) p. 92.

The question must be asked: Which perspective was confirmed by subsequent historical development: the Stalin-Bukharin theory of "socialism in one country" or Trotsky's refutation of the possibility of establishing socialism on a national basis? Which perspective anticipated the trajectory of economic development: Stalin's autarkic conception of national socialism or Trotsky's insistence on the primacy of global economic processes?

The history of the Soviet Union, taken as a whole, establishes that the campaign against Trotsky and Trotskyism, which began in the Politburo in 1923, marked the onset of a right-wing and essentially Russian nationalist reaction against the revolutionary internationalist program on which the October Revolution had been based. Within little more than a decade, the expulsion of the internationalists within the Soviet Communist Party developed into an unrestrained campaign of political genocide aimed at the physical extermination of all the representatives of Marxist politics and culture within the socialist intelligentsia and working class.

The Soviet Union emerged from the anti-socialist terror of the 1930s a politically scarred society. Stalin's campaign of mass murder, which included the destruction of virtually the entire officer corps of the Soviet Union, abetted the Nazis and facilitated their subsequent invasion. The horrifying human losses suffered by the USSR between 1941 and 1945 were attributable, to a great extent, to the impact of the Stalinist purges. The Soviet victory in World War II could not, in the long run, reverse the disastrous political trajectory of the USSR. All the frantic reform efforts of the Soviet bureaucracy, after Stalin's death in 1953, developed on the basis of the nationalist program that formed the basis of the Stalinist regime. The system left behind by Stalin staggered from crisis to crisis until its collapse less than 38 years after the dictator's death. And the form of that collapse—the dissolution of the USSR by the bureaucracy, the conversion of nationalized property into private property, and the transformation of sections of the bureaucracy into capitalist multi-billionaires—proceeded along the lines anticipated by Trotsky in the 1930s.

In conclusion, I would like to address the relevance of Trotsky today. What is Trotsky's place in history? As a writer, orator, strategist of revolutionary insurrection, military leader and political thinker, Trotsky represents the summit of socialist politics and culture in the 20th century. Before 1917 Trotsky elaborated the strategy of the Russian Revolution. During the years of revolution and civil war, he personified the proletariat's will to victory. And later, in the face of political defeat and isolation, as a hunted exile, Trotsky rose to still greater political and moral heights—as the implacable opponent

of the Stalinist counterrevolution and the strategist of the future world socialist revolution.

In a way unequalled by any other figure, Trotsky defined what it meant
to be a revolutionary socialist in the 20th century. That Lenin was a towering
figure in the history of socialism is beyond dispute. But his life and work are
embedded in the Russian Revolution, with all its contradictions. His death
in January 1924 came as the reaction against the October Revolution, within
the party that he had created, was only beginning to unfold. In the final weeks
of his conscious political life, beset with anxiety over the fate of the revolution, Lenin—as documented in his final writings—turned to Trotsky for
support. In the struggle against Stalinism, Trotsky's political work acquired a
world historical significance. The Russian Revolution was a great episode in
Trotsky's life—an episode in his struggle for the victory of the international
working class. Trotsky personified and represented the world socialist revolution. Moreover, in the fight against Stalinism, Trotsky rescued socialism from
the abyss into which it had been dragged by the Kremlin gangsters and their
political accomplices.

No political tendency that calls itself socialist can define its program, can
define its relationship to Marxism today, except through the political conceptions and political struggles developed by Trotsky. The Fourth International,
which he founded in 1938, has endured and developed as the political expression of genuine Marxism. Seventy years after his death, Trotsky, the greatest
political figure of the last century, remains the most important teacher of socialists in the new century.

Leon Trotsky and the Defense
of Historical Truth[1]

I would like, first of all, to thank the Partei für Soziale Gleichheit for inviting me to speak this evening in Leipzig, which is one of the historic centers of the German socialist workers' movement. In the years before World War I, as the right-wing and opportunist tendencies within the Social Democratic Party (SPD) were exercising ever greater influence inside the SPD, the *Leipziger Volkszeitung* was the principal newspaper through which the revolutionary wing of the party, led by Rosa Luxemburg, defended the principles of genuine Marxism. Two decades later, in the critical years prior to the Nazi takeover in 1933, Leipzig was a major center of Trotskyist activity in Germany. The German Trotskyists were affiliated with the International Left Opposition that had been founded by Trotsky to fight against the disastrous policies of the Stalinist regime within the Soviet Union and internationally. In 1931, Trotsky, who had been expelled from the USSR and was living on the Turkish island of Prinkipo, declared that Germany was the "key" to the international situation. The growing power of the Nazi party, Trotsky warned, posed a mortal threat to the German, Soviet and international working class. He declared that a Nazi victory would be a catastrophe of unprecedented dimensions. It would be a staggering defeat of the most powerful socialist movement in Western Europe, would result in the establishment of a barbaric dictatorship, and would set into motion a chain of events leading to the outbreak of a second world war.

---

[1] Lecture at the University of Leipzig on March 16, 2012.

And yet, despite the colossal political stakes, the two mass parties of the German working class, the Social Democratic Party and the Communist Party (KPD), were pursuing policies that were removing all obstacles to Hitler's victory. The SPD, Trotsky explained, was clinging desperately to the rotting corpse of the Weimar regime, depending on the bourgeois state to bar the Nazi Party's path to power. The KPD, following the instructions it received from Stalin, pursued the mindless policy of "social fascism." That is, the KPD declared that there existed no significant differences between the Social Democracy, a mass party of the working class, and the NSDAP (Nazis), the mass party of the reactionary German petty-bourgeoisie. On this basis, the KPD leaders rejected Trotsky's call for a united front of the two mass working class parties against the Nazi danger.

Between 1931 and 1933, Trotsky sought to arouse the most politically conscious sections of the German working class and the socialist intelligentsia to the immense danger posed by fascism and the urgent necessity for a unified struggle of the proletariat to prevent a Nazi victory. Trotsky's writings on German fascism rank among the greatest works of political literature in the twentieth century. No one else wrote with such prescience, precision and passion on the German events and their world historic implications.

This is how Trotsky defined fascism in his pamphlet *What Next?*, written in January 1932:

> Fascism is not merely a system of reprisals, of brutal force, and of police terror. Fascism is a particular governmental system based on the uprooting of all elements of proletarian democracy within bourgeois society. The task of fascism lies not only in destroying the Communist vanguard but in holding the entire class in a state of forced disunity. To this end the physical annihilation of the most revolutionary section of the workers does not suffice. It is also necessary to smash all independent and voluntary organizations, to demolish all the defensive bulwarks of the proletariat, and to uproot whatever has been achieved during three-quarters of a century by the Social Democracy and the trade unions. For, in the last analysis, the Communist Party also bases itself on these achievements.[2]

In the same pamphlet, Trotsky brilliantly characterized the political bankruptcy of the SPD:

---

[2]   See, http://www.marxists.org/archive/trotsky/germany/1932-ger/next01.htm

The present crisis that is convulsing capitalism obliged the Social Democracy to sacrifice the fruits achieved after protracted economic and political struggles and thus to reduce the German workers to the level of existence of their fathers, grandfathers, and great-grandfathers. There is no historical spectacle more tragic and at the same time more repulsive than the fetid disintegration of reformism amid the wreckage of all its conquests and hopes. The theatre is rabid in its straining for modernism. Let it stage more often Hauptmann's *The Weavers*: this most modern of modern dramas. And let the director of the theatre also remember to reserve the front rows for the leaders of the Social Democracy.[3]

Nothing written during that period on the subject of fascism is comparable to the work produced by Trotsky. The renowned journalist Kurt Tucholsky expressed his amazement that Trotsky, living in exile more than one thousand miles away, understood the political situation in Germany more clearly and profoundly than anyone else. Berthold Brecht, in discussion with Walter Benjamin and Emil Hesse-Burri, remarked that Trotsky could justly be described as the greatest European writer of his time.

But Trotsky's writings and the activities of Trotskyists in Germany could not forestall the consequences of the betrayal of the Social Democratic and Stalinist parties. Hitler came to power in January 1933, and the tragedy foreseen by Trotsky came to pass.

More than 30 years later, during the political radicalization of the 1960s, Trotsky's writings were essential reading for workers and students who wanted to understand how it was possible for fascism to come to power in Germany. I belong to a generation, born in the aftermath of World War II, which found in the writings of Leon Trotsky an incomparable analysis of the political causes of the greatest catastrophe of the twentieth century. Trotsky's writings made clear that the victory of fascism was not inevitable. Hitler's rise to power could have been prevented. Fascism was neither the irresistible outcome of the "Dialectic of Enlightenment," as claimed by Adorno and Horkheimer, nor the product of repressed sexuality, as argued by Wilhelm Reich. Fascism, the most barbaric form of bourgeois rule, came to power as a result of the failure and betrayals of the political leadership of the working class.

Trotsky's writings on Germany were only part of his extraordinary political legacy. The defense of Trotsky against lies and distortions, which continue

---

[3] Ibid.

unabated more than 70 years after his death, is necessary because of his central role in the history of the past century. All the critical events of the first four decades of the twentieth century were mirrored in his life's work. He was, next to Lenin, the most important figure in the Russian revolutionary movement, which culminated in the Bolshevik seizure of power in October 1917. The perspective and program that inspired the October Revolution was based on Trotsky's theory of permanent revolution, which he developed in the aftermath of the Russian Revolution of 1905. In the civil war that followed the October 1917 Revolution, Trotsky became the commander of the Red Army. Under his leadership, the Soviet Union was defended against counter-revolutionary forces which were backed by all the major imperialist powers.

Trotsky played a decisive role in the victory and defense of the socialist revolution in Russia. But his place in history is determined, above all, by his achievements as the foremost exponent and strategist of world socialist revolution. As far back as 1905 Trotsky had analyzed the Russian Revolution as part of a world revolutionary process. Earlier than anyone else, Trotsky had foreseen the possibility of the Russian working class coming to power in a socialist revolution. But he insisted that the fate of socialism in Russia depended, above all, on the victory of the working class in the advanced capitalist countries—above all, in Europe and the United States. The socialist revolution, Trotsky explained, may achieve its first victory in a national arena. But its survival is possible only to the extent that the revolution expands beyond the national boundaries within which it conquered power. The final victory of socialism is achieved with the overthrow of capitalism on a world scale.

In the final analysis, the central political issue that underlay the conflict that erupted inside the Russian Communist Party in the 1920s was the relationship between the building of socialism in the Soviet Union and the program of world socialist revolution which had formed the basis of the revolutionary strategy of the Bolshevik Party, under the leadership of Lenin and Trotsky, in 1917. In October 1923, Trotsky's criticism of the growth of bureaucratism within the Bolshevik Party and Soviet state led to the formation of the Left Opposition. This was a critical month in not only Soviet, but also German history. The immense crisis that had erupted in Germany in the spring of 1923, with the French occupation of the Ruhr, led rapidly to the development of a revolutionary situation. Against the background of hyper-inflation and the disorientation of the bourgeois regime, an unprecedented opportunity arose for a successful revolutionary uprising by the German working class. But what was lacking was a determined revolutionary leadership. The German Communist Party's preparations for an uprising were haphazard and indecisive. The Soviet Communist Party, increasingly dominated by Trotsky's political opponents in the party leadership, provided the KPD with contradictory advice. In the last minute, the KPD called off its plans for a nationwide insurrection. In the confusion that followed, local insurrectionary outbreaks were suppressed and the bourgeois government recovered its nerve. The German working class suffered a blow from which it never fully recovered, and which set into motion a chain of events that facilitated the explosive growth of the Nazi party.

The defeat in Germany strengthened the conservative bureaucratic tendencies within the Soviet Communist Party. As the civil war came to a conclusion, the state and party bureaucracy grew rapidly—consisting of tens of thousands of functionaries for whom a position in the apparatus meant personal security and privileges. These functionaries formed the social basis of Stalin's rapidly growing power as the general secretary of the Communist Party. The "secret" of Stalin's power lay in his attentiveness to the material interests of the growing caste of bureaucrats, who came to identify their own interests with the Soviet Union as a national state, rather than as the new center of world socialist revolution. The increasingly nationalist and conservative orientation of the bureaucracy found expression when Stalin unveiled, in 1924, the program of "socialism in one country."

This program legitimized—theoretically, politically and in practice—the separation of the development of socialism within the USSR from the cause of international socialist revolution. It sanctioned the subordination of the interests of the international working class to the national interests of the ruling bureaucracy within the Soviet Union. This separation led rapidly to bitter attacks on Trotsky's theory of permanent revolution. Trotsky's insistence that the fate of socialism in the USSR depended on the victory of the working class beyond its borders became anathema to the Soviet bureaucrats, who were concerned, above all, with their own income and privileges. As Trotsky later wrote in his autobiography, the attacks on permanent revolution were motivated by the bureaucracy's self-conscious egotism. "Not everything for world revolution," thought the petty Soviet official as he denounced Trotsky and the program of permanent revolution. "Something for me too."

Nothing is more historically absurd and politically untenable than the claim that the conflict between Stalin and Trotsky was merely a subjective fight between two individuals over personal power. The struggle that erupted inside the Soviet Communist Party in the mid-1920s was between two irreconcilably opposed programs—the nationalist pseudo-socialism of the Soviet bureaucracy led by Stalin versus the socialist internationalism of the Left Opposition led by Trotsky. The outcome of this struggle was to determine the fate of the socialist revolution in the twentieth century and, ultimately, that of the Soviet Union itself.

The shift in the program of the Soviet Communist Party was not easily achieved. The ideas and ideals of socialist internationalism were deeply ingrained in the Soviet working class. Moreover, Trotsky occupied in the minds of the advanced Soviet workers and, indeed, among socialists throughout the world, a position of respect and prestige equaled only by Lenin. In contrast, when the factional struggle began in the early 1920s, Stalin was virtually unknown. For Stalin and his allies in the party and state bureaucracy to abandon the revolutionary internationalist program, it was necessary to destroy Trotsky's political influence. But this could not be achieved without rewriting history with the aim of denying Trotsky's preeminent role in the victory of the October Revolution. Herein lay the origins and political source of the campaign of historical falsification that began in 1923.

It is not possible, in the time available to us tonight, to trace in the necessary detail all the stages of this insidious process of falsification. The lies began with the distortion of old factional disputes in the pre-1917 revolutionary movement. It proceeded through the twisting of quotations and the selective citation and misinterpretation of documents. With astonishing speed an entirely new and grotesque persona was attached to Trotsky in the Soviet press. The slanders against Trotsky and his many supporters prepared the ground for expulsion and exile. Trotsky was deported from the USSR in January 1929. In 1932, he was formally deprived of citizenship. Within the Soviet Union, the Trotskyist movement was subjected to increasingly violent repression. The bureaucracy's war against Trotskyism set the stage for a campaign of political genocide directed against all representatives of the international socialist program and culture within the Soviet working class and Marxist intelligentsia.

The three anti-Trotskyist trials held in Moscow between August 1936 and March 1938 marked the climax of the relentless process of historical falsification that had begun in 1923. In the course of these trials, the principal leaders of the Bolshevik Party were accused of plotting terror against Stalin, committing acts of sabotage within the USSR, and forming treasonous alliances with the fascist regimes in Germany and Japan. All the defendants—old revolutionaries who had devoted their entire adult lives to the cause of socialism—confessed to the most horrible crimes. But aside from their confessions, the prosecution did not produce a single piece of evidence in support of the accusations.

As has long been established, the confessions were extorted from the defendants through physical and psychological torture and threats against their families. Stalin secured the defendants' cooperation with cynical and empty promises to spare their lives and those of their loved ones if they played their assigned roles in the terrifying Moscow spectacle.

Many years later, in the early 1990s, I spoke to the daughter of Mikhail Boguslavsky, a defendant in the second trial, held in January 1937. Rebecca Boguslavskaya recalled visiting her father in the Lyubianka Prison in Moscow several weeks before the trial began. Mikhail Boguslavsky looked like a ghost—emaciated, with dark rings around his eyes. He was in pain, and moved uncomfortably in his chair. Rebecca realized that her father had been severely beaten, and that he found it difficult to place the weight of his body upon the seat. Boguslavsky looked at his daughter and cried out in agony: "You must renounce me. You must forget that I ever lived." Rebecca replied, "Papa, I will never renounce you."

At the trial itself, Boguslavsky looked somewhat better. He had been fed by his jailers, and Rebecca surmised that drugs had been administered to improve his appearance. But within hours of the trial's conclusion, Boguslavsky was shot. As for Rebecca, she was arrested soon afterwards and spent nearly two decades in a Siberian labor camp. She died in 1992 at the age of 79.

When the first of the Moscow Trials was staged in August 1936, Trotsky was living in Norway. In order to prevent Trotsky from answering the incredible charges being made against him in Moscow, the Norwegian government, controlled by the Social Democratic Party, placed Trotsky and his wife, Natalia Sedova, under house arrest. In December 1936, Trotsky was deported from Norway and placed on a freighter bound for Mexico.

In Mexico, Trotsky was finally able to reply publicly to the accusations of the Stalinist regime. He denounced the trials as a political frame-up and called for the organization of an "international counter-trial" to expose the "true criminals who hide behind the cloak of the accuser."

It must be recalled that in Europe and the United States, substantial segments of "left" public opinion—supporters of the "Popular Front" alliance of bourgeois liberals with the Stalinist parties—were willing to accept the accusations hurled against the defendants in Moscow without objection. They bitterly opposed Trotsky's call for the establishment of an independent commission of inquiry into the Moscow trials, fearing that an exposure of the lies of the Kremlin would undermine the liberal-Stalinist populist front against fascism—as if the struggle against fascism could be served through the legalized murder of revolutionaries.

Despite the opposition of liberals and Stalinists, a Commission of Inquiry into the trials was established in the spring of 1937 under the chairmanship of the greatest living American philosopher, John Dewey. The Commission traveled to Mexico in April, where for more than one week it questioned Trotsky on all matters related to the accusations against him. Trotsky's testimony consisted of a defense of his activities and his ideas over a period that spanned 40 years, beginning with his entry into revolutionary politics as a 17-year-old youth in 1897.

The climax of the Commission's work in Mexico was, undoubtedly, Trotsky's closing speech. He spoke for four and a half hours in English. I am not merely speaking as a Trotskyist partisan when I state that this oration ranks among the very greatest in world history. In one of the many remarkable passages to be found in the text, Trotsky explained the origins and significance of the lies upon which the Moscow Trials were based. The lies of the Soviet regime were not merely the product of Stalin's pathological personality. Rather, they were rooted in the material interests of the bureaucracy of which Stalin was the chief representative:

> One can understand the acts of Stalin only by starting from the conditions of existence of the new privileged stratum, greedy for power, greedy for material comforts, apprehensive for its positions, fearing the masses, and mortally hating all opposition.
>
> The position of a privileged bureaucracy in a society which that bureaucracy itself calls Socialist is not only contradictory, but also false. The more precipitate the jump from the October overturn—which laid bare all social falsehood—to the present situation, in which a caste of upstarts is forced to cover up its social ulcers, the cruder the Thermidorean lies. It is, consequently, a question not simply of the individual depravity of this or that person, but of the corruption lodged in the position of a whole social group for whom lying has become a vital political necessity.[4]

Herein lay the key to understanding not only the lies of the Moscow Trials, but, more generally, the significance of all historical falsifications. There is a

---

[4] See, http://www.marxists.org/archive/trotsky/1937/dewey/session13_c.htm

well-known saying: "If geometric axioms impinged on material interests, an attempt would be made to refute them." Similarly, to the extent that the ruling class sees the historic record as a threat to the legitimacy of its dominant position in society, it must resort to distortions and outright falsifications. The Stalinist bureaucracy resorted to the most brazen and monstrous lies to cover up its betrayal of the principles of the October Revolution, and to conceal the ever-more glaring contradiction between the real goals of socialism and the bureaucracy's defense of its own material interests as a privileged caste.

An understanding of the objective significance and social function of historical falsifications allows us to answer a highly important question: Why is it that we are still compelled to deal with lies about the historical role of Leon Trotsky? Seventy-five years have passed since the Dewey Commission, which concluded its work with an unequivocal declaration that Trotsky was innocent of all the charges leveled against him, and that the Moscow Trials were a frame-up. Fifty-six years have passed since Soviet Premier Nikita Khrushchev, in his famous "secret speech" of February 1956 before the 20th Congress of the Communist Party, denounced Stalin as a criminal and all but acknowledged that the Moscow Trials were based on lies. Twenty years have passed since the dissolution of the Soviet Union, an event that vindicated Trotsky's life-and-death struggle against the Stalinist bureaucracy. He justified his struggle against Stalinism as politically necessary if the Soviet Union was to be saved from destruction by the bureaucratic regime.

It would seem to be obvious that Trotsky is a major historical figure. Even after he lost power, he continued to exercise immense influence through his writings. Not even his assassination in August 1940 could free the bureaucracy of the specter of international Trotskyism. The publication of Isaac Deutscher's three-volume biography led to a resurgence of interest in Trotsky throughout the world. A measure of the Soviet bureaucracy's never-ending fear of Trotsky was the fact that of all the Bolshevik revolutionaries murdered by the Stalinist regime, Trotsky was the only figure who was never officially rehabilitated.

It is to be expected that Trotsky must remain, given the nature of his political aims, an intensely controversial figure. But can there be any question that his activities and his ideas deserve the most intellectually conscientious study? But if this has not happened—if, instead, we have witnessed over the past decade a renewal and intensification of the campaign of lies—it is necessary to uncover and explain the political and social necessity that motivate the unrelenting falsification of virtually every aspect of his life.

I believe that the campaign against Trotsky derives its momentum from two inter-related factors of a historical and political character. First, let us deal with the historical factor. The collapse of the Stalinist regimes in Eastern Europe and the dissolution of the USSR gave rise to an outburst of bourgeois triumphalism. Prior to 1989, predictions that the Stalinist regimes were heading toward a shipwreck could be found only in Trotskyist publications. Not a single prominent bourgeois historian or journalist had anticipated the dissolution of the East European and Soviet regimes. However, once the regimes no longer existed, bourgeois politicians, academics and journalists proclaimed that their collapse had been inevitable. The dissolution of the USSR in 1991 "proved" that the October Revolution of 1917 had been doomed from the start. From the very beginning, the socialist revolution of 1917 could lead only in one direction: to the restoration of capitalism. That this process unfolded over a period spanning nearly three-quarters of a century did not call into question the inevitability of the outcome. No other course of development was possible. The Stalinist regime was not the betrayal of the October Revolution. It was the unavoidable historical blind alley created by the events of 1917, and from which the only exit was the restoration of capitalism.

This mechanical interpretation of Soviet history demanded the denial of the very possibility of a different, non-totalitarian and socialist evolution of the USSR. No alternative path of development was to be taken seriously. This position determined the treatment of Trotsky. The struggle he waged against Stalinism was to be minimized, if not entirely ignored. On no account was he to be presented as a viable alternative to Stalin.

But, by the turn of the new century, the historical issues that demanded the denial of Trotsky's significance as an alternative to Stalinism were compounded by new political anxieties. The triumphalism evoked by the dissolution of the USSR had already begun to dissipate as the twentieth century drew to a close. The economic shocks that began with the Asian crisis in 1998 made all too clear that the end of the USSR had not cured capitalism of its own deep-rooted maladies. The conditions of life of broad sections of the working class, even before the collapse of 2008, steadily worsened in the last decade of the twentieth century and the first decade of the twenty-first. Against the backdrop of deteriorating economic conditions, the increasingly unrestrained militarism of the imperialist ruling elites—institutionalized in the aftermath of the events of 9/11 as the "war against terror"—encountered steadily mounting popular opposition. With social tensions becoming ever more palpable, bourgeois strategists such as Zbigniew Brzezinski began to voice alarm about the potentially revolutionary implications of a rapidly growing global population of well-educated but disaffected youth, unable to find decent jobs and economic security.

In these uncertain conditions, the bourgeoisie recalled the political atmosphere of the 1960s, when the writings of Trotsky—which had been suppressed for decades—suddenly became essential reading material for radicalized youth. In the far more uncertain economic environment of the new century, as workers and youth began to look for alternatives to capitalism, did there not exist the danger that Trotsky might again provide theoretical and political direction and inspiration for a new generation entering into revolutionary struggle? After all, the academic guardians of bourgeois interests asked, how many of Trotsky's damned books were in print? Works such as *The History of the Russian Revolution, The Revolution Betrayed,* and, worst of all, Trotsky's enthralling autobiography, *My Life.* What could be done to counter the revolutionary narrative of Trotsky's literary masterpiece?

The new age of pre-emptive war produced a new literary genre: the preemptive biography! In the space of little more than five years, no less than three such pre-emptive biographies of Trotsky were published. The first biography, by Professor Ian Thatcher, was published in 2003. The second biography, by Professor Geoffrey Swain, was published in 2006. I wrote a lengthy reply to these two books that was published in 2007. I exposed in detail the crude falsifications, based largely on the old lies concocted by the Stalinists, retailed by the two British historians. Whatever hope that I entertained of having silenced the anti-Trotsky enterprise of the British academic establishment was soon disappointed. Robert Service's biography appeared in 2009.

Thus, I found myself obligated to write a detailed refutation of yet another volume aimed at discrediting Trotsky. Together with my earlier analysis of the biographies of Thatcher and Swain, and two other shorter essays in which I sought to explain the contemporary relevance of Trotsky's work, the critique of Service was published in a volume entitled *In Defense of Leon Trotsky.* There is no need for me to review in detail my refutation of the works of Thatcher, Swain and Service. I believe that the quality and integrity of my effort have been substantiated by a lengthy review written by historian Bertrand Patenaude that was published last June in *The American Historical Review.* Professor Patenaude unambiguously endorsed my description of Service's biography as a piece of "hack work." Moreover, I welcome the open letter to the Suhrkamp publishing house, written by 14 distinguished European historians, endorsing my exposure of Service's book and opposing the publication of a German-language edition. That 14 outstanding historians should feel compelled to protest the publication of Service's book testifies decisively to the utterly appalling character of Service's work.

One might have thought that the open letter from 14 distinguished historians would have so discredited Robert Service that no serious historian would have intervened in his behalf. After all, the central charge against Service's biography was that it violated the most basic standards of scholarship. There were numerous factual errors. Service advanced arguments that lacked any documentary foundation. He attributed to Trotsky opinions and positions that he did not hold, including those that were the exact opposite of what Trotsky had actually written. Moreover, the historians concurred with my objections to Service's treatment of Trotsky's Jewish ancestry in a manner that tended to legitimize the anti-Semitic stereotypes and slanders that were frequently used against him.

Moreover, Suhrkamp, while not replying to the historians, has delayed publication of Service's book while retaining an "outside expert" to examine the biography and correct the most glaring factual errors. In this way, Suhrkamp is attempting to salvage what it can of a publishing disaster with the literary equivalent of plastic surgery. But the intractable nature of the problem it confronts is indicated in the promotional introduction for Service's book that is posted on the Suhrkamp web site. Suhrkamp refers to "the man born in 1879 in the southern Ukraine under the name of Lev Davidovitch Bronstein." But this statement contradicts Service's claim that Trotsky's real first name was Leiba, and that he was known by this Yiddish name throughout his youth. For the first 40 pages of the English-language edition of his biography, Service refers to the young Trotsky only as "Leiba." Service then claims that it was only after he turned eighteen that the young Bronstein decided to assume the name Lëva, in order to have a Russian-sounding name like his comrades in the revolutionary movement. In order to stress the significance of this change in Trotsky's first name, Service writes: "Semantically it had nothing to do with the Yiddish name Leiba..."

As I have already explained at length, this entire story is an invention of Service. Trotsky's first name was Lev, and he was known by this name (or a diminutive such as Lyova) from his earliest childhood. However, the false attribution of the name Leiba to the young Trotsky plays a central role in Service's biography. First, it serves to magnify Trotsky's Jewish identity in a manner frequently used by his anti-Semitic opponents. Second, Service claims that Trotsky's effort to conceal his real first name was not only an example of his recurring efforts to play down his Jewish origins, but also one of the significant inaccuracies that Service claims to have uncovered in Trotsky's autobiography.

However, it appears that Service's error in attributing the name Leiba to the young Trotsky may have been corrected by the expert hired by Suhrkamp. Thus, we are left with an interesting literary paradox. The subject of Service's biography will have been born with one name in the English edition and a quite different one in the German edition!

Suhrkamp's web site states that the Service biography will be released in July. But the open letter of the 14 historians and the long delay in the publication of the book have provoked alarm in right-wing circles and among a layer of anti-Marxist historians. The extreme right-wing newspaper *Junge Freiheit* has come to Service's defense, praising his work for repudiating any sort of sympathetic portrayal of Trotsky. The newspaper praises Service's remark at a book launch in London, "If the icepick didn't quite do its job killing him off, I hope I've managed it," as "an attractive comment."

One can hardly be surprised by the defense of Service in the pages of *Junge Freiheit*. Of greater interest are two articles in support of Service that have appeared in the pages of the *Neue Zürcher Zeitung*. Their author is Professor Dr. Ulrich M. Schmid, who teaches at the University of St. Gallen and who has written widely on matters relating to history, philosophy, literature and culture. His curriculum vitae, posted on the university web site, list more than 600 articles—a quite astonishing number. His essays appear frequently in the *Neue Zürcher Zeitung*.

The first article appeared in the *Neue Zürcher Zeitung* on December 28, 2011. Its title, somewhat predictably, was "No Alternative to Stalin." It begins by deploring that Trotsky was viewed by the '68 Generation as a viable alternative to Stalin:

> If after Lenin's death it had not been Stalin but rather Trotsky who took over the leadership of the Soviet Union—so goes the argument—then the experiment in a socialist form of society would not have relapsed into an inhumane dictatorship.
>
> Many western socialists allowed themselves to be blinded by Trotsky's intellectual brilliance, and concluded too quickly from his hostility to Stalin that Trotsky was motivated by the ideal of socialism with a human face.

Following Service's approach, Schmid attempts to refute this favorable view of Trotsky by portraying him as a sort of monster, capable of the worst abominations. He writes:

Right from the beginning of his career as commissar of war Trotsky demonstrated his utter monstrousness. He obtained the obedience of tsarist officers by taking their families as hostages.

When one reads such furious denunciations of Trotsky's actions as a military commander, one might almost believe that prior to the appearance of Trotsky on the stage of history, civil wars were non-violent and bloodless affairs, in which the opposing sides treated one another with mutual affection and unblemished kindness. And yet, as we all know, history tells a very different story. But Schmid prefers to avoid placing Trotsky's actions in a broader historical context that might explain, and even justify, his actions.

Between 1918 and 1921, as Trotsky defended the Soviet regime against the forces of counterrevolution, he knew very well the likely consequences of a Bolshevik defeat. He belonged to a generation of revolutionaries for whom the events that followed the suppression of the Paris Commune in May 1871 were still part of living memory. In the week that followed the defeat of the Commune, the victorious National Guard commanded by the bourgeois regime slaughtered somewhere between 30,000 and 50,000 workers. Adolph Thiers, president of the bourgeois regime, said of the communards: "The ground is strewn with their corpses. May this terrible sight serve as a lesson."

But Trotsky did not need the example of the Paris Commune to remind him what awaited the Bolshevik regime and the Soviet working class if the counterrevolution was victorious. The Bolsheviks and masses of workers and peasants remembered very well the bloodbath that had followed the defeat of the 1905 Revolution. The tsarist regime sent its army on punitive expeditions into towns and villages where the population had evinced support for the revolution. Tens of thousands of people were murdered in cold blood by the tsarist troops as the towns and villages in which they lived were destroyed.

Schmid, like Service, fails to note one other not entirely insignificant fact: the October Revolution occurred against the backdrop of World War I, which had begun in the summer of 1914. By the time the Bolsheviks came to power, approximately 1.7 million Russian soldiers had already been lost in the senseless bloodbath. Millions more died on the various fronts of World War I, a conflict which, in the words of one historian, "produced the most extensive cultural devastation and mass killing in Europe since the Thirty Years War." The violence of the Russian Revolution was in no small measure determined by the horrifying social and economic conditions created by Russia's participation in the World War. In his book *The Dynamic of Destruction: Culture and Mass Killing in the First World War*, historian Alan Kramer (the author of the sentence cited above) wrote:

> ... To say that the Russian Revolution of October 1917 and the nature of the Soviet Union were profoundly affected by Russia's experience in war would be an understatement: it was a seven-year catastrophe of war, political upheaval, and civil war, which shaped the entire political culture of the Bolshevik regime for the following decades.[5]

Determined to discredit Trotsky on moral grounds, Schmid offers further examples of Trotsky's alleged "monstrousness." He writes:

> When his Red Army unit on the Kazan front in 1918 retreated before the enemy, Trotsky summarily ordered the commander and 40 soldiers to be shot and had their corpses thrown into the Volga.

It is true that Trotsky, at a critical moment when the fate of the newly organized Red Army hung in the balance, ordered the execution of soldiers who had deserted under fire. Trotsky took this extreme measure in order to maintain discipline, and recounted the incident in his autobiography. In the context of war, Trotsky's actions were justified. As Schmid must certainly know, the death penalty was employed against deserters in the German, French and British armies during World War I. Perhaps because he doubts the effectiveness of his condemnation of Trotsky's use of the death penalty, Schmid adds a strange and disturbing detail: that Trotsky ordered the corpses of the executed deserters to be thrown into the Volga.

This statement evokes in the mind of the reader a frightening image. Trotsky not only shot deserters, but denied them a proper burial. He dumped their corpses into a river! I have never come across this gruesome detail before. What is the documentary evidence upon which Schmid bases this allegation? Professor Schmid should let us know where he discovered this alleged act of inhumanity.

Schmid cites other well-known indictments of Trotsky's alleged cruelty, such as the suppression of the Kronstadt uprising in 1921. Once again, these events are presented without reference to, let alone serious analysis of, the political and historical context within which they occurred. This form of presentation makes no contribution whatever to an understanding of the events,

---

[5] Alan Kramer, *The Dynamic of Destruction: Culture and Mass Killing in the First World War*, (New York: Oxford University Press, 2007) p. 3.

or Trotsky's role in them. Their sole purpose is the advancement of Schmid's own politically motivated anti-communist agenda. In the final paragraph of his first article, Schmid again complains that:

> Although there can no longer exist any doubts about Trotsky's dictatorial inclinations, there are still "Communist Nostalgists" who wish to regard him as having been martyred by a conspiracy orchestrated by Stalin and world capitalism. The absurd assumption of such an alliance itself makes clear how far removed these authors are from common sense.

This supposedly absurd assumption is substantiated by the fact that Trotsky and his supporters were persecuted simultaneously by Stalinist, fascist and bourgeois democratic governments. Following his expulsion from the USSR, Trotsky was denied asylum by both the British and German governments. He was later allowed to enter France only after accepting severe restraints on not only his political activity, but also his physical movement within the country. In 1936, as I have already mentioned, the Norwegian government placed Trotsky in confinement in order to prevent him from publicly exposing the frame-up trial in Moscow. The widespread support for the Moscow Trials among bourgeois liberals in Europe and the United States flowed from their political alliance with the Stalinist parties, which formed the basis of the "Popular Front" movement of the 1930s. By mocking those who write of a Stalinist-imperialist alliance against Trotskyism, Schmid betrays his own ignorance of the political dynamics of the 1930s.

In a second article by Schmid, published in the *Neue Zürcher Zeitung* on February 21, 2012, he acknowledges that my critique of Service's book has been substantiated by Professor Bertrand Patenaude of Stanford University. He also takes notice of the letter from the fourteen historians, mentioning by name Helmut Dahmer, Hermann Weber, Bernhard Bayerlein, Heiko Haumann, Mario Kessler, Oskar Negt, Oliver Rathkolb and Peter Steinbach. Schmid certainly knows that all these historians are immensely respected scholars. Schmid could not help but be troubled to find the name of Professor Heiko Haumann on the list of signatories protesting against the publication of Service's biography. Professor Haumann assisted Schmid in the preparation of his *habilitationsschrift* [post-doctoral dissertation] in 1998–99, a service for which Schmid publicly expressed his gratitude. But now Schmid finds himself in the embarrassing position of challenging the judgment of one of his own mentors.

Schmid adopts a curious strategy in his defense of Service's book. He admits that there are mistakes, but he dismisses these errors as inconsequential. Schmid refers to them disingenuously as "little mistakes," which include "false dates of death ... the inexact description of historical events ... unreliable footnotes ... the mixing up of family relationships ... the truncation of citations ... the selective preference for memoirs that show Trotsky in an unfavorable light ..."

One can only read this list of Service's departure from basic standards of scholarship with amazement. Any one of these faults would be considered out of place in a book written by a professional historian. To find all these errors in a historical work published in the United States under the imprimatur of Harvard University Press is nothing short of a major intellectual scandal. An academic who produces such a work forfeits all right to be taken seriously as a scholar. A publishing house that produces such a work is violating its professional and ethical responsibility to uphold the integrity of intellectual discourse.

Professor Schmid cannot be unaware of the seriousness of Service's failure to observe academic norms. He writes prolifically and, as far as I can tell from a brief review of a portion of his published academic work, seeks to observe professional standards. And yet he seems to believe that Service should be allowed to violate the rules of scholarly work with impunity. Schmid would have readers believe that the factual errors that appear in Service's biography—which are so numerous that Suhrkamp has been obligated to hire an independent expert to review the entire text—is a problem of no great significance. Of course, an occasional factual error may be found in the work of even the most diligent historian. But the discovery of numerous factual errors in a single work is another matter entirely. The presence of such errors is evidence that the author is not in command of his subject matter, and his interpretation of events loses all credibility.

But despite the exposure of all the errors in Service's work, Schmid insists that its publication must go forward. He writes:

> The German translation is to be published in a corrected version at the beginning of July 2012—but there will not be far-reaching changes in the structure of the text. The decision of the publishing house is correct: neither North nor Patenaude have been able to advance arguments that undermine Service's fundamental critique of Trotsky's revolutionary fanaticism and his willingness to use violence.

As this passage makes all too clear, the sole basis of his defense of Service is Schmid's ideological and political commitments. Despite the errors, falsifications and violations of scholarly standards, Service's book satisfies the only criterion that is of importance to Schmid: it is against Trotsky and against socialist revolution. Nothing else matters.

More than 70 years after Trotsky's assassination, his legacy remains the subject of the fiercest controversy. He has been denied the right to pass into the realm of dispassionate historical scholarship. Trotsky remains an intensely contemporary figure. He lives in history, not only as the leader of the greatest revolution of the 20th century, but as a political and intellectual inspiration of the revolutions of the future.

More than 20 years after the dissolution of the USSR, capitalism is mired in crisis. The End of History promised by Francis Fukuyama has not been realized. What we are witnessing is the return of history—that of economic crisis, the relentless assault on democratic rights, and the eruption of imperialist wars. In this situation, the working class must study history in order to understand the present-day reality. The defense of Trotsky's legacy against historical falsification is an essential component of the political education of the working class and its preparation for the political demands of a new epoch of revolutionary struggle.

In Defense of Leon Trotsky[1]

I welcome the opportunity to participate in the Historians' Convention at the University of Mainz, and I am especially pleased to share the platform this evening with Professor Mario Kessler, who, as a scholar of international stature, is no stranger to historical controversies. He has made a significant contribution to the study of the political pathology of anti-Semitism and the complex relationship between the development of the socialist workers' movement and the Jewish people. By virtue of his field of interest, Professor Kessler knows in advance that whatever he publishes will certainly offend somebody—including, at times, even his friends. This is a problem with which I can sympathize.

I wish also to express my gratitude to my comrades at Mehring Verlag, and especially Wolfgang Weber, for all they have done to bring my book, *In Defense of Leon Trotsky*, to the attention of such a wide audience in Germany. A second edition of this book is now in preparation. This is something of a new experience for me. Over many decades in the socialist movement, I have become somewhat accustomed to waiting quite a few years for the size of the readership for my books and pamphlets to catch up with the initial press run. With *In Defense of Leon Trotsky*, and especially its German edition, I have not had to wait all that long.

There is a well known saying, *Habent sua fata libelli*—"Books have their destinies." Actually, as I recently learned upon consulting the contemporary world's incomparable source of information, Wikipedia, this phrase is a

---

[1] Lecture given at the Historians' Convention at the University of Mainz in Germany, September 27, 2012.

231

shortened and simplified version of the more profound statement, attributed to the ancient grammarian Terentianus Maurus. He wrote: "*Pro captu lectoris habent sua fata libelli*" (literally, "According to the capabilities of the reader, books have their destiny")[2]

In other words, the reader is an active agent in the shaping of a book's destiny. It is through its readers that a book makes its way in the world.

Fortunately, *In Defense of Leon Trotsky* attracted the attention of a number of highly principled scholars. Professor Bertrand Patenaude wrote the joint review of my book and Robert Service's biography of Trotsky, published in June 2011 in *The American Historical Review*, which attracted so much attention. His review was followed by the Open Letter to Suhrkamp that was signed by Professors Hermann Weber, Mario Kessler, Helmut Dahmer, Bernhard Bayerlein, Heiko Haumann, Wladislaw Hedeler, Andrea Hurton, Hartmut Mehringer, Oskar Negt, Hans Schafranek, Oliver Rathkolb, Peter Steinbach, Reiner Tosstorff and Rolf Wörsdörfer.

It is likely that there exists between me and the signatories, and among the signatories themselves, divergent views on the causes of the Russian Revolution, the social basis of the Bolshevik-led insurrection of October 1917, the nature of the Soviet regime, and the political conceptions and historical role of Leon Trotsky. A biography of Leon Trotsky written by Professor Kessler would, I am quite sure, be a very different work than one that I would produce. How could that not be the case? Our efforts would reflect our different viewpoints, different interests, and different experiences—in short, our different lives. But we would both be working from a real historical record.

All genuine history is a reconstruction of an objective process. The interpretative process strives to clarify, not distort, history. Trotsky was a real participant in an objective social and historical process. His actions and ideas are recorded in a massive archival record. There are documents from innumerable and varied sources. It is hard to think of another man who provoked such utterly divergent reactions. There exist the recollections and testimonials of those who followed Trotsky; there exist the denunciations of those who hated him. Trotsky was among the most prolific writers of his time. Not even the largest archival collection—that which is housed at the Houghton Library at Harvard—contains all his written work. A significant portion of his writings remains unpublished. Trotsky's ideas—as they found expression in his many books, essays, newspaper articles and even transcripts of discussions—have

2 See, en.wikipedia.org/wiki/Habent_sua_fata_libelli

exerted immense and enduring influence on the political and intellectual life of countless countries.

The historian who undertakes the gigantic task of writing a biography of a historical figure of Trotsky's magnitude must be prepared to immerse himself in the archival record. He or she must be prepared to devote the years and even decades—not a few months—necessary to acquire the appropriate level of understanding of the man and the times in which he lived.

The point I am trying to make is that the historian is obligated, by the nature of his discipline, to immerse himself in a vast objective record. Every biographer has, of course, a "standpoint." But he should not see it as his task to lecture, harangue and denounce his subject for pursuing aims, holding views and living in times different than his own. If a politically conservative historian undertakes to write about a Russian Communist, he must still attempt to understand the historical and social context which shaped the ideas and determined the actions of his subject. The historian has, and, indeed, must have, ideas of his own. If he did not, he could not produce an interesting work. However, he must grapple with the ideas of his subject and be prepared to accept their legitimacy, at least in the sense of understanding the historical circumstances and conditions of which they were an expression. To borrow a phrase from the historian R.G. Collingwood, as recalled by E.H. Carr, "the historian must re-enact in thought what has gone on in the mind of his dramatis personae..."[3]

It should not be necessary to add that the historian must exhibit an absolutely unyielding honesty in his treatment of the archival record and all that falls under the broad category of what is generally termed the "facts." Of course, despite the popularity of the phrase, no historian has ever "read everything that can be read" on any substantial subject. But he or she will make a good faith effort to locate and examine all that is necessary to achieve a multi-faceted reconstruction of the historical subject. The selection of facts must not be arbitrary and tendentious, and their presentation must be accurate. Nothing is so irreparably damaging to the reputation of a historian and the credibility of his work than the discovery that he has gotten his facts wrong, that the claims and assertions of a historian are not supported by the documents he cites, or that he has, in one way or another, falsified the historical record to fit preconceived needs of a predetermined narrative.

It has been irrefutably established over the past three years, since I wrote my first analysis of Service's biography, that his work is a travesty of historical

---

[3] E.H. Carr, *What is History?* (New York: Random House, 1961), p. 25-26.

writing. His book is, as the letter of the 14 historians so precisely stated, a "defamatory lampoon." Even though I substantially expanded my critique in the course of additional lectures, including two in Berlin and one in Leipzig, I could not fully catalog the errors, falsifications and misrepresentations that Service somehow managed to pack into a single volume. The pattern of dishonesty is so deeply woven into the fabric of Service's narrative that he apparently felt compelled to misrepresent historical documents even when there was no apparent reason for doing so.

For example, as I was preparing my remarks for today's meeting, I once again looked through the Service biography. I selected a chapter at random, knowing that I was likely to find at least one error on whatever page I looked. I turned to Chapter 14, entitled "War on War." It deals with the impact of the outbreak of World War I on Trotsky's life. On page 137, Service describes an encounter between Trotsky and the German Social Democrat Hermann Molkenbuhr on a Zurich street, in which the latter predicted a speedy end to the conflict. Immediately following the quoted words of Molkenbuhr, Service adds the following sentence: "Molkenbuhr regarded Trotsky's apocalyptic prognosis as the ranting of a 'utopian.'"[4]

The entire account is taken from Trotsky's *My Life*, and Service includes a footnoted reference.

Upon turning to the referenced passage, we find that Service did manage to reproduce correctly Molkenbuhr's words, as recalled by Trotsky. But the subsequent passage—"Molkenbuhr regarded Trotsky's apocalyptic prognosis as the ranting of a 'utopian'"—significantly alters Trotsky's account. Nowhere does Trotsky state that Molkenbuhr "regarded Trotsky's apocalyptic prognosis as the ranting of a 'utopian.'" He tells the story quite differently. Following the quote from Molkenbuhr, Trotsky writes:

> Molkenbuhr was stating, of course, not his own estimate of the situation; he was simply expressing the official opinion of the Social Democracy. At the same time, the French ambassador to St. Petersburg wagered Buchanan five pounds sterling that the war would be over before Christmas. *No, we 'utopians' foresaw things a little better than these realistic gentlemen from the Social Democracy and the diplomatic circles.*[5] [Italics added]

---

[4] Service, p. 137.

[5] Leon Trotsky, *My Life* (Mineola, NY: Dover, 2007), pp. 237-38.

Service's account creates a very different image in the mind of the reader than that which emerges from what Trotsky actually wrote. In the former, the reader is presented with an imagined scene in which the aged Social Democratic leader observes before him a "ranting" Trotsky, spouting apocalyptic phrases. Trotsky is reduced to a political caricature. But in the original text, Trotsky does not say anything about his immediate reply to Molkenbuhr. Rather, Trotsky adopts an ironic tone in recalling the wildly misguided political calculations of the opportunists and diplomats. Who, he is asking the reader, were the "utopians"? The revolutionists who foresaw the catastrophic implications of war or the so-called "realists" who believed all would be restored to normal within a few months? Service not only distorts the historical scene, he misses the political point of the entire passage.

Just a few paragraphs later, Service writes: "For the first time in his [Trotsky's] career he entered into polemics with Plekhanov, whom he now regarded with utter contempt."[6] The sentence is footnoted. Service informs us that he is citing a letter from Trotsky to the much older revolutionist, Pavel B. Akselrod, dated December 22, 1914. It is part of the famous Nicolaevsky Collection that is housed at the Hoover Institute at Stanford University in Palo Alto, California, where Service did almost all his research for the biography. When I first read this passage, I was taken aback. While Trotsky certainly deplored Plekhanov's support of the war, it was surprising to read that Trotsky regarded the "father of Russian Marxism" with "utter contempt." After the Bolsheviks came to power, Trotsky affirmed in several moving essays his intense and enduring admiration of Plekhanov. So what did Trotsky actually write to Akselrod in December 1914? Did Trotsky, in a private letter to an older comrade, give vent to an inner rage provoked by Plekhanov's political betrayal?

Trotsky's letter to Akselrod consists of three brief paragraphs. Only the first paragraph makes any reference to Plekhanov. It reads:

> Have you read Plekhanov's pamphlet? I have begun a series of articles about it. For the first time in my life I am polemicizing against Plekhanov. He is not as secure as he had seemed to me.[7]

Most readers, lacking access to the source material, would assume that Service has accurately interpreted the content of the letter that he is citing. But

---

[6] Service, p. 138.

[7] Translated by Frederick S. Choate.

it would be a mistake to extend such credit to Service. There is nothing in the referenced paragraph that suggests that Trotsky's attitude toward Plekhanov had become one of "utter contempt." That sentiment, which would reflect on Trotsky's own character, is simply invented by Service. In reality, this short letter conveys a sense of regret and sorrow over Plekhanov's evolution, sentiments far more appealing in the circumstances than that suggested by Service.

Just two pages later, after reporting Trotsky's arrival in Paris during the spring of 1915, Service writes:

> Both Trotsky and his wife were to claim that they lived frugally in Paris. There is no evidence for this. In 1914 he dispatched six substantial articles to *Kievskaya Mysl*. Such were their success that the newspaper continued to employ him throughout 1915–16; and since the French and the Russians were allies in the war he could rely on money being transferred quickly to his bank account in Paris. The Trotskys were not hard up in wartime France.[8]

Service implies that Trotsky and his wife, Natalia Sedova, lied about their conditions in Paris. "There is no evidence," he writes categorically, that the couple lived frugally in the midst of the war. How then did they live? Lavishly? Did they enjoy the comforts of an affluent middle-class life? The only information that Service provides about Trotsky's personal resources is 1) that he wrote six articles for the liberal newspaper *Kievskaya Mysl* in 1914; and 2) that Trotsky was still employed by the newspaper in 1915–16. Service offers no precise information about Trotsky's remuneration. Instead, Service claims, without supporting evidence, that Trotsky "could rely on money being transferred quickly to his bank account in Paris." What is the factual basis of Service's assumption that this was actually the case?

Unfortunately for Service, his self-assured claims about Trotsky's wealth and easy access to money are contradicted by the text of a letter that is referenced in a footnote just one page earlier. Trotsky wrote to Akselrod on December 11, 1915:

> I have a favor to ask of you. On the 20th, Nat. Iv. Trotskaya has a large payment to the printshop. Somewhere at the consulate there is 200 rubles for us which simply cannot be found. I wrote to "Kievskaya Mysl" asking them to send money by telegraph. But I fear that the money will not be received in time. With your help

---

[8] Service, pp. 140–41.

could she not get a loan—for a maximum of 10–12 days? This would help her avoid unpleasantries. Where is Martov: in Zurich or has he already left?[9]

In this letter, Trotsky is asking Akselrod for a loan. His wife owes a substantial amount of money to the printshop. Clearly, they are using their personal income to support political work. Contrary to Service's claim, transfers of money from Russia to France are not problem-free. The 200 rubles that Trotsky and his wife desperately need in order to "avoid unpleasantries" have gone missing in the consulate. Once again, Service has both misrepresented and withheld from his readers important pieces of information contained in the archives because they contradict his dishonestly constructed and tendentious narrative.

Is there anything that we actually know about the conditions of life that Trotsky and his wife endured during the decade they spent as political exiles in Western Europe following Trotsky's astonishing escape from Siberia in 1907? Trotsky provided this short description of his circumstances in Vienna, where he lived for seven years (1907–1914):

> My earnings at the *Kievskaya Mysl* were quite enough for our modest living. But there were months when my work for the *Pravda* left me no time to write a single paying line. The crisis set in. My wife learned the road to the pawn-shops, and I had to resell to the booksellers books bought in more affluent days. There were times when our modest possessions were confiscated to pay the house-rent. We had two babies and no nurse; our life was a double burden on my wife. But she still found time and energy to help me in revolutionary work.[10]

Trotsky's account is substantiated by the recollections of Russian revolutionary Moisseye Olgin, who included in the 1918 preface to an early collection of Trotsky's writings a description of the latter's life as an exile:

> His house in Vienna was a poor man's house, poorer than that of an ordinary American workingman earning eighteen dollars a week. Trotzky[11] has been poor all his life. His three rooms in

---

[9] Translated by Frederick S. Choate.

[10] *My Life*, p. 232.

[11] The English transliteration of Trotsky's name with a "z" was common in the immediate aftermath of the Revolution.

a Vienna working-class suburb contained less furniture than was necessary for comfort. His clothes were too cheap to make him appear "decent" in the eyes of a middle-class Viennese. When I visited his house, I found Mrs. Trotzky engaged in housework, while the two light-haired lovely boys were lending not inconsiderable assistance. The only thing that cheered the house were loads of books in every corner, and, perhaps, great though hidden hopes.[12]

I have drawn these examples of historical falsification from just four pages that I chose at random from Service's biography. I could find, without difficulty, dozens more. Some of these errors may appear, when viewed in isolation, relatively minor. But their cumulative effect, spread over 500 pages of text, is to create a monstrous parody of the real historical personality. The reader is presented with a "Trotsky" drawn to the specifications of a contemporary anti-communist.

In a review posted on the web edition of the *Neue Zürcher Zeitung*, historian Ulrich Schmid, who praises Service's work, argues that the factual errors pertain only to minor details—he uses the term "Monita"—which do not significantly detract from the overall value of the work. He justifies this position with the following declaration: "Neither North nor Patenaude have brought forward arguments that detract from Service's fundamental criticism of Trotsky's revolutionary fanaticism and his willingness to use violence. Trotsky directed the Red Terror in 1918 with an iron fist and ordered the bloody suppression of the Kronstadt sailors' uprising in 1921."[13]

Schmid is arguing not as a historian but as a petty-bourgeois moralist. His position is, in effect, that the exposure of Service's factual errors and fabrications do not detract from his condemnation of Trotsky on ethical grounds. The obvious reply to this sort of tendentious argument is that Service should have simply written a pamphlet entitled, "Why I Hate Trotsky," and marketed this work not as a historical biography, but rather as a statement of his own personal ethical, political and, perhaps, religious convictions. Ulrich Schmid fails to explain why Trotsky's support for the Red Terror in 1918 (which began after the assassination of Bolshevik leaders and the nearly successful attempt on Lenin's life) and the suppression of the Kronstadt uprising absolve Service of the responsibility to deal scrupulously with the historical record, and, moreover, make some attempt to understand and explain the historical

---

[12] See, www.marxists.org/archive/trotsky/1918/ourrevo/ch01.htm

[13] "Streit um Trotzki," February 21, 2012.

circumstances and political pressures that shaped the actions of Trotsky and the Bolshevik regime.

A serious historian is not indifferent to moral issues. But if a moral condemnation is in order, it should emerge with compelling force out of the logic of the narrative itself. The historian should not feel the need to conceal or falsify the historical record in order to make his "moral" point. A genuine historian like Ian Kershaw does not need to wag his finger at Hitler and remind his reader again and again how awful he was. Hitler's criminality and the horror of the regime he led emerge out of the historian's narrative. Kershaw's command of the archival record and a vast body of secondary literature is never in doubt. Moreover, as a historian, Kershaw is interested in Hitler not simply as an individual. He seeks to understand and explain how such a man could rise to power and become the subject of mass adulation.

Of course, Kershaw's choice of a subject simplified, in a certain sense, the moral issue. An honest and scrupulous treatment of the historical record leads inexorably to the conclusion that Hitler led a criminal regime. Those who seek to justify the regime, like the notorious David Irving, are the ones who must distort, falsify and lie.

Herein lay the source of the problem for Service. He could not extract from the historical record the materials he needed to sustain his efforts to portray Trotsky as an odious and even criminal political figure. Thus, to achieve his aim, he had to resort, as Stalin did in the 1930s, to fabrications, half-truths and outright lies.

In a candid moment, Service declared that he hoped that he had successfully completed what the assassin had failed to accomplish: the destruction of Trotsky's reputation. But this effort has failed completely. The only reputation that has been completely destroyed by Service's biography is that of its author.

Leon Trotsky in Coyoacan

Part V

Appendices

Trotsky with V.I. Lenin and Lev Kamenev in 1923

Review by Bertrand M. Patenaude in
The American Historical Review

Robert Service. Trotsky: A Biography.
David North. In Defense of Leon Trotsky.
Author(s): Bertrand M. Patenaude
The American Historical Review, Vol. 116, No. 3 (June 2011), pp. 900-902
Publisher: The University of Chicago Press on behalf of the American
Historical Association

Robert Service, who authored biographies of V. I. Lenin and Joseph
Stalin and a history of world communism, has now published a biography
of Leon Trotsky. "This book's purpose," Service announces at the start, "is to
dig up the buried life" (p. 4). It appears that he set out thoroughly to discredit
Trotsky as a historical figure and as a human being. His Trotsky is not merely
arrogant, self-righteous, and self-absorbed; he is a mass murderer and a terrorist, a cold and heartless son, husband, father, and comrade, and an intellectual
lightweight who falsified the record of his role in the Russian Revolution and
whose writings have continued to fool generations of readers—a hoax per-
petuated by his hagiographer Isaac Deutscher. In his eagerness to cut Trotsky
down, Service commits numerous distortions of the historical record and
outright errors of fact to the point that the intellectual integrity of the whole
enterprise is open to question.

Enter David North. North is an American Trotskyist whose book col-
lects his review essays of Service's volume and of earlier biographies of Trotsky
by Ian Thatcher and Geoffrey Swain. (He does not mention my 2009 book,

243

Trotsky: Downfall of a Revolutionary.) Given North's Trotskyism, he might reasonably be suspected of hyperbole in his brief against Service. But a careful examination of North's book shows his criticism of Service to be exactly what Trotsky scholar Baruch Knei-Paz, in a blurb on the back cover, says it is: "detailed, meticulous, well-argued and devastating."

Service, in his attempt to indict Trotsky, makes Exhibit #1 Trotsky's autobiography, *My Life* (1930), which Service calls "a masterpiece of political fudging masked by the artifices of a literary alchemist" (p. 403). Service has examined what he says in one place is the "first draft" of Trotsky's memoir in the Hoover Institution Archives, "which has much information he excluded from the printed version" (p. xix). Elsewhere he writes,

"By examining the drafts and proofs, we can catch glimpses of aspects of his upbringing that have long lain hidden" (p. 12).

Here, in the discussion of Trotsky's youth, Service targets Trotsky's alleged embarrassments about his parents' wealth (Trotsky's father was a prosperous farmer in southern Ukraine) and his Jewish origins (Trotsky was born Lev Davidovich Bronstein). Yet neither here nor anywhere else is Service able to provide a single example of a significant discrepancy between the published memoir and the draft. In fact, in his depiction of Trotsky's youth, Service relies almost entirely on the published version of *My Life*, not on earlier drafts. Service accuses Trotsky the memoirist of being "selective, evasive and self-aggrandizing" (p. xxi) (as if most memoirs do not fit this description), yet he reads other memoirs completely uncritically (for example, those of Gregory A. Ziv and Clare Sheridan) when they show Trotsky in an unfavorable light.

Service's animus toward Trotsky is on clearest display in his treatment of Trotsky's relationship with Alexandra Sokolovskaya, a comrade whom he married in prison in 1899 and whom he left behind with their two infant daughters when he escaped from Siberian exile in 1902. Trotsky later said that it was with her blessing that he fled Russia to join up with Lenin and other Russian Marxists in Western Europe. But in Service's telling, "Bronstein was planning to abandon her in the wilds of Siberia . . . No sooner had he fathered a couple of children than he decided to run off. Few revolutionaries left such a mess behind them. Even so, he was acting within the revolutionary code of behaviour" (p. 67). Service felt it necessary to soften his criticism with that final sentence, yet later in the book he says outright that Trotsky "ditched his first wife" (p. 112).

In fact, Trotsky's family in Russia helped support Sokolovskaya and their daughters, and she went to her death in the Great Terror as a Trotskyist.

Not only does Service fail to furnish a single piece of evidence that contradicts Trotsky's account, he tampers with the available evidence. He produces what he wants to present as a damning quote from Trotsky's memoir: "'Life,' [Trotsky] said as if it was a simple matter of fact, 'separated us'" (p. 67). In Service's account, this amounts to a callous Trotsky shrugging his shoulders: Stuff happens. But as North notes, Service has cut off Trotsky's sentence, which reads as follows: "Life separated us, but nothing could destroy our friendship and our intellectual kinship" (p. 125). So here we find Service excising inconvenient text from the autobiography he accuses Trotsky of having edited in order to suppress embarrassing passages.

The number of factual mistakes in Service's book is, as North says, "astonishing" (p. 167). I have counted more than four dozen. Service mixes up the names of Trotsky's sons, misidentifies the largest political group in the first Duma in 1906, botches the name of the Austrian archduke assassinated at Sarajevo, misrepresents the circumstances of Nicholas II's abdication, gets backward Trotsky's position in 1940 on the United States' entry into World War II, and gives the wrong year of death of Trotsky's widow. Service's book is completely unreliable as a reference.

At times the errors are jaw-dropping. Service believes that Bertram Wolfe was one of Trotsky's "acolytes" living with him in Mexico (pp. 441, 473), that Andre Breton was a "surrealist painter" whose "pictures exhibited sympathy with the plight of the working people" (p. 453), and that Mikhail Gorbachev rehabilitated Trotsky in 1988, when in fact Trotsky was never posthumously rehabilitated by the Soviet government.

Service fails to examine in a serious way Trotsky's political ideas in his writings and speeches—nor does it appear that he has always bothered to familiarize himself with them. A striking case in point is his brief discussion of Trotsky's *Literature and Revolution* (1923). In trying to summarize what he dismisses as a "patchy survey of contemporary prose and poetry," Service writes: "Like fellow communist leaders, Trotsky wanted a high culture subordinate to the party's purposes. It would take many years, he assumed, before a 'proletarian culture' would be widely achieved" (p. 317). In fact, Trotsky emphatically rejected the concept of "proletarian culture," which was his main purpose in taking up his pen against the communist radicals of Proletcult.

But Service is not about to let the facts get in the way of his exposing the "crudity of Trotsky's judgements" (p. 318) about culture. He leaps from statements that Trotsky was "no liberal in affairs of culture" (p. 315) and "no advocate of complete artistic freedom" (p. 316) to a hard conclusion: "When all is said and done, though, it was Trotsky who laid down the philosophical foundations for cultural Stalinism" (p. 318). Nothing in Service's book justifies such a statement.

With no way to prove his case, Service relies on cheap shots and slanderous asides to keep his readers convinced that Trotsky is a despicable man. Examining Trotsky's marked-up copy of a book on Marxism by Sidney Hook, Service decides that "the exclamation marks he made in the margins testify to angry self-righteousness and intellectual self-regard" (p. 6). At times it is unclear to what degree Service's writing is informed by ignorance or malice. His discussion of the Dewey Commission, the independent investigation into the veracity of the Moscow trials led by philosopher John Dewey in 1937, is an example. In Service's error-strewn account, the Dewey Commission was a put-up job, with Trotsky manipulating the proceedings and engineering the eventual not-guilty verdict. The members of the commission, Service writes, were "blind to Trotsky's contempt for their values . . . Like spectators at a zoo, they felt sorry for the wounded beast" (p. 466). This is a travesty of the actual facts. In reality, most members of the Dewey Commission, liberals together with socialists, had no sympathy for Trotsky's ideas, but they believed he deserved a fair hearing after the sham justice handed down in the Moscow trials, which had effectively condemned Trotsky to death in absentia.

Service is on a crusade to place Trotsky alongside Stalin as one of the great bloodthirsty tyrants of the twentieth century. Because of the way the story turned out—Trotsky was assassinated by a Stalinist agent in Mexico in 1940—Service has to huff and puff to try to convince his readers. "It is true that Stalin did things of a monstrosity which only a few dictators in the twentieth century matched," Service writes. "But Trotsky was no angel" (p. 4). Indeed, "He was close to Stalin in intentions and practice. He was no more likely than Stalin to create a society of humanitarian socialism even though he claimed and assumed that he would. Trotsky failed to work out how to move from party dictatorship to universal freedom. He reveled in terror" (p. 497).

Service assures his readers that although Trotsky may have paid attention to Soviet culture, "This did not mean that he had gone soft in his politics. What still counted for him was world revolution, and no human price [sic!] was too great to pay in the interests of the cause" (p. 313). But insinuation and non sequiturs can get Service only so far, so he must fabricate evidence. Service writes of Trotsky: "He displayed his complete moral insouciance when telling his American admirer Max Eastman in the early 1920s that he and the Bolsheviks were willing 'to burn several thousand Russians to a cinder in order to create a true revolutionary American movement.' Russia's workers and peasants would have been interested to know of the mass sacrifice he was contemplating" (p. 313).

Here North catches Service in an act of outright falsification. A look at Eastman's memoir, Service's source for the anecdote, reveals that Trotsky was reacting to Eastman's lament that the American Communist movement was dominated by ex-Menshevik Russian Americans. Trotsky's response to Eastman had nothing to do with Russian workers and peasants and was spoken in jest. But Service, pretending that he has found a spine-tingling passage about the monster Trotsky, delivers a solemn clincher: "If the ends were desired, the means had to be willed" (p. 313).

Service seeks to portray Trotsky as a man who was coldly indifferent to the births of his children and whose political obsessions make him ultimately responsible for the suffering and deaths of his family members. Trotsky, not Stalin, is the culprit here. Of the suicide in Berlin of Trotsky's mentally ill daughter Zina in January 1933, Service writes: "Trotsky's attempt to politicize the death was not his finest moment" (p. 386). Yet Service fails even to mention that the Kremlin had recently revoked Zina's citizenship, cutting off the possibility for her to return to her mother, her daughter, and her husband—a fact that Trotsky had uppermost in mind in blaming Stalin for her death.

Meanwhile, the archival citations pile up in the back of Service's book, lest anyone be inclined to question whether the biographer has hard proof of Trotsky's moral and political bankruptcy. These citations are mostly from Moscow archives and the Hoover Institution Archives: oddly, there is very little from Harvard, where Trotsky deposited his papers on the eve of his assassination. Instead, Service has decided that this, the most important collection of Trotsky's papers in the world, has been "mined long ago" (p. xix). Mined by whom? Surely Service does not assume that Deutscher, the man he says "worshipped at Trotsky's shrine" (p. xxi), or Pierre Broué, whom he calls a Trotsky "idolater" (p. xxi), can be trusted to have researched the Harvard collection honestly and thoroughly. Service informs his readers: "The Houghton Library at Harvard University too contains letters in its holdings which have merited reconsideration, and I thank [name of research assistant] for obtaining the ones I requested" (pp. xix-xx). And how did Service decide which letters "merited reconsideration"?

North calls Service's biography a "piece of hack-work" (p. 140). Strong words, but entirely justified. Harvard University Press has placed its imprimatur upon a book that fails to meet the basic standards of historical scholarship.

BERTRAND M. PATENAUDE
Stanford University

Letter from Historians to German Publisher Suhrkamp on Robert Service's Biography of Trotsky

Berlin, 30 July 2011
Re: Publication of Robert Service's Trotsky biography

Dear Ms. Unseld Berkéwicz,

Your publishing company is preparing a German edition of Robert Service's biography of Trotsky. This project has provoked surprise and consternation on the part of professional historians. Trotsky expert David North undertook a thorough analysis shortly after the book was published two years ago by Harvard University Press. He came to the conclusion that Robert Service had violated basic standards of historical scholarship and his publisher had failed to exercise the necessary editorial oversight. A recent review of the book by the Trotsky biographer Bertrand Patenaude in *The American Historical Review* has completely confirmed the criticisms raised by North.

North and Patenaude have pointed out a host of factual errors by Service (including false information regarding biographical facts and historical events, incorrect names of places and persons, up to blatant misrepresentations—e.g., Trotsky's position regarding autonomy and "partiality" in art and literature). Service's sources are unreliable. Sources that are very difficult to access and hardly verifiable for most readers often have nothing to do with the claims made, or demonstrate the opposite. Contrary to the announcement of the book made by Suhrkamp, Service has not sought to deal with Trotsky and

Stalin in an "impartial and genuine" manner. Instead, the aim of his work is to discredit Trotsky, and unfortunately he often resorts to the formulas associated with Stalinist propaganda.

The Service biography is a pasquil. The *Evening Standard* of 23 October 2009 reports on a presentation of the book and quotes Service as follows: "There's life in the old guy Trotsky. If the *ice pick* didn't finish him off, I hope my book does."

Trotsky's origins from a Jewish peasant family have always played a prominent role in the countless polemics against him. Service also treats these origins—which, he claims, Trotsky underplayed—as of great significance. The passages in which he deals with this theme have repugnant connotations. We quote in German translation from the original English edition:

"Russian anti-Semites had picked out Jews as a race without patriotic commitment to Russia. By becoming the foreign minister for a government more interested in spreading world revolution than in defending the country's interests, Trotsky was conforming to a widespread stereotype figure of the 'Jewish problem'. The truth was that he would inevitably become a figure of hatred among ultra-nationalist political groups in Russia and abroad if he accepted any prominent job in the revolutionary administration. As things stood he had already become the most famous Jew on earth. America's Red Cross leader in Russia, Colonel Raymond Robins, put this with characteristic pungency. Talking to Robert Bruce Lockhart, head of a diplomatic mission in Moscow, he described Trotsky as 'a four-kind son of a bitch, but the greatest Jew since Jesus Christ.'" (Robert Service, *Trotsky*, page 192)

"He was brash in his cleverness, outspoken in his opinions. No one could intimidate him. Trotsky had these characteristics to a higher degree than most other Jews emancipated from the traditions of their religious community and the restrictions of the Imperial order.... But he was far from being the only Jew who visibly enjoyed the opportunities for public self-advancement. In later years they were to constitute a model for Jewish youth to follow in the world communist movement when, like communists of all nationalities, they spoke loudly and wrote sharply regardless of other people's sensitivities." (202)

"The party's leadership was widely identified as a Jewish clique.... Jews were widely alleged to dominate the Bolshevik party." (205)

Robert Service also believes—without providing any evidence—he has discovered that Trotsky's forename was not Lev but rather "Leiba", something that Trotsky later denied. (Amongst the book's illustrations, Service includes an anti-Semitic caricature [No. 11]. The original text accompanying the portrait reads: "War and Navy Commissar Leiba Trotsky-Braunstein...the real dictator of Russia." Service's own commentary reads: "In reality, his real nose was neither long nor bent and he never allowed his goatee to become straggly or his hair ill-kempt.")

We are of the opinion that the book by Service is misplaced in your highly regarded publishing house and ask you to reconsider your options.

Vienna, 30 July 2011

Professor for Sociology, Dr. Helmut Dahmer (Technical University, Darmstadt)

Mannheim, 30 July 2011

Professor for Political Science and Contemporary History, Dr. Hermann Weber (Mannheim University)

Further Signatories:

Bernhard Bayerlein, Centre for Contemporary Research, Potsdam

Heiko Haumann, Professor for East European History, University of Basel

Wladislaw Hedeler, Historian and author, Berlin

Andrea Hurton, Historian and author, Vienna

Mario Kessler, Professor at the Centre for Contemporary Research, Potsdam

Hartmut Mehringer, Institute for Contemporary History, Berlin

Oskar Negt, Professor for Sociology, University of Hanover

Hans Schafranek, Historian and author, Vienna

Oliver Rathkolb, Professor at the Institute for Contemporary History, University of Vienna

Peter Steinbach, Professor at the University of Mannheim, Director of The German Resistance Memorial Center

Reiner Tosstorff, University of Mainz

Rolf Wörsdörfer, Technical University of Darmstadt

Index

W

Weber, Hermann viii, 228, 232, 251
Weber, Wolfgang 231
What Is History? 85
White, James D. 57, 110, 195
Wilde, Oscar 31
Wise, Rabbi Stephen 146
Witte, Count Sergei Yulievich 72
Wolfe, Bertram 245
Wolf, Erwin 4, 133
Wörsdörfer, Rolf viii, 232, 251

Y

Yakir, Iona Emmanuilovich 89

Yakubovich, Pyotr 152
Yegorov, Aleksandr Ilyich 89
Yeltsin, Boris Nikolaevich 6
Young Socialists 105

Z

Zinoviev, Grigory Evseevich 32, 41, 44, 46, 51, 61, 65, 66, 69, 70, 76, 131, 132, 146
Zipperstein, Steven J. 120
Ziv, Gregory A. 121–123, 144, 145, 244